COURTING KIDS

ALTERNATIVE CRIMINOLOGY SERIES

General Editor: Jeff Ferrell

Pissing on Demand: Workplace Drug Testing and the Rise of the Detox Industry
Ken Tunnell

*Empire of Scrounge: Inside the Urban Underground of Dumpster Diving,
Trash Picking, and Street Scavenging*
Jeff Ferrell

Prison, Inc.: A Convict Exposes Life inside a Private Prison
by K. C. Carceral, edited by Thomas J. Bernard

The Terrorist Identity: Explaining the Terrorist Threat
Michael P. Arena and Bruce A. Arrigo

Terrorism as Crime: From Oklahoma City to Al-Qaeda and Beyond
Mark S. Hamm

Our Bodies, Our Crimes: The Policing of Women's Reproduction in America
Jeanne Flavin

Graffiti Lives: Beyond the Tag in New York's Urban Underground
Gregory J. Snyder

Crimes of Dissent: Civil Disobedience, Criminal Justice, and the Politics of Conscience
Jarret S. Lovell

The Culture of Punishment: Prison, Society, and Spectacle
Michelle Brown

Who You Claim: Performing Gang Identity in School and on the Streets
Robert Garot

5 Grams: Crack Cocaine, Rap Music, and the War on Drugs
Dimitri A. Bogazianos

Judging Addicts: Drug Courts and Coercion in the Justice System
Rebecca Tiger

Courting Kids: Inside an Experimental Youth Court
Carla J. Barrett

Courting Kids

Inside an Experimental Youth Court

Carla J. Barrett

NEW YORK UNIVERSITY PRESS
New York and London

NEW YORK UNIVERSITY PRESS
New York and London
www.nyupress.org

References to Internet websites (URLs) were accurate at the time of writing.
Neither the author nor New York University Press is responsible for URLs
that may have expired or changed since the manuscript was prepared.

LIBRARY OF CONGRESS CATALOGING-IN-PUBLICATION DATA
Barrett, Carla J.
Courting kids : inside an experimental youth court / Carla J. Barrett.
p. cm. — (Alternative criminology series)
Includes bibliographical references and index.
ISBN 978-0-8147-0946-7 (cl : alk. paper)
ISBN 978-0-8147-0945-0 (pb : alk. paper)
ISBN 978-0-8147-6004-8 (ebook)
ISBN 978-0-8147-8946-9 (ebook)
1. Juvenile courts—New York (State)—New York County. 2. New York (State). Supreme Court. 3. Juvenile courts—New York (State)—New York. 4. Manhattan (New York, N.Y.) I. Title.
KFN6196.B37   2012
345.747'1081—dc23   2012026194

New York University Press books are printed on acid-free paper,
and their binding materials are chosen for strength and durability.
We strive to use environmentally responsible suppliers and materials
to the greatest extent possible in publishing our books.

Manufactured in the United States of America

c 10 9 8 7 6 5 4 3 2 1
p 10 9 8 7 6 5 4 3 2 1

For the kids

CONTENTS

ACKNOWLEDGMENTS

There are many people I wish to thank for helping to make this book possible. My time with two organizations—Save Our Sons and Daughters (SOSAD) in Detroit and the Harlem Writers Crew in New York—set me on this path originally. Thanks to Clementine, Terry, Greg, Andy, Avery, and all the kids for sharing your worlds with me.

This book would not have been possible without the help and generosity of so many people who work in and around the Manhattan criminal courts. I am truly grateful to the attorneys, the personnel of alternative-to-incarceration programs, court advocates, and court staff (whom I wish I could acknowledge here by name) who were overwhelmingly willing to share their time, expertise, and insights with me. Judge Michael Corriero opened his court to me for more than five years. He and his staff were tremendously generous with their time and endlessly patient with my repeated questions and requests for still more information. It was an inspiration to spend time with folks who work so tirelessly, and often thanklessly, to try and make a difference. Dean Mauro of the New York State Division of Criminal Justice Services provided much of the quantitative data on Juvenile Offender indictments (and kindly put up with my repeated requests for more).

Numerous colleagues, friends, and mentors read early drafts, helped work out theoretical and methodological concerns, commiserated, questioned, and inspired along the way. Thank you to Nina Aledort, Claudio Benzecry, Avi Brisman, Lynn Chancer, Michael Coyle, Caroline DeBrovner, Megan Doherty, Celeste Donovan, Joanna Dreby, Trevor Milton, Rafik Mohammed, Jayne Mooney, Richard Ocejo, Elizabeth Perea, Carolyn Pinedo Turnovsky, Diana Rickard, Michelle Ronda, Austin Sarat, Greg Snyder, René van Swaaningen, Rebecca Tiger, Jonathan Wynn, and Jock Young. If I have achieved any level of skill in the craft of ethnography it is because I had the privilege of being trained by some of the best: Angela Gilliam, Bill Kornblum, Mitchell Duneier, Alisse Waterston, and Terry Williams. Thank you—for doing and for teaching.

Special thanks go to Susan Will for being my Sociology of Law guru, and to Michael Jacobson for talking me out of going to law school and providing a wealth of other cogent advice. I am especially grateful for the time I have spent with the Common Studies Programme in Critical Criminology—my participation in the common sessions has informed and transformed my scholarship and my worldview in powerful ways. Alternative Criminology Series editor Jeff Ferrell's insistence on the value of this project helped sustain me through the rough spots. NYU Press editor Ilene Kalish provided consistent support, impeccable attention to detail, and gracious good humor. I am especially indebted to my anonymous reviewers for their thoughtful and thorough comments and suggestions, and to David Updike for copyediting the manuscript.

On a more personal note, grand thanks to Janan Cargile, Leonard Rosenblum, Cristina Livingstone, Michelle McDaniel, and Jen Adams for being part of my eclectic New York family. To my dear sister Ronda and all my family out west, thank you for your continuous love and support—you are the great heart that stands me by.

There can be no keener revelation of a society's soul than the way in which it treats its children.

—Nelson Mandela

Introduction

An Experiment in Youth Justice

SUPREME COURT OF NEW YORK, NEW YORK COUNTY, PART 73,
FRIDAY, 11 A.M.

Terell, a 15-year-old black Juvenile Offender, made his way hesitantly through the low gate in the courtroom when his name was called. Judge Michael Corriero looked over the notes in front of him. Terell had not been meeting the requirements of the alternative-to-incarceration (ATI) program to which the court had assigned him. The judge wasted no time getting to the point.

"You need to cooperate with the project, you understand?" the judge said to Terell in a stern voice. "And you need to cooperate with school authorities. And his curfew will remain at 7 p.m.," the judge added, his voice getting more terse.

The judge looked back at the paperwork in front of him. "Now listen to me young man. You need to cooperate with these people and do what they say, you understand?"

"Yes," Terell answered.

The judge then looked Terell directly in the eyes and raised his voice to just below a full yell: "If you so much as SPIT ON THE SIDEWALK I'll put you in jail. Do we understand each other?"

"Yes," replied Terell.

The judge then put the case on for a "short date"—meaning that he wanted to see Terell again in two weeks, hoping that the youth would heed his warning and turn things around. Judge Corriero didn't often yell in court, but he knew the stakes were high for Terell and wanted to make sure he got through to the kid. Terrell had been arrested two months earlier for his alleged involvement, with others, in a robbery involving a fake gun. Because of his age and the nature of the alleged offense, New York State law required that Terell be prosecuted as an adult in the criminal court, not as a juvenile in Family Court. The presence of a gun—even a fake one that wasn't in Terell's possession at the time of the alleged crime—meant that Terell was charged with first-degree robbery and was facing three to ten years of incarceration and a lifetime felony record if convicted. The judge knew that Terell's only hope of avoiding that future was to cooperate fully with the ATI

1

program and earn the right to receive an alternative sentence of probation. The judge hoped that the threat of jail might wake Terell up to that reality.

Because Terell was 15 years old and facing a first-degree robbery charge, state law required that he be prosecuted in the adult criminal court system rather than the juvenile court system. Because his alleged crime had taken place in Manhattan, Terell's case was handled in the Manhattan Youth Part. Courtrooms are called "parts" in New York, and the Manhattan Youth Part is the one courtroom set aside in the borough for criminal cases involving youths who are required by law to be prosecuted as adults. This specialized part was established in 1992 to address the special legal issues related to youths charged as adults. Judge Corriero presided over the part from its creation until his retirement in 2007. During those fifteen years, this unique criminal court undertook an experiment in youth justice. Working within the statutory constraints of retributive law, court actors, led by a dedicated and activist judge, created a system of justice that sought to hold young defendants, nearly all of them black and/or Hispanic males between the ages of 14 and 18, accountable for their alleged crimes while acknowledging their adolescence and attempting to divert them away from the full force of the adult sentences they were facing. This book details the unique experiment in justice undertaken by the Manhattan Youth Part.

In the culture of the Manhattan Youth Part, although the defendants were legally required to be labeled "adults," they were never really treated as such in courtroom interactions. Instead, the court chose to respond to the young defendants by openly acknowledging their youthfulness from their first appearance in court. Defendants' adolescent status was reinforced by paternalistic treatment from the judge, the important role given to the parents, and the heavy use of ATI programs that privileged staying in school, getting good grades, abiding by curfews, and obeying elders. This was the first step in the court's effort to deal realistically, and humanely, with adolescent defendants. The court chose to apply the principles and "child-saving" ideals of the early American juvenile court, actively devising rehabilitation-based case-processing mechanisms focused on individualized justice. Recognizing that kids whom the legal system labeled as "adults" were in fact not adults, the court developed a system of case processing that sought, when and where appropriate, to treat defendants like Terell as redeemable, salvageable kids. Toward that goal, dedicated court actors employed creative and sometimes problematic strategies in their efforts to divert as many deserving youths as possible away from the full force of adult felony convictions.

Operating as it did, the Manhattan Youth Part openly acknowledged the contradictions inherent in prosecuting youths as if they were adults and deliberately designed court practices to overtly counteract—some might even say subvert—the punitive dictates of New York State law as much as was legally possible. Beyond this, the part worked to develop a humanizing form of justice that treated the often troubled kids before it in a manner that allowed space for patience, dignity, respect, and communication. In a time when state after state was passing harsher laws in response to transgressive youth, the Manhattan Youth Part undertook a modern-day experiment in child-saving. This book examines how that experiment operated and analyzes the questions that it raises and insights it offers about the proper legal responses to youth offenders, about the tenability of the practice of prosecuting youths as adults, and about the ongoing criminalization of youth—particularly urban youth of color.

The Prosecution of Juveniles in Adult Courts

The increased prosecution of juveniles in criminal (i.e., adult) courts is one of the most important criminal justice trends of recent decades. The practice of prosecuting youths as adults is often referred to as "transfer" or "waiver" because it traditionally involved the transfer, or waiver, of young defendants from the jurisdiction of a juvenile court system to that of a criminal court. Juvenile court judges in many states had the discretionary right to transfer certain delinquents to adult court, but this practice was limited and was generally reserved for particularly heinous offenses or for individual chronic repeat offenders.[1] The 1990s, however, saw sweeping legislative changes, as nearly every state and the District of Columbia passed new transfer laws allowing for, and in many cases requiring, the criminal prosecution of younger and younger defendants for a growing list of crimes, sometimes even nonviolent ones. This legislation was an abrupt shift from individual transfer decisions to moving whole categories of offenders into the criminal courts.[2] The goal was to label certain juveniles legally as "adults," strip away their claims of "childness," and deny them the differential and rehabilitation-centered treatments traditionally provided within juvenile court settings. The very concept of trying youths as adults carries within it the implication that those designated for transfer simply cannot be rehabilitated.[3] The increase in punitive transfer legislation during the 1990s occurred within a political, legal, and social environment already devoted to retributive policies such as mandatory sentencing, mass incarceration, and so-called three strikes laws. The proliferation of condemnatory transfer legislation was also facilitated by a racialized moral panic over media hype about a generation of "superpredators" supposedly on the rise in cities across the United States. During this time, conceptualizations of juvenile justice moved away from the rehabilitation-based, "child-saving" models of earlier decades and toward a more retributive, punishment-focused system.

Juvenile Justice Prior to the 1990s

The emergence of the juvenile court as a concept at the end of the nineteenth century was borne out of a dual motivation—a concern for the welfare of neglected and abused "children in need," and the desire to quell socially transgressive youth behavior.[4] Dedicated to the idea that youth are fundamentally different from adults and as such deserve a separate style of justice, the early juvenile court movement touted a philosophy known as *parens patriae*. Under this guiding principle, the state, in response to law-breaking children, was to act "in the best interests of the child" in a non-adversarial environment structurally different from that of adult courts. Championing a belief in the redemptive power of rehabilitation, juvenile courts were to focus more on the offender than the offense, and to utilize an individualized model of justice dedicated to child-saving outcomes. Grounded in the belief that most transgressive youths were "salvageable," juvenile courts were designed to hold closed proceedings and to seal the records so that rehabilitated kids could enter adulthood without the stigma of a criminal record.[5]

This informal *parens patriae* model of juvenile justice prevailed until the late 1960s and the early 1970s, when a number of Supreme Court decisions altered the legal structure of juvenile courts.[6] The informality of traditional juvenile court proceedings allowed tremendous discretion, which could lead to either benevolence or abuse. A system that allowed judges to deal with young offenders in flexible, individualized, and nonlegalistic ways came to be seen as an arbitrary system in which youths had little, if any, of the legal protections available to adults. Three Supreme Court cases changed all this: *Kent v. United States* (1966), *In re Gault* (1967) and *In re Winship* (1970). Each case, in its own way, challenged the informality and nonlegalistic nature of juvenile court proceedings and introduced requirements of due process. Taken together, these three cases brought about what is generally referred to as the "due process revolution" in juvenile justice and served to formalize procedural guidelines in juvenile court proceedings.

Kent v. the United States originated in the District of Columbia over the procedures by which the juvenile court there could transfer cases to criminal court jurisdiction. The juvenile court had transferred 16-year-old Morris Kent, who had been arrested on housebreaking, robbery, and rape charges, to adult court without holding a hearing prior to the transfer. Such a transfer hearing with a full investigation was required under District law. In its decision, the Supreme Court raised questions about the constitutional legitimacy of the existing system:

> While there can be no doubt of the original laudable purpose of juvenile courts, studies and critiques in recent years raise serious questions as to whether actual performance measures well enough against theoretical purpose to make tolerable the immunity of the process from the reach of constitutional guaranties applicable to adults.[7]

A year later, the Supreme Court heard *In re Gault*. The best-known and most significant of the three cases, *Gault* involved 15-year-old Gerald Gault, who had been sentenced in Arizona to a state industrial school until the age of 21 for making an obscene phone call, a misdemeanor offense. The maximum penalty allowed for such a crime if committed by an adult would have been a $50 fine and a maximum of two months jail time.[8] The challenge, first heard by the Arizona Supreme Court, centered on the fact that such harsh punishment had been applied through the juvenile court without the defendant having been given the right to counsel, the right to cross-examine witnesses, or the right against self-incrimination—all rights guaranteed to defendants in the criminal court. The Arizona Supreme Court held that "due process did not require that an infant have a right to counsel."[9] The U.S. Supreme Court, however, disagreed and stated that a hearing resulting in such stiff penalty required the application of due process rights. The Court questioned the constitutionality of the *parens patriae* doctrine and instituted the right to counsel, the right to question and cross-examine witnesses, and the right against self-incrimination for offenders adjudicated in juvenile courts.[10] In its review of the relevant case law, the Court stated that "neither the fourteenth Amendment nor the Bill of Rights is for adults alone."[11] *Gault* was a watershed event in the history of juvenile justice in the United States. In his book *Bad Kids: Race and the Transformation of the Juvenile Court*, law professor Barry Feld claims that *In re Gault* "transformed [the juvenile court] from a social welfare agency into a legal institution."[12]

Three years later, the Supreme Court further formalized juvenile court proceedings with its decision in *In re Winship* (1970). At 12 years of age Samuel Winship had been sentenced through a juvenile court to a state training school for allegedly stealing money from a woman's purse in a retail store. Although there had been "reasonable doubt" of Winship's guilt, he was adjudicated delinquent under the civil court standard of "a preponderance of evidence." The lower courts ruled that the lesser standard of evidence was adequate given the child-saving, rather than punishing, goals of juvenile courts.[13] The Supreme Court rejected this finding, stating, "In sum, the constitutional safeguard of proof beyond a reasonable doubt is as much required during the adjudicatory stage of a delinquency proceeding as are those constitutional safeguards applied in *Gault*."[14]

The constitutional guarantees brought forth by *Kent*, *Gault*, and *Winship* served to formalize the juvenile court legally as it never had been. The legal structure of juvenile courts began to resemble more closely the criminal courts in which adults were prosecuted. This due-process revolution, which corrected the deficiencies and abuses of the early juvenile justice model, also served to distance the system from its child-saving *parens patriae* mandate and paved the way for what has been called the "criminalization" of the juvenile system.[15] The adoption, within juvenile courts, of legal structures that resembled and often mimicked adult criminal courts served to blur the real and philosophical distinctions between juvenile and criminal courts. These legal changes altered juvenile court practices in ways that often moved them toward more punitive and less rehabilitative outcomes. They did not, however, directly challenge the basic concept of a separate legal jurisdiction for non-adults. Those challenges came in 1990s.

The 1990s Transfer Law Boom

Just as the due-process revolution fundamentally altered the structure of the juvenile court, the proliferation of retributive transfer law during the 1990s significantly altered the nature of legal responses to adolescent offenders. In that decade forty-nine states passed new transfer laws making it easier to try young offenders as adults.[16] In addition, several states amended the statutory language of their juvenile justice laws to include more emphasis on the protection of "public safety" and on the "punishment" rather than rehabilitation of delinquent youths.[17]

There are different legal pathways through which youths under the age of 18 can end up in criminal courts, and the laws vary from state to state. Young people can end up in criminal court simply because their age places them outside the jurisdiction of the juvenile court. Each state decides the age at which juvenile court jurisdiction ends. For example, in New York the upper age of juvenile court jurisdiction has always been 15. This means that anyone 16 or older charged with any offense in New York is prosecuted in the criminal courts, while juvenile court jurisdiction is reserved for those under age 16. Historically, most states have had an upper age of 17 for juvenile court jurisdiction. Youths who are above the cut-off age in their state are not technically transferred from juvenile to criminal court—their cases simply originate in criminal court.[18] Nonetheless they are still juveniles (under 18) who are being prosecuted as adults.

Beyond these age-of-jurisdiction mechanisms, many youths are prosecuted in criminal courts through different specific transfer laws. There are three basic categories of transfer laws, or waiver provisions, as they are often called. *Judicial Waivers*, in general, put the transfer decision-making power in the hands of juvenile court judges. Different kinds of judicial waivers allow juvenile court judges different levels of discretion in transfer decisions: *Discretionary Judicial Waivers* authorize, but do not require, a juvenile court judge to transfer a case to criminal court under specific circumstances; *Presumptive Judicial Waivers* require that the juvenile defendant bear the burden of proof as to why the case should *not* be transferred to criminal court; and *Mandatory Judicial Waivers* require that a juvenile court judge transfer all cases that meet certain criteria. The only role of the juvenile court judge under this type of waiver is to determine if the specific transfer criteria have been met. Although these three types of judicial waivers offer different levels of judicial discretion, they all maintain the transfer decision-making process within the juvenile courts. *Prosecutorial Waiver* or *Direct File* provisions, in contrast, leave the decision to transfer up to the prosecutor. Prosecutors' decisions to transfer, unlike those of judges, are not subject to appeal.[19] Lastly, *Statutory Exclusion* laws legislatively mandate that cases meeting certain basic criteria be sent to the criminal courts. Under these laws, qualifying juveniles are automatically transferred to criminal court; in effect, their cases originate in criminal court.[20] All fifty states and the District of Columbia have different transfer laws, with many states utilizing a complex and confusing combination of these different waiver mechanisms, depending upon the age of the offender and/or the nature of the alleged offense.[21]

In addition to moving significantly larger numbers of kids into the adult system, the transfer laws passed in the 1990s also marked a clear shift away from judicial discretion–based transfer mechanisms and toward more prosecutorial-discretion and statutory-exclusion mechanisms. The Supreme Court's ruling in *Kent v. United States* may well have facilitated this shift. In *Kent* the Supreme Court reinforced the requirement of proper transfer hearings within the juvenile court before a case could be transferred to criminal court. However, this requirement only holds in cases of judicial waivers. Direct-file and statutory-exclusion provisions simply eliminate the need to satisfy this hearing requirement because such cases are not actually transferred from within the juvenile court. Since the 1990s, the power to decide whether an alleged young offender should be prosecuted as an adult has increasingly been taken away from the juvenile judiciary in favor of automatic transfer (i.e., required by legislation) or prosecutorial discretion.

The actual number of youths under 18 prosecuted in criminal courts is hard to assess because no comprehensive national data collection exist on the practice. Best estimates, however, suggest that around 200,000 kids under the age of 18 are prosecuted as adults each year in criminal adult court systems in the United States, comprising approximately 20–25% of all offenders under age 18.[22] These young defendants are quite diverse given that states have very different transfer laws. In some states one can be tried as an adult as young as age 10; others set the age as high as 15. Some states set no minimum age at all. It is often thought that laws allowing for or requiring the transfer of youths to adult courts pertain only to young people charged with violent felonies. This is not the case. The Office of Juvenile Justice and Delinquency Prevention's assessment of transfer laws in 1998 concluded: "A surprising number of [transfer laws] authorize criminal prosecution for nonviolent offenses."[23] An overview of states' transfer provisions by the National Center for Juvenile Justice found that as of 2008, twenty states allowed for or required criminal prosecution for drug offenses, twenty-two states required or allowed for criminal prosecution for "certain property offenses," and eleven states allowed for or required criminal prosecution for such offenses as "escape," "soliciting a minor to join a street gang," "auto theft," or "perjury."[24] The practice of criminally prosecuting juveniles in adult court systems is clearly not reserved for serious or violent offenders.

Retribution, Moral Panic, and the Criminalization of Youth

Two related forces help explain the rapid proliferation of retributive transfer legislation and the criminalization of youth throughout the 1990s—the increasing popularity of retributive criminal justice policies in general, and the "superpredator" moral panic that arose in the late 1980s and early 1990s. In many ways, the transfer legislation that proliferated in the 1990s was just one in the long list of punitive penal trends in the United States in the last three decades, including three-strikes laws, determinate sentencing, and the abolishment of parole. It is within this larger social, political, and legal context, including a thirty-plus-year trend toward mass incarceration and the fading of the "rehabilitative ideal,"[25] that the criminalization of youth was able to become normalized. Criminologists Franklin Zimring and Jeffrey Fagan, editors of a collection of writings on transfer law titled *The Changing Borders of Juvenile Justice: Transfer of Adolescents to the Criminal Court*, explain that harsh new transfer legislation was simply the latest in a long line of retributive trends: "Transferring from juvenile to criminal court was attractive in the 1990s because it meant removing cases from the only courts that had not joined the incarceration boom into a criminal court system that more accurately reflected the punitive temper of the times."[26] The proliferation of transfer legislation was part and parcel of a larger trend toward retribution that began across all institutions of social control during the 1970s, moving through the 1980s and 1990s and continuing today.

Within this larger "get tough" context, a spike in youth violence in some urban areas in the late 1980s and early 1990s spurred a moral panic that dramatically accelerated the pace and reach of transfer legislation and the criminalization of youth, particularly of male urban youth of color. Sociologist Stanley Cohen first defined "moral panic" in 1972 as when "a condition, episode, person or group of persons emerges to become defined as a threat to societal values and interests."[27] The late 1980s and early 1990s saw a limited uptick in violent crime attributable to juveniles in the United States, particularly an increase of gun violence among young black urban males. This upsurge in gun violence was localized and mainly attributable to the upheavals surrounding the introduction of crack cocaine in many cities around the country.[28] Alarming as this increase in violence must have been for residents of the affected urban communities, there was no evidence of a nationwide increase in overall juvenile crime or widespread violence, a fact that has been well-documented by several researchers.[29] Regardless of the reality, a moral panic took hold, focused on a so-called new generation of young "superpredators." Political scientist John DiIulio, in his now infamous 1995 article, struck the loudest "superpredator" alarm bell. He wrote in the *Weekly Standard*:

> The youth crime wave has reached horrific proportions from coast to coast . . . on the horizon, therefore, are tens of thousands of severely morally impoverished juvenile super-predators . . . the demographic bulge of the next 10 years will unleash an army of young male predatory street criminals who will make even the leaders of the Bloods and Crips . . . look tame.[30]

In their 1996 book *Body Count*, DiIulio and his co-authors William Bennett and John Walters wrote of "vicious, unrepentant, predatory street criminals."[31] A *New York Times* article that same year quoted law enforcement officials' concern over a "ticking time bomb" of rampant youth violence.[32] Other news stories focused on immoral young urban thugs traveling in "wolf packs" and "wilding in the streets."[33] David Myers, author of *Boys among Men: Trying and Sentencing Juveniles as Adults*, argues that "by 1995, at the height of the superpredator panic, it appeared to many that the only thing that could save society was the further punishment and incarceration of morally depraved youths who were violently taking over the nation's streets."[34] This discourse of fear fueled the fire of punitive transfer legislation. Two important features of the superpredator moral panic must be noted. First, political and media discourse at the time tended to conflate the concept of *juvenile crime* with the concept of serious *youth violence*.[35] Juvenile delinquency experts know well that the vast majority of offenses committed by youths involve property and public disorder crimes, not violent crime. They also know that most offending youths eventually "age-out" of criminal behaviors and do not go on to become adult offenders. Thus, while there is and always has been a segment of the young offender population involved in serious violent crime, it does not represent the majority of such cases. This differentiation was almost wholly absent from the superpredator discourse.

The second important feature of the superpredator moral panic is that it was, in both covert and overt ways, a racialized moral panic, highly attentive to a perceived threat of hyperviolence perpetrated by poor urban black and Hispanic young males. These two features of the panic tended to mutually reinforce one another. The "problem of youth violence" became code for "dangerous young black or brown men." This, in turn, engendered fear-soaked demands for harsh and swift polices of retribution and incapacitation. The conflation of "youth violence" with all other types of juvenile crime tended to expand these fear-infused demands for harsh punishment to all delinquent youth, violent and nonviolent alike.[36]

These mutually reinforcing forces encouraged and legitimized transfer legislation in the 1990s, and they continue to shape the discourse regarding transgressive youth today. The petty, misdemeanor, and nonviolent acts of delinquency by juveniles—the majority of crime attributable to youth—rarely make the news or garner the attention of publicity-seeking politicians. The statistical, linguistic, and symbolic conflation of the vast array of petty juvenile offenders that the system encounters with the real but limited number of hardened, violent repeat adolescent offenders was, and is still, annoyingly common.[37] Zimring reminds us that "more than 80 percent of all juvenile law violations are not violent,"[38] yet "youth crime" and "youth violence" often become linguistically and symbolically interchangeable, resulting in political rhetoric and policy initiatives that, while couched in terms of a response to the perceived threat of youth *violence*, result in broad policy written for all juvenile crime. This practice serves to criminalize all transgressive youth as members of one group of irredeemable, violent predators. The further conflation of ideas regarding youth crime with images of violent urban males of color tends to inappropriately criminalize all male youth of color as a cohesive, menacing group. In his article "The Racial Politics of Youth Crime," sociologist Victor Rios cites the racist legacy of the moral panic: "The superpredator thesis exacerbated the youth crime problem leading to the hypercriminalization of black and Latino youth."[39]

Impact of Transfer Laws on Case Processing

Punitive transfer legislation flourished in a time of misconception about the amount and percentage of crime attributable to young people, compounded by mounting fear of the urban nonwhite male teenager, all set within a larger trend of retributive justice policy and the resulting mass-incarceration movement. Despite the marked drop in youth crime since those years[40] and the refutation, even by DiIullio, of the supposed impending threat of the superpredator, these laws and their influence on ideas of youth justice remain largely intact. Across the 1990s, changes to transfer laws substantially rewrote legal and social policy in regard to youth, which in turn has altered the legal, social, and criminological discourse on appropriate or inappropriate responses to youth violence, juvenile delinquency, the degree of culpability among the young, and their perceived amenability to treatment. Although some states have begun to rethink their transfer laws and to focus more resources and attention on the rehabilitation of court-involved youths, the policy changes ushered in during the 1990s are still very much with us. They have served to routinize the criminal prosecution of youth, making it a common institutional practice across the country. Laurence Steinberg and Elizabeth Cauffman, leading researchers on adolescent culpability, have called this criminal court net-widening "a fundamental challenge to the very premise on which the juvenile court was founded: that adolescents and adults are different in ways that warrant their differential treatment under the law."[41]

This normalization of the prosecution of youth in adult courts has created a unique category of defendant in criminal courtrooms—what I prefer to call the "adult-juvenile." An adult-juvenile is a person under the age of 18 caught in legal limbo: legally labeled within the justice system as an adult for the purposes of criminal prosecution, yet still defined as a minor in all other legal and social settings. Regardless of which of the various transfer mechanisms described above are at work in a given jurisdiction, the criminal prosecution of adolescents produces a range of challenges for judges, defense attorneys, prosecutors, and other criminal-court personnel assigned to handle such cases.[42] Aaron Kupchik's *Judging Juveniles: Prosecuting Adolescents in Adult and Juvenile Courts*, published in 2006, provides unique insight into these challenges. Kupchik sought a better understanding of the criminal prosecution of adolescents, but rather than focusing solely on outcome measures such as recidivism rates, he compared the actual day-to-day operations of a juvenile court in New Jersey and a criminal court in New York City. Because of the different laws that prevail in each state, the two courts handled cases of youths of about the same age charged with comparable offenses. Utilizing court observations, interviews with different court actors, and multivariate analysis, he investigated how court actors in each of the jurisdictions responded to young offenders and examined the attitudes court actors had regarding notions of youthfulness and adolescent culpability.

In the juvenile court he studied, Kupchik discovered a juvenile-justice model of case processing with a focus on individualized justice and rehabilitation. In the criminal court, however, he found that the court utilized both a juvenile-justice model and a criminal-court model focused on due process and punishment. In this hybrid model of case processing, which Kupchik refers to as a "sequential model of justice," the criminal court he observed utilized a criminal-justice model during the initial phases of case processing, and then employed a juvenile-justice model during the sentencing phase. Kupchik found that the court actors in both the juvenile and criminal court jurisdictions held similar attitudes regarding young offenders, their "youthfulness," and their degree of criminal culpability. Thus, the adolescent defendants in the criminal court, although legally labeled as adults, nonetheless retained their social status as adolescents—a reality that court actors could not simply ignore. Kupchik concludes that the court actors in the criminal court developed case-processing methods that accommodated their own social understandings of the "youthfulness" of young defendants, regardless of the legal requirement that they be prosecuted as adults.

From these findings, Kupchik theorizes that court actors involved in the criminal prosecution of adolescents modify their case processing to accommodate their understanding of adolescent offenders and youth culpability. Regardless of the mandates of transfer laws, criminal-court actors must find ways to try to reconcile the inherent contradictions at work in the criminal prosecution of kids. He speculates that courts with different philosophies and cultures, in different jurisdictions, and with different prevailing transfer laws, will find different mechanism through which to cope with these contradictions. That is, different courts will find different ways to "filter" transfer laws.[43]

My ethnographic account of the Manhattan Youth Part extends Kupchik's research by documenting the particular way the Youth Part chose to "filter" New York's transfer law. Through a comparison of Kupchik's findings with my own, I am able to show the similarities and differences between the case processing in the different criminal courts we studied and thus confirm Kupchik's assertions that criminal courts must wrestle with the contradictions inherent in the criminal prosecution of adolescents, and that different courts will do this in different ways. While I found many similarities in case-processing styles between the Manhattan Youth Part and the criminal court Kupchik observed, I also found numerous differences. Thus, this ethnography, in dialogue with and expanding upon Kupchik's research, furthers our understanding of how criminal courts grapple with the reality of trying youths as adults in the day-to-day practice of law.

Researching the Manhattan Youth Part

I came to the Manhattan Youth Part by accident. When I told a graduate school advisor that I was interested in issues related to youth and the criminal justice system, he put me in touch with a colleague of his, a professor at another university. That professor, after meeting with me and suggesting several books and articles, invited me to join her class on an upcoming visit to the courts. I knew nothing of the court system in New York and how it treated young offenders, nor did I know about the Manhattan Youth Part, the court we visited. I understood little of what legally transpired in those first three hours I was in the court, but I left knowing that something important was taking place there, and that I had to come back. A phone call to the judge's office a few months later led to an in-person meeting with him, during which he quickly granted me permission to observe the court formally.

My first formal observations of the Manhattan Youth Part took place between April 2001 and March 2003, during which time I sat in on twenty-five "calendar days," the one day a week (usually Fridays) set aside for general case processing. I was given a seat in the jury box, which served as overflow seating for the cramped courtroom, in order to observe and stay out of the way. Calendar-day sessions generally ran for three to four hours, with anywhere from fifteen to forty cases before the court. More extensive field research took place throughout 2005, during which time I observed an additional twenty-five calendar days and conducted open-ended interviews with various courtroom actors—defense attorneys, ATI program representatives, a representative from the district attorney's office, the judge, and members of the judge's staff.

My original plan to conduct open-ended interviews with juvenile defendants involved with the Youth Part had to be abandoned as the field research unfolded. Initially, no defense attorneys trusted me to interview their clients. This obstacle was eventually overcome as I established rapport with many attorneys and other court actors over my considerable time in the Youth Part. However, it also became quite clear that interviewing defendants I might later encounter in court during observation could have possible undue influence on their cases. Judge Corriero noticed almost everything that went on in his court, and I could easily imagine a scenario in which the judge could ascertain that I had interviewed a particular kid. Thus, I chose not to attempt any interviews with defendants during the time of my court observations. After court observations were completed, I attempted to interview kids who had previously been through the Youth Part. This line of research also, unfortunately, had to be abandoned when coordination with the necessary city agencies proved too difficult. It is a regrettable limitation of this study that the voices of the young people involved could not be more prominent. In order to remedy this deficit, I have endeavored to highlight, as often as possible, defendants' voices from their time in court. I was able to trace many defendants' progress through the court and create "courtroom narratives" of their time there. Such narratives allowed for an understanding of the progress of different defendants' cases and the individualized justice approaches employed by the court.

No recording devices are permitted in New York courts, so I relied on extensive note-taking. As court ethnographer M. A. Bortner has pointed out, an observer can sit scribbling notes in a courtroom without eliciting much attention or suspicion.[44] Despite developing a shorthand specific to the types of action and dialogue common in the courtroom, I was often unable to document verbatim the sometimes lengthy exchanges that took place between the judge and the defendants and others in the court. For many of these instances I obtained court transcripts in order to provide more accurate renderings of discourse and interactions. While court transcripts often contained details of verbal exchanges not in my field notes, there were occasions when my field notes contained parts of conversations that did not make it into the official transcripts. By combining the "official" information contained in court transcripts with my field-note data, including details of nonverbal interactions, I was able to provide a fuller account of courtroom events than either my field notes or court transcripts could offer alone.

Although the Manhattan Youth Part is an open criminal court whose proceedings are a matter of public record, I have, nonetheless, taken measures to protect the identities of the people written about, most especially the young defendants. Many youths who came before the court had the possibility of obtaining an alternative sentence and a sealed conviction. This would mean that they would not carry the stigma of a felony record into adulthood. I wanted to make sure that the reporting of my research would not reveal any stigmatizing information about the youths I observed. I have tried as much as possible to represent the look and feel of courtroom interactions but have purposely left out dates and specifics such as the names of schools or particular agencies. Judge Corriero has generously given me explicit permission to use his real name. All other names used are pseudonyms.

In addition to Kupchik's research, which was especially instructive, both methodologically and theoretically, this ethnography has been richly informed by prior ethnographies done in juvenile and criminal court settings by Robert Emerson, Mark Jacobs, and M. A. Bortner, as well as the detailed court research done by journalists Edward Hume and Steve Bogira.[45] In addition, Caroline DeBrovner's examination of specific therapeutic justice practices in the Manhattan Youth Part helped frame my discussion of court interactions in chapter four.

Terminology

While it is common among criminal justice researchers and practitioners to refer to court-involved youths using terms such as "offenders," "juvenile offenders," or "young offenders," I have chosen to avoid much of this terminology when writing about the youths in the Manhattan Youth Part. I opt instead for the more descriptive term "defendant" because it best describes the role of the adolescents observed within the legal setting of the court. Technically, *offender* means "one that commits an offense," whereas *defendant* means "the party against whom a criminal or civil action is brought."[46] *Defendant* is a descriptive legal term, while *offender* implies, and by definition assumes, criminal wrongdoing. This distinction is important because, as justice studies scholar Michael Coyle argues, the "*language habits* of multiple 'criminal justice' discourses" all too often go unexamined and un-interrogated as to their potential impact and meaning.[47] Given the overwhelming tendency—in the criminal justice system, in academia, and in news and popular media—to criminalize urban youth of color and to assume that any youth caught up in the criminal justice system must be, by nature of that involvement, an "offender," careful attention to the nuances of terminology is not only warranted but required.

In addition, while many terms could be used to describe the young defendants who come before the Youth Part—adolescents, juveniles, children, teenagers—I most frequently use "kid" or "kids," simply because this is the way that court actors most commonly referred to Youth Part defendants. Phrases such as "these kids," "our kids," or "I have a kid" were used repeatedly in conversations by the judge, attorneys, court officers, detention facility personnel, program representatives, and parents. Also, "kid" is what the average person would use if he or she saw any one of these youngsters on the street, as in, "Yesterday I saw this kid who was wearing a t-shirt that came down to his knees." By using common descriptors, rather than those inscribed by the criminal justice system, it is my intention to stand in contrast to the majority of criminal justice research on court-involved youths, which tends to depict them more as criminal justice system objects than as real human subjects.

Race, Gender, and Class

It should come as no surprise that, like other retributive criminal justice policies (mandatory minimums, determinate sentencing, three-strikes laws, and the war on drugs), transfer laws have had an alarmingly disproportionate impact on poor youth of color. Several studies since the transfer law boom of the 1990s have documented the racial disparity in the practice of trying youths as adults at all stages in the process and across a variety of transfer mechanisms.[48] In his survey of the available data on the disproportional impact of transfer on youth of color, David Myers found that "virtually all studies that measure the race of waived offenders find that nonwhites (especially African Americans) are highly overrepresented, usually making up 50% to 95% of transferred youth."[49] A 1999 study in Florida found that black youth were 2.3 times as likely to be transferred as white youth.[50] Another study found that in 1996 minority youth in Los Angeles County were 2.5 times more likely to be transferred to adult court than white youth, even when controlling for the seriousness of the crime.[51] A study of Illinois transfer law found that in Cook County in 1999–2001, 99.6% of all automatic transfers were of nonwhite youth.[52] A 1992 study of New York City, which is governed solely by statutory exclusion provisions, showed that 96% of the juveniles required by law to be prosecuted as adults that year were nonwhite.[53] My field research supports this finding. In all the days that I observed, I saw exactly one white defendant come before the court.

Nearly all of the young defendants who came before the Manhattan Youth Part during my observations, and all whose court experiences are accounted for in this book, were black and/or Hispanic males between the ages of 13 and 19 who came largely from poor families and often live in distressed urban communities. While there were girls who came before the court, they made up a very small percentage of cases. Thus, this book is fundamentally an examination of the Youth Part's experiment in attempting to provide legal alternatives for black and Hispanic boys from poor urban communities facing felony charges and possible incarceration. The racial and class disparities encountered in the Manhattan Youth Part reflect the glaringly disproportional representation of poor urban black and Hispanic men and boys more generally throughout criminal justice systems in the United States.[54]

Given these realities of race and class, any examination of criminal justice systems, particularly in urban jurisdictions, must remain cognizant of the function of race within any and all courtroom settings. One cannot, should not, research, theorize, or write about judicial processes in U.S. courts without researching, theorizing, and writing about race. The very real danger for academics, researchers, and those who work in such settings is that we may become so accustomed to seeing the black and brown faces of criminal defendants and their families that it becomes a given, nothing much to note, simply routine. It is for these reasons that particular attention is paid to race in the descriptions of the court throughout the text.

The Law in Action

In a 1955 book titled *Youth and the Law*, Frederick Ludwig offered a simple yet compelling statement:

> Serious consideration of what the law ought to be cannot begin without comprehension of what the law is. Existing law cannot be understood merely from collections of statutes in books. It must be explored in action, especially in the light of the exercise of the vast discretion vested in administrators.[55]

This ethnography of the Manhattan Youth Part's experiment in justice is an account of the law in action. It is an account of the inherent contradictions imbedded within punitive transfer laws. It is an account of how one court developed case-processing strategies to respond realistically to those contradictions. It is an account of the creativity that lives within discretion. It is an account of child-saving, of giving troubled kids a second, sometimes even a third, chance at rehabilitation. It is an account of how, with an emphasis on the now passé ideals of the rehabilitation of wayward youth, one court choose to exemplify the best promise of the early juvenile court movement a century after its founding. It is an account of an attempt by one group of legal actors, amidst two decades of retributive transfer policies and the ongoing criminalization of urban youth of color, to try to bring a dose of humanity, dignity, and rationality into the daily practice of transfer law. If successful, this ethnography provides an opportunity to reconsider what the appropriate legal response to adolescent offending ought to be.

Chapter one provides a description of a typical calendar day in the Manhattan Youth Part courtroom and shows how delay, routinization, and drama characterize the court on a daily basis. I also explain New York's transfer law, how this specialized court came into being, and the occasionally would the "assigned assistant," the ADA assigned to prosecute a particular case, appear for that specific case on the calendar.

Defense attorneys, on the other hand, came and went as their clients' cases were called—carrying legal-size folders in their arms or in briefcases, temporarily taking up residence at the defense table where their client sat. Most defense attorneys in the court were from the public defender agencies in the county—the New York County Defender Services, the Legal Aid Society, and Neighborhood Defender Services of Harlem—or from the pool of private lawyers who take on indigent cases. In addition to defense attorneys, ATI and other social service program representatives often stepped forward when a defendant's case was called. Since these representatives didn't have an assigned space in the court, they tended to occupy the area between the defense lawyer's table and the ADA's table, carrying all their paperwork in their arms.

Three more wooden desks in varying sizes along the courtroom's left wall were home to the head court officer, the court clerk, and an assistant to the court attorney. A few padded chairs were available for use by the Spanish interpreter or by one or more of the five or six uniformed court officers whenever they were not escorting, cuffing, or uncuffing incarcerated defendants, passing paperwork, or directing traffic.

The judge's bench at the front of the room was made of dark polished wood. Behind it stood two flagpoles—one with a U.S. flag, the other a New York State flag—and on the wall, the words "In God We Trust" were raised in dark wooden letters. The judge's law clerk sat on his right, and on the judge's left was the witness box, which sat empty on calendar days. In the far right corner of the courtroom, a wooden door provided passage to the unused jury room and to the heavy, locked metal door through which the court officers escorted incarcerated defendants.

Other than the paneled wall behind the judge's bench, the top half of the courtroom's walls were a bright, glaring white, while the bottom halves were all a dark, polished wood. Overly bright fluorescent lighting created a glare off of everything: the white walls, the polished wood, the court officers' badges. The floor was not carpeted and the acoustics were less than ideal, resulting in a slight yet constant echo. Summer or winter, the room tended toward the cool side. The jangle of the court officers' keys was an omnipresent sound in the cramped courtroom, as was the frequent clanging of the metal door in the back and the intermittent clicking of handcuffs being put on or taken off. The shuffling of paper and of people continuously coming and going and moving around the court added to the din of controlled chaos on calendar days.

Calendar days were full of mundane legal case-processing activity, such as ordering reports from the probation department, making arrangements for a youth to have an intake appointment with an ATI program, or waiting for the court officers to "bring up" the next remanded kid. These were the kids who were detained, not released on bail or on their own recognizance (ROR). These kids were held at one of the secure juvenile facilities in the city and needed to be transported to the court whenever their cases were on the docket. Court workers often had to wait for kids to be delivered to the courtroom from holding cells located in the interior of the court building. Waiting was simply part of the culture of the court for all participants. While waiting in the hard benches in the audience area, some family members would read the free newspapers handed out at the subway stations or whisper among themselves. Younger children often fell asleep on shoulders or in laps or tucked up under a mother's or grandmother's arm. There was a good deal of yawning and the occasional nap. Many of the lawyers and ATI program representatives who had to wait for their clients' cases to be called would work on the daily crossword puzzle or read a novel. Waiting was just part of the job.

In addition to the normal delays that are part and parcel of the mundane routine of a working court, calendar days in the Youth Part were often marked by further instances of frustrating bureaucratic delay:

- A defendant's case gets called but his lawyer hasn't arrived yet, so the case has to be recalled.
- A remanded defendant is brought from the back in cuffs, escorted to his chair and uncuffed, only to be informed that his lawyer is busy with another case and that the court has to put the young man's case over for another three weeks, after which he is recuffed and led back out.
- A case is brought before the court four weeks after a series of reports were ordered only to learn that the department that prepares the reports needs more time. The case is adjourned for a future date.
- A case is called and the defense attorney reports that no movement has been made since the last date because the ADA assigned to the case has not returned her calls.
- The assigned ADA on a case no longer works for the district attorney's office and a new assistant has to be assigned.

by 5 o'clock, so if you come in and you take the time to talk to a kid about how they are doing in school and everything, it's time-consuming. So you wouldn't ordinarily do that in a part where you just have enormous numbers. So [the kids] get lost, and that's why I thought the youth part would be of value in itself, in that it would commit us to focus more time on this very, very vulnerable category of offender.

In his desire to make the Youth Part court more intimate and less intimidating, the judge dispensed with the formality of having everyone stand when his arrival was announced. Instead, he began a court session simply by walking into the courtroom and saying, "Good morning, everybody," as he took his seat at the bench. From the moment he arrived in the courtroom, Corriero was aware of what was going on and who was in the room. He was very attentive to the details of what went on in his court. At the beginning of a session, he would survey the jury seats and the audience to see who was in attendance. Over the course of the day, he would notice if Ramon, a 16-year-old Hispanic boy with a case before the court, had his girlfriend with him in the audience. Or he would notice if a kid had fallen asleep in the audience while waiting for his case to be called. The judge might even call out to the kid by name, asking him what time he had gone to bed the night before.

One calendar day, the judge was standing in the back entrance to the court before taking the bench, and he saw a particular defendant sitting in the audience.

"Malik, how are you feeling?" the judge called across the courtroom to him.

"A little sore but alright," the young black man responded. The judge nodded. Later, when the young man's case was called, it was revealed that Malik had recently been released from the hospital after having been shot in the same incident in which his brother had been shot and killed.

On another calendar day, a Hispanic mother was waiting in the audience with her young daughter, who looked to be about 10 or 11 years old. They had been sitting there for a couple of hours when the mother left the courtroom, leaving the young girl sitting in the audience. During some down time between cases, the judge asked the young girl who she was there for. She sat up straight in her seat and said her brother's name. The judge then asked, "And where is your mother?"

"She went downstairs to get a drink," the girl replied.

"Isn't today a school day?" the judge asked in a steady and patient voice. The young girl nodded.

"Shouldn't you be in school then?" the judge asked.

"My mom has to find me a school," the girl replied. Given that it was the very start of the school year and many kids were still working out placement with the city's education department, the judge accepted the girl's statement, nodded, said, "Okay," and went back to the business of the court.

One day, my own actions caught the keen attention of the judge. I always attempted while observing the court to remain as stoic as possible and not telegraph any immediate reactions I might have to activity in the room. On one particularly tough calendar day, characterized by several difficult cases and emotional ups and downs, the judge saw me inadvertently rub my forehead after an especially challenging case.

"That one give you a headache too, Carla?" he said aloud, smiling across the courtroom. I returned his smile and nodded, startled at his ability to keep track of such nuances amid the borderline chaos of a typical calendar day.

Race, Class, and Gender in the Court

Manhattan Youth Part defendants and their family members were almost never white. As stated earlier, I saw one white kid come before the court in all the time I observed the part. A seasoned defense attorney with twenty years' experience defending kids in the county told me that in all her years she has had only one white defendant. Data on indictments bears this racial disparity out—between 1984 and 2004, white defendants made up no more than 4% of total JO indictments in Manhattan. The vast majority of defendants in the Youth Part were also male, although girls did come before the court from time to time.[13]

In contrast to the predominately black and/or Hispanic kids and family members, defense attorneys, the ADAs, and ATI representatives tended to be white and, by the definition of their jobs, well-educated and middle-class. While there was diversity among this group of professionals, over the time that I observed the court they ran about 80% white and close to 50% female. There was considerably more racial, gender, and ethnic diversity among the court's civil servants, such as the court reporters, court clerks, the judge's staff, and the court officers (COs).

The physical space of the court and the movements of the various people within it reinforced the race and gender dynamics. It was common to have an audience full of low-income people of color and a jury box full of predominately white and/or middle-class educated professionals. Kids were allowed to pass through the gate that separated the audience from the main part of the courtroom only when their cases were called, and were required to quickly pass back out. Family members were never allowed to pass through the gate. The predominately white professionals were able to come and go quite freely through the gate. In this way, the low walls that demarcated the spaces in the courtroom reproduced the lines of separation in class, race, and prestige found outside the courthouse. Because of these physical demarcations of space and the racial and gender dynamics of the court, it was not at all uncommon to witness scenes like these from my field notes:

> In the inner part of the court, a young [remanded] black male kid is surrounded by three white male court officers, his white female lawyer, a white female ATI rep, a white female district attorney, a white male judge, and a white female law clerk while his black mother looks on from behind the low wall in the audience.

> A black male defendant's attorney asked if they could approach as soon as the case was called. The white male ADA, the white female Legal Aid defense attorney, the white female ATI representative and the white female Legal Aid social worker were all huddled around the bench discussing the case with the white male judge and his white female law clerk. The young black kid sat slumped, alone in his chair watching the group of adults huddled around the bench deciding his fate. No family members were standing for him today.

While not all cases before the court were as starkly racially polarized as these, an overall fact of the court was that it was largely white professionals, along with a handful of nonwhite middle-class professionals, who decided the fate of poor, black, and/or Hispanic youth within the court.

The INs and the OUTs

The kids that came before the court on calendar days were either "IN" or "OUT." OUT was the shorthand term for those who had been released from custody and enrolled in ATI programs. IN defendants were those kids who were remanded, incarcerated. Many kids would spend time both IN and

OUT before their cases were finally resolved. Some never did any time IN and those with the most serious charges, of course, never got OUT.

When an OUT defendant's case was called ("Calendar Number 14, indictment number 9909 of 2004, Jeremy Sanchez," the clerk would call), kids who knew the ropes would walk through the low wooden gate and take their place next to their attorney and ATI representative with the ease and confidence of a regular. After several months of interaction with the court, these kids had learned the basic rules—to look at the judge when he was speaking to them, to answer loudly enough to be heard, to say "yes" instead of "yeah," and to not chew gum in court. They knew the judge would ask the parent standing in the audience how the kid was doing at home and that the answer would be important. They knew that the report from the ATI or drug treatment program or their report card from school would be scrutinized, and that the judge would praise or admonish them accordingly. If a kid was doing well in a program, the judge might say: "Keep up the good work. Keep doing well and you'll get probation." If all reports were good, he might say, with sincerity, "I'm proud of you," before scheduling the next control date—generally a month away, sometimes longer if a kid was doing particularly well. If the judge wanted to keep a close watch on a kid, he would schedule a shorter date—one or two weeks away. If an ATI program report reflected problems such as a positive drug test, missed curfews, or missed days in school, the judge might change his tone: "Do we have a problem here?" he might ask, or "Do you want me to have to lock you up? Then do what you are supposed to do."

An IN defendant, on the other hand, entered the courtroom through the back door in handcuffs. He was escorted to his seat by two court officers, one in front and one behind. Sometimes, a kid who was IN was facing more serious charges than those who were OUT, but often he was just in the early stages of his case processing and would be released into an ATI program as soon as all the reports were in, necessary arrangements were made, and the court thought that he had spent enough time IN. Some kids were IN because of mental health concerns, or due to delays in arranging appropriate program placement or establishing stable living arrangements. Very occasionally, an IN defendant would be awaiting trial.

Those kids new to being locked up were always easy to spot. When escorted into the courtroom by the court officers, these novices tended not to take a single step unless directed to; they waited for instruction from a court officer at every turn. They had to be told by a court officer to sit down once the handcuffs were taken off; they had to be told to pull the chair all the way in toward the table when they sat down. A tinge of fear was often noticeable on their young faces, even as they attempted to be stoic. When they were done, they again had to be told to stand and put their hands behind their backs for the cuffs to be put back on, to be directed where to walk, when and where to stop. They often appeared intimidated, overwhelmed.

Those kids who had been IN awhile moved through the courtroom with more ease. These more experienced kids appeared less intimidated, less overwhelmed. They may not have known all the rules yet, but they were more accustomed to the court officers telling them what to do. They had learned to take their hands out of their pockets when they were standing before Judge Corriero. They knew to say "yes" instead of "yeah." They knew to say "no" not "nah." They knew to look at the judge when he addressed them. There was less hesitancy in their movements.

There were also some "veterans" among the INs. These seasoned young men knew exactly how and where to walk, how fast to walk, where to stop. They knew to pull their chair in and did it unconsciously. They would automatically put their hands behind their backs when they stood to go, lifting their right wrist slightly away from their body, which made it easier for the court officer to slide the first of the cuffs on. Many of these young veterans assumed a "prison stance" even when it was not required of them: even when uncuffed, they would automatically put their hands behind their backs whenever they were standing. They naturally fell into the posture that cuffing creates—a slightly forward shoulders and chest—even when no physical apparatus constricted their movements, their young bodies silently broadcasting their carceral conditioning.

Judge Corriero was always adamant that the handcuffs had to be taken off whenever an IN kid was in the courtroom. Even if a kid was being brought in just to be told that his case would have to be put over for another time—a process that takes no more than thirty seconds—because his lawyer was working on a trial, the judge would make sure that the cuffs were taken off for that brief time. When I asked why he took so much care in this regard he explained it this way:

> I want to make the point of treating a young person with dignity, even those who may be guilty because they're coming back at some point. And you never know what it is that will ignite that, perhaps,

little flicker of consciousness or conscientiousness or whatever. That's me. . . . As a general rule I want the handcuffs off, I want to be able to communicate with them, I want them to feel that—I mean it's very hard to communicate with someone where you're the boss and they're in handcuffs. And especially when you think of all the racial aspects of what we're doing, I mean, my God, a little sensitivity to that reality.

On those rare occasions when an IN defendant was brought before the court in shackles, the judge would insist that they be taken off in the back room. When asked directly about the use of shackles by some correctional agencies, he said that while there were rare occasions when a kid was violent or when shackles may be necessary, in general,

I think it is totally dehumanizing . . . and what we are really trying to do is uplift so many of these kids, let them get a sense of self-respect so that they would respect themselves and respect others. That's what we are trying to do in many ways. . . . I mean this is America, you are coming here with a presumption of innocence. I just don't think that's the way to do things in a courtroom where you have kids and families and poor people who always are up against the bureaucracy, always up against the government, and I want them to feel that there can be a firm yet compassionate response to the situations that they find themselves in.

IN defendants' brief time in the courtroom was often marked by creative attempts to communicate with family members in the audience. IN defendants and their families were not allowed any physical or verbal contact in the courtroom. Nonetheless, an amazing amount of communication took place between these kids and those who came to stand for them. As IN defendants were being lead in and out, they had a brief opportunity to make eye contact with family members. Mothers, grandmothers, or aunts would often say phrases out loud such as "I love you" or "Te Amo" or nod or smile as their son was being led in or out of the courtroom. Often the kid would make eye contact and nod by throwing his head back a bit and jutting his chin forward a little. Sometimes he would say out loud, "I love you" or "Call me" or "Mama, don't cry" as he was being led out. Sometimes he would simply mouth the words "I love you" or blow a quick kiss back to a family member. Sometimes family and kid simply held eye contact for as long as they could. Sometimes there were smiles; sometimes there were tears, on one or both sides.

By the time a defendant had reached the metal door in the back of the room, his eyes were forward again, minding the directions of the court officers. Family members would often linger, watching until the last moment they could see the back of their child's head, sometimes a little while longer, staring into the space where the child had just been. Younger brothers, sisters, nieces, nephews, or cousins, less inclined to restraint, would often smile and wave energetically to an IN defendant as he was brought in or out of the courtroom.

Many family members whose kids had been IN for some time learned that if they sat off to the right side of the audience, they would be in the line of sight with the back hallway where IN defendants waited for their turn before the judge. From this vantage point, families could see and interact nonverbally with kids for a longer time. The space I normally occupied when observing court, located in the back row of the jury box, often put me directly in this line of sight, so I had to be mindful of not blocking it. I witnessed some court officers purposefully shift their position slightly in one direction or another so that a kid and family could see each other. As defendants were still cuffed when they were in the chairs by the back door, they had only their facial expressions, the set of their shoulders, a tilt of the head, or the mouthing of short phrases to convey information. Defendants would smile to their families, or sometimes frown as if asking a question that only a family member could comprehend. Many family members, especially mothers, were adept at reading their kids; meanings I could only guess at often appeared clear as day between a mother and her son.

Sometimes a family member would mouth the words "How are you?" to which a kid would nod his head up and down as if to say "I'm OK." Twice I saw a mother question the bruise on a young defendant's face by raising her hand up to her own face, brushing it along her own eye or cheekbone with a questioning expression on her face. Both times, in an unsuccessful attempt to alleviate a mother's concern, the kid shook his head back and forth as if to say, "Don't worry about it, I'm fine." Gestures of reassurance were common and went both ways—family reassuring kids, kids reassuring family.

Occasionally a kid would not make any eye contact with his people during his visit to court—purposefully not looking up when brought in and keeping his eyes straight ahead or aimed at the floor as he was led out. Sometimes family members would leave quickly before their kid had left the courtroom. Sometimes there was only a long, stoic stare between family and kids, or a frown, or a quick glancing away, evidence of anger, disappointment, frustration, loss of hope, hardenings.

All these personal, familial exchanges of love, joy, sorrow, anger, worry, and resignation took place with little or no words, without privacy, in the glaring light of this public, institutional space. In creative, adaptive ways, both IN kids and their family members engaged in an abundance of communication in a place where they were not officially allowed to communicate. In so doing, they developed ways to maintain familial ties and human connection and to claim, if only temporarily, a space for their family within the court.

Judge Corriero often noticed these nonverbal exchanges. One Friday, he seized upon a family's nonverbal interaction as an opportunity for what he would describe as a "teachable moment."

Calvin, a 14-year-old black boy, IN, was waiting in a chair by the back door of the court for his case to be called. His mother, seated within his line of sight in the audience, held up a very newborn baby, dressed in blue for her son to see. Calvin, still in handcuffs, grinned widely. A few minutes later, when Calvin's case was called, the judge asked him about the newborn.

"Is that your baby brother?" the judge asked.

"Yes," Calvin answered.

"Fourteen years from now do you want him to be standing where you are?" the judge asked in a slightly stern tone.

"No," the boy said.

"Well, who's gonna teach him?" the judge asked. "You're gonna have to be a role model for him. You see, this isn't just about you. You think it's easy for your mother to have to come down here after just having had a baby? You think it is good that this is where your baby brother has to come in his first days of life, with you in handcuffs? You think that is a good thing?" the judge asked, his voice growing louder as he spoke.

"No!" Calvin whimpered.

"I want you to think about that," the judge said before scheduling the next control date for the young man and moving on to the next case. Court officers then put the handcuffs back on and Calvin was led out of the courtroom with his mother, his newborn brother in her arms, looking on.

The JOs and the Non-JOs

Although not immediately obvious, not all defendants in the Youth Part were Juvenile Offenders as defined by New York State Law. This is one of the more confusing details of the Youth Part. The part handled cases of 13-, 14-, and 15-year-olds charged as JOs as well as those of their codefendants, regardless of age. Young people, more so than adults, are prone to co-offend, committing crimes in groups, often with people of a similar age. Many cases before the Youth Part were co-offender cases.[14] For example, if three young men, one 14, one 17, and one 18, were arrested and indicted for robbery, all of them would come to the Youth Part even though the 14-year-old was the only JO under state law. Since New York State has long set the age of legal "adulthood" at 16, the other two youths are already technically, legally "adults." In contrast, if three 17-year-olds were to be indicted for the same crime, their cases could end up in any of the all-purpose parts in the criminal court. In an even more complicated scenario, if a 12-year-old, a 14-year-old, and a 17-year-old were arrested as codefendants on a robbery charge, the 12-year-old would be processed as a Juvenile Delinquent in the Family Court, the 14-year-old as a JO in the criminal court, and the 17-year-old as a "non-JO" adult in the criminal court.

The Youth Part, then, handled cases of Juvenile Offenders (13–15 years old) and some non-JOs (generally ages 16–21).[15] According to Judge Corriero, the Youth Part had, "on average, about 125 new Juvenile Offender cases —individuals who fall into that category—a year. Plus triple that number perhaps for co-defendants." This complicated division of legal categorization resulted in a unique population in the Youth Part. The cases being handled here were all serious cases; regardless of age or legal status, all defendants who came before the Youth Part had been indicted for one of the JO-listed crimes: murder, arson, kidnapping, aggravated sexual abuse, attempted kidnapping, attempted murder, burglary, manslaughter, rape, criminal sexual act, robbery, assault, and criminal possession of a weapon. Unlike in the Family Court or the other criminal courts, you wouldn't find a simple case of marijuana possession, vandalism, or trespassing in the Manhattan Youth Part.

To look at any given male defendant standing before the judge on a calendar day, one was hard-pressed to know whether he was a JO or a non-JO. They almost all wore the same baggy street clothes, popular sneaker brands, and hairstyles (although some did arrive in suits or shirts and ties). Since adolescents mature at varying rates, signs of physical maturity such as height, facial hair, or a deep voice could be highly misleading.[16] Over my time in the court, I repeatedly attempted to guess the age of a kid by his physical appearance—and I was repeatedly wrong. There were baby-faced 18-year-olds, 14-year-olds with full beards, exceedingly tall, mature-looking 16-year-olds, and 15-year-olds who didn't look a day over 12.

JOs and non-JOs have different sentencing structures under the law, are allowed very different plea-bargaining options, are housed in different types of detention facilities, and are often diverted into different types of ATI programs. This was another confusing aspect of the Manhattan Youth Part. The sentencing structure for JOs is an indeterminate one in which the court imposes a sentence of a range of time within the dictates of the law. In contrast, for those over 16 convicted of similar felonies there is a determinate sentencing structure in which the court imposes a sentence of fixed duration.[17] Table 1.1 shows the possible sentences allowed by law for JOs and non-JOs for the full list of JO offense categories.

As the table shows, the minimum sentence that a JO can receive for a conviction of assault in the first degree is 1–3⅓ years, while the minimum sentence a person 16 or over can receive for the same conviction is 5 years. So, although New York State law designated 13-, 14-, and 15-year-olds charged with certain crimes to be prosecuted as adults, it also mandated a separate sentencing structure from that required for those 16 and older. This difference was just one of the many contradictions imbedded within the practice of prosecuting youths as adults under New York State law.

JOs and non-JOs also have significantly different plea bargaining options available to them. This had a profound impact on how their cases could be handled. Non-JOs had all the usual options for pleading guilty to a lesser charge. The nature of the Juvenile Offender Law, however, meant that similar options were not available to JOs because the lesser charges a JO defendant might plead down to are not within the purview of the criminal court.[18] The part's law clerk explained the confusing limits on plea bargaining created by the JO legislation:

> Say you are 16, an adult in the eyes of the law, and you are arrested for robbery in the first degree [a B class felony]. A plea offer to a 16-year-old can be to a C [lesser] felony. [The DA] can offer a C violent and 3½ years as a minimum. Now, say a JO is charged with robbery in the second degree [a C class felony]. Now say the DA's office wants to plea him out to an *attempted* ROB II, which is a D felony. They can't do it; they can't do it because he is not *criminally* liable

for *attempted* robbery in the second degree. If you take away the top charge that makes him responsible in criminal court, then he would be in Family Court. It's very strange, the whole nature of plea bargaining is very different for JOs. Because if they plea down—they wouldn't be JOs anymore!

The common practice in criminal courts of pleading guilty to a lesser charge wasn't an option for many JOs because the law does not allow for

Table 1.1

JO vs. Non-JO Sentencing Structures for JO Offenses

JO		"A" CLASS FELONY	Non JO
INDETERMINATE			DETERMINATE
MIN.	MAX.		
5-9	LIFE	MURDER 2 (13 year olds)	15-LIFE
7½-15	LIFE	MURDER 2 (14/15 year olds)	
4-6	12-15	ARSON 1	15-LIFE
4-6	12-15	KIDNAPPING 1	15-LIFE

JO		"B" CLASS FELONY	Non JO
INDETERMINATE			DETERMINATE
MIN.	MAX.	AGGRAVATED SEXUAL ABUSE 1	
1-3⅓	3-10	ARSON 2	5-25
		ATTEMPTED KIDNAPPING 1	
		ATTEMPTED MURDER 2	
		BURGLARY 1	
		MANSLAUGHTER 1	
		RAPE 1	
		CRIMINAL SEXUAL ACT 1 (previously 'sodomy')	
		ROBBERY 1	
		ASSAULT 1	

JO		"C" CLASS FELONY	Non JO
INDETERMINATE			DETERMINATE
MIN.	MAX.	BURGLARY 2	
1-2⅓	3-7	ROBBERY 2	3½-15
		CRIMINAL POSSESSION OF A WEAPON 2	
		(ON SCHOOL GROUNDS FOR JOs)	

JO		"D" CLASS FELONY	Non JO
INDETERMINATE			DETERMINATE
MIN.	MAX.	CRIMINAL POSSESSION OF A WEAPON 3	
1-1⅓	3-4	(ON SCHOOL GROUNDS FOR JOs)	2-7

Sources: New York Penal Law article 70, §§ 70.02, 70.05; Eric Warner, The Juvenile Offender Handbook (Flushing, NY: Looseleaf Law, 2004).

them to plead down to non-JO charges. Changing a charge from a JO offense to a non-JO offense was much more complicated and required a formal process to "remove" the case to the Family Court. Given these legal limitations, the chance to earn an alternative sentence of probation was vital to the case-processing model the Youth Part set up. It provided those JOs with limited plea-bargain options an alternative means to lessen the full impact of their original felony charges.

Beyond these complications, JOs and non-JOs were detained in different types of facilities both before and after sentencing, if they were sentenced. JOs were detained at one of the three secure juvenile detention facilities run by the Department of Juvenile Justice, paradoxically named Horizons, Crossroads, and Bridges.[19] Non-JOs (those 16 or over) were held at Rikers Island, the city's jail.[20] If sentenced to terms of incarceration, JOs and non-JOs were sent to different detention facilities as well. Non-JOs would enter the state prison system managed by the Department of Correctional Services and get placed in an upstate prison, while JOs would be assigned to one of the state's secure juvenile detention facilities through the Office of Children and Family Services (OCFS), the agency that places youths from the Family Court. Although prosecuted as adults, JOs were housed as youth. I am not suggesting that these youths should have been housed with adults in prisons; however, I am suggesting that this practice underscores, once again, the basic contradiction at work in the criminal prosecution of youth—that they are not adults.

JO versus non-JO status mattered for youths enrolled in ATI programs as well. The Youth Advocacy Project (YAP), an ATI run by the Center for Community Alternatives (CCA), was specially designed and funded to handle JO cases, while the Center for Alternative Sentencing and Employment Services (CASES) program generally took older kids. So, while both JOs and non-JO in the Youth Part were legally labeled as adults for prosecution, they were actually two distinct categories of "adult" defendants under New York State Law. Regardless of this difference in legal status, the Manhattan Youth Part preferred to see all the defendants, whether JO or non-JO, as kids. As Judge Corriero described it, the court's philosophy of how to deal with them was consistent: "We don't discriminate [between JOs and non-JOs] about the concept of offering alternatives." At the same time, he readily acknowledged that legal status restricted the options of what was legally possible for a given kid.

Negotiating the complexity of these different layers of legal rules, categories, and sentencing structures was a confusing and often daunting task for any and all involved in the Youth Part. The judge once likened the navigation of the sentencing structures alone to "landing a 747 in the dark." Several defense attorneys in the court were seasoned experts on the minutiae of these laws. The Legal Aid Society went so far as to establish a JO Team in the 1990s in order to create a group of lawyers with expertise on the laws that effect Juvenile Offenders and their codefendants. These specialists had a constant presence in the Youth Part on calendar days. As one of them said, "Most lawyers don't understand JO cases . . . the law is different, it's jerry-rigged, it's bizarre, it's very counterintuitive."

Within the confines of these bizarre, complex, and often contradictory legal circumstances, a dedicated judge, court staff, specially trained and experienced lawyers, and social-service personnel worked to carve out a unique form of rehabilitative justice for New York City kids charged with serious felonies. Amid the delay, bureaucratic mundanity, and barely controlled chaos of calendar days, the Manhattan Youth Part worked to create a method of responding to troubled and troublesome kids (JO and non-JO) in a manner that did not risk public safely, but that also sought rehabilitative justice with a certain humility and humanity.

Creating the "Juvenile Offender"

New York's 1978 Juvenile Offender Law was the first in the country that allowed criminal prosecution of youth under age 16 without juvenile court oversight. As such it represented a significant moment of rupture in the history of the American juvenile justice system.[1] Fox Butterfield, Pulitzer Prize–winning author of *All God's Children: The Bosket Family and the American Tradition of Violence*, called the passage of the Juvenile Offender Law "a watershed in American juvenile justice policy."[2] The law was a statutory exclusion law, requiring that qualifying cases be brought directly before the criminal courts, completely bypassing Family Court. Juvenile Offender cases, under the new law, were not to be *transferred* up from the Family Court but were to *originate* in the criminal courts. The statutory exclusion law removed Family Court judges' discretion and, as Judge Corriero has written, "prevented individual assessment of each juvenile before exposure to adult procedures and penalties."[3] New York's harsh legislation foreshadowed the kinds of transfer laws that would become popular in many states two decades later. To understand why New York passed such harsh legislation decades before the rest of the states, it is necessary to know something of the history of state law related to youthful offending and to examine certain significant events of 1978. It was an election year in New York State, and the issue of juvenile crime and violence became a hotly contested campaign issue, fueled in large part by two murders committed by 15-year-old Willie Bosket that spring. The convergence of these forces—election year politics and a sensational case of juvenile violence—facilitated New York's harsh legislative action. Examining these events provides insight into the role of politics and media in the creation of law.

New York's Juvenile Justice History

In 1824, decades before the establishment of the first juvenile court in Chicago in 1899, New York established "the first formal state institution for juveniles," called the New York House of Refuge, which provided for separate detention in New York City for delinquents under the age of 16.[4] In 1840 such differential treatment of those under 16 was mandated statewide. The law stated:

> Whenever any person under the age of sixteen years, shall be convicted of any felony or other crime, the court, instead of sentencing such person to imprisonment in a state prison, or county jail may

order that he be removed to and confined in the house of refuge, established by the society for the reformation of juvenile delinquents.[5]

The year 1902 saw the establishment of the first children's court in New York City, a separate part of the magistrate's court for those under 16. By 1910 many areas of the state had similar institutions. Originally, these were not separate courts for juveniles but rather just a special part within the criminal court. By 1922 separate juvenile courts had been set up across the state, and by 1924 the legislature established formally independent children's courts separate from the existing criminal courts.[6] The Family Court Act of 1962, which still governs today, maintained the 16-year-old age distinction and "maintained the provision of exclusive original jurisdiction over crimes committed" by those younger than 16 to the newly named Family Court.[7] At the time, New York was one of only four states to set the age of jurisdiction as low as 16.[8]

In 1975, New York's governor, Democrat Hugh Carey, set up a Panel on Juvenile Violence for the purpose of recommending changes to the state's laws on juvenile justice. The panel's main recommendation was that "older juveniles found to have committed any one of a certain class of designated felonies would be subject to a separate and somewhat harsher set of penalties."[9] The following year, the state legislature took up this recommendation with the passage of the Juvenile Justice Reform Act. This 1976 act created a new category of delinquency, the "designated felony," and allowed kids as young as 14 who had committed certain violent crimes (homicide, first-degree robbery) to be detained in secure juvenile facilities for longer periods than had previously been allowed.[10] Those convicted of class A felonies were required to be committed to secure detention for five years. Prior to the new law, the longest possible sentence for class A felonies was eighteen months for juveniles under age 15 and three years for 15-year olds.[11] Although the law created this new category of serious offenders and increased the possible sanctions against them, it still kept all such cases under the jurisdiction of the Family Court and all of its governing statutes.[12] However, the act also added new language that instructed the court to consider "the needs and best interests of the respondent *as well as the need for protection of the community*" (emphasis added),[13] signaling a deliberate movement away from the traditional *parens patriae* model. The 1976 Juvenile Justice Reform Act is an often underappreciated legal step in the process of the criminalization of youth under 16 in New York. As researchers Simon Singer, Jeffrey Fagan, and Akiva Liberman suggest in their case study of the Juvenile Offender Law: "To ignore the 1976 act is to assume mistakenly that the 1978 *Juvenile Offender Law* was a complete and radical shift in New York's system of juvenile justice."[14] In passing the Juvenile Justice Reform Act of 1976, the New York State legislature laid the groundwork for easier passage of the Juvenile Offender Law two years later.

The Point of Rupture: The 1978 Juvenile Offender Law

As Singer, Fagan, and Liberman suggest, the Juvenile Offender Law passed in 1978 was built upon prior "jurisprudential rationale[s]" including due-process reforms, the traditionally low age of criminal court jurisdiction in New York, and the 1976 Juvenile Justice Reform Act.[15] But it was also passed in 1978 because of political forces at work in New York at the time, and because of Willie Bosket. On March 19, 1978, Willie, a 15-year-old black kid from Harlem, robbed and then shot and killed Noel Perez, a male passenger on a New York City subway. Four days later, Willie shot and wounded Anthony Lamorte, a subway workman who discovered Willie and his cousin in the train yards illegally. Four days later, Willie shot and killed another subway passenger, Moises Perez, again in the course of a robbery on the subway. Willie was arrested on March 31, 1978, and charged with two counts of murder and one of attempted murder.[16]

Laws protecting the identity of juveniles dictated that Willie's identity not be made public and that the facts of the case be kept confidential. Nonetheless, information was quickly leaked to the press: a poor black kid from Harlem with a history in the juvenile courts, a father in prison, and the apparent ability to murder in cold blood, Willie Bosket made good front-page press. What most outraged many at the time was the inability of the Family Court system to punish Willie in a manner that seemed appropriate to his crimes. Had he been 16 years of age, Willie would have faced a possible sentence of life imprisonment; as the law read in 1978, however, the stiffest sentence allowable, even under the recently passed Juvenile Justice Reform Act, was a maximum of five years in a secure juvenile detention facility. Such punishment seemed woefully inadequate given the supposedly cold-blooded nature of Willie's crimes. In and out of Family Court and juvenile reformatories since he was six, Willie also quickly became a poster child for those claiming the abject failure of the entire juvenile justice system. Willie's high-profile case became ready ammunition for those advocating for harsher treatment of violent juveniles and for those who believed the juvenile justice system no longer tenable in the face of a much-touted and feared new generation of violent urban youth.

Governor Carey was running for a second term in office in 1978, and even prior to the Bosket case, crime—particularly juvenile crime—was one of the most hotly contested campaign issues that season.[17] According to Walter Collier's 1984 thesis analyzing the implementation of the Juvenile Offender Law, halfway through the 1978 New York State legislative session, "128 juvenile justice bills [were] introduced by democrats and republicans."[18] Governor Carey had already come under attack by the law-and-order right early in 1978 when he vowed to veto a death penalty bill being pushed through the state legislature.[19] Carey's Republican opponents used his anti–death penalty stance to claim that he and the rest of the state's Democrats were "soft on crime."[20] In a climate where no politician wanted that distinction, political debates quickly centered on whose program was the harshest. Governor Carey won his veto of the reinstitution of the death penalty, but came under increasing political fire as the Willie Bosket saga played out in the headlines. Perry Duryea, Carey's Republican opponent in the gubernatorial race, sponsored a bill, which later became the Juvenile Offender Law, requiring the transfer of certain juveniles to criminal court jurisdiction.

Willie Bosket was sentenced to the maximum allowable sentence—five years in a secure juvenile detention facility—on June 27, 1978.[21] Two days after the sentencing, Governor Carey, who had been adamantly opposed to transfer legislation of any kind, said that he would consider measures that would allow for some youths to be prosecuted in adult courts. The *New York Times* reported on its front page: "In an abrupt shift, Governor Carey said today that under certain circumstances, he would support giving prosecutors the discretion to try juveniles in adult courts."[22] Signaling the direct connection between his swift turnaround and the high-profile Bosket case, the governor stated that the new law would guarantee that Willie Bosket "never walks the street again."[23]

By July 14th, in the wake of Bosket case publicity, Carey agreed to accept the Republican version of the bill, which called for the statutory exclusion of certain categories of youth offenders from the Family Court altogether. The *New York Times* reported Carey's change of heart this way:

> Mr. Carey was willing to make concessions to reach a compromise, according to those familiar with his thinking, because he needed a tough anticrime package to bolster his re-election drive and did not want the Republicans to get political mileage from portraying him as blocking a program that was, in many respects, similar to his own.[24]

That same day the *New York Times* also ran an editorial titled "Criminals Yes, Adults No." While agreeing that some reform of the laws dealing with violent juveniles was in order as no one was thrilled with the status quo, the authors wrote: "Given the clamor for stiffer penalties, one would think that New York State is lax on juvenile criminals. Quite the contrary. New York has been in the vanguard of the 'get tough' movement."[25] The Juvenile Offender Law was passed six days later.[26] The vote in the Republican-led State Senate was 50 to 2, while the vote in the Democratic-led State Assembly was 125 to 10.[27] A Senate sponsor of the bill stated: "A most important purpose of this bill is to deal with juvenile offenders who presently terrorize our communities by placing them on notice that firm sanctions will be applied for their vicious and violent criminal conduct."[28]

During the brief debate over the bill in the Assembly, an assemblyman opposed to the new law argued that it was "a war on people, not on crime . . . there is not one line in this bill to strengthen the family and community structures which we know will bring people away from crime."[29] Democratic Assemblyman Arthur O. Eve of Buffalo argued: "We're putting 13-year-olds away for life—for life! That's unbelievable. I don't think anyone else is doing anything comparable."[30] The assemblyman was correct: no state was doing anything comparable—not yet anyway. In reporting the law's passage, the *New York Times* wrote: "The hard-line anticrime legislators voted for it because it reflected most of their wishes . . . the more liberal legislators with reservations voted for it because, like the Governor, they hoped to counter some of the pressure on them for voting again the death penalty, which is being made a major campaign issue."[31] The new law required that all 13-year-olds charged with murder in the second degree, and all 14- and 15-year-olds charged with any of the offenses shown in Table 2.1 be criminally prosecuted in adult courts as Juvenile Offenders, and if convicted, be sentenced to the corresponding indeterminate sentences. The law also required that Juvenile Offenders serve their "entire sentences in secure facilities."[32]

The sentencing structure put in place for JOs under the new law was different from that in place at the time for offenders over the age of 16. Both groups were subject to indeterminate sentences, but the maximum and minimum sentencing ranges were higher for those over 16.[33] This differential-sentencing scheme implies an acknowledgment on the part of lawmakers, even in the heat of the Bosket backlash, of the reality that younger kids were somehow different from older kids.

Changes to New York State penal law since 1978 have altered the Ju-

Table 2.1

Juvenile Offender (JO) Offenses and Sentencing Guidelines, 1978

	Indeterminate sentence Requirements	
	Minimum	Maximum
Class A Felony		
Murder 2	5-9	Life
Kidnapping 1	4-6	12-15
Arson 1	4-6	12-15
Class B Felony		
Assault 1	1-3⅓	3-10
Manslaughter 1	1-3⅓	3-10
Rape 1	1-3⅓	3-10
Sodomy 1	1-3⅓	3-10
Burglary 1	1-3⅓	3-10
Robbery 1	1-3⅓	3-10
Attempted murder 2	1-3⅓	3-10
Attempted kidnapping 1	1-3⅓	3-10
Class C Felony		
Burglary 2	1-2⅓	3-7
Robbery 2	1-2⅓	3-7

Source: 1978 New York Laws, Chapter 481, §§ 27–32.

venile Offender Law in a few ways from its original form. The minimum sentence range for 14- and 15-year-olds (but not 13-year-olds) charged with second-degree murder has been increased to 7½–15 years, and two new Class D felonies were added to the list of JO crimes in 1998—criminal possession of a weapon in the second and third degree when the weapon is possessed on school grounds.[34] Changes in legislation have further bifurcated the sentencing structures for JOs and youths 16 and older. In the late 1990s, New York required determinate sentencing for a number of adult offenses but left the indeterminate structure in place for JOs.

The Juvenile Offender Law came under criticism from numerous sources as soon as it was passed. The frontline critique was that the law, as a statutory exclusion provision, completely bypassed the juvenile court system. In 1979, the Citizens' Committee for the Children of New York, a child-advocacy organization, reported findings from its study of the law: "in our interviews with court personnel, including court administrators and several judges of the various courts, it was suggested that the Family Court be the court of original jurisdiction, with a waiver or transfer to the Criminal Court."[35] In his 1981 analysis of the Juvenile Offender Law, legal scholar Merril Sobie's number-one recommendation was that "every juvenile offender case should be filed initially in the Family Court."[36] Two years later, the Association of the Bar of the City of New York's Juvenile Justice Committee also stated that the law should be modified, suggesting that "the better practice would be to begin all proceedings against juveniles charged with serious crimes in the Family Court, and to permit the Family Court judge to waive jurisdiction to the adult court in appropriate cases."[37] Despite these and many other critiques, the Juvenile Offender Law has remained in place for more than thirty years. Once considered a law on the extreme end of the transfer law spectrum (which it was), its requirements for criminal prosecution of adolescents have since been met or exceeded by laws in many other states. Writing on the profound impact of the Juvenile Offender Law on American jurisprudence, Fox Butterfield asserts:

> The new law represented a sharp reversal of 150 years of American history, dating to the founding of the New York House of Refuge in 1825. It was the first break with the progressive tradition of treating children separately from adults. . . . The new law also marked a departure from the cherished American ideal of rehabilitation—the notion that kids could be changed and saved.[38]

Because it had historically set the age of criminal court jurisdiction at 16, New York had long been in the business of the criminal prosecution of adolescents. The passage of the Juvenile Offender Law in 1978, however, marked the creation of a new category of offender—the Juvenile Offender. At a time when most states left transfer decisions in individual cases to the discretion of juvenile court judges, New York State mandated that all members of a certain class of young offenders be prosecuted as adults. In passing this statutory exclusion legislation, New York set a clear and early precedent for the normalization of the criminal prosecution of adolescents and for the ongoing criminalization of youth that was to come in the 1990s.

Characteristics of New York's Juvenile Offenders

So who are these Juvenile Offenders? The characteristics of JOs in New York have remained consistent for over thirty years—they are mostly nonwhite, predominately male, largely from New York City, and mainly charged with robbery. In 1979, the Citizens' Committee for the Children of New York reported that in the first six months after the Juvenile Offender Law was passed, of the 754 JO arrests made, less than 10% were of female youth. The report also found that 5% lived in foster care group homes, 76% were black, 21% "had Spanish surnames," and 3% were white.[39] Of these early JO arrests, 79% were for first- or second-degree robbery. Data from the first year of the law's implementation found similar trends—most JO cases were in New York City and the vast majority were for the crime of robbery in the first or second degree.[40]

Indictment data for 1984–2004 show that these early trends have continued.[41] The typical JO is a black and/or Hispanic male prosecuted within New York City on a first- or second-degree robbery charge. While no solid data are available on how many JOs are first-time offenders—meaning they have had no prior criminal or Family Court case—Judge Corriero put the estimate for his court at about 50%.[42] In the first three years after the law's passage, 86% of the 5,298 JO arrests made across the state took place in New York City.[43] The data for 1984–2004 show that, although the percentage of New York City JO indictments has steadily declined since 1990, the city has accounted for the vast majority of JO indictments in the state each year (Table 2.2). Within New York City, JO indictments are distributed

Table 2.2

New York State Juvenile Offender (JO) Indictments, State and New York City, 1984–2004

	STATE TOTAL	NYC TOTAL	NYC Percentage of State Total
1984	447	373	83%
1985	503	402	80%
1986	428	357	83%
1987	297	258	87%
1988	412	353	86%
1989	504	455	90%
1990	705	661	94%
1991	774	681	88%
1992	801	701	88%
1993	781	681	87%
1994	797	666	84%
1995	660	552	84%
1996	567	457	81%
1997	531	434	82%
1998	488	415	85%
1999	459	384	84%
2000	325	244	75%
2001	304	223	73%
2002	289	197	68%
2003	332	237	71%
2004	389	292	75%

Source: New York State Division of Criminal Justice Services, Indictment Statistical System, August 2005.

evenly across all boroughs except Staten Island, which has consistently had a much lower percentage than the other four boroughs (see Table 2.3). As already noted, in the first six months after the Juvenile Offender Law was implemented, only 10% of JO arrests were of female youth.[44] As Table 2.4 shows, this trend has clearly held.[45]

Table 2.3

Juvenile Offender (JO) Indictments (and SCIs), New York City by County, 1984–2004

	Bronx		Kings (Brooklyn)		New York (Manhattan)		Queens		Richmond (Staten Is.)	
	#	%	#	%	#	%	#	%	#	%
1984	91	24	123	33	96	26	61	16	2	1
1985	85	21	153	38	96	24	65	16	3	1
1986	77	22	126	35	84	24	65	18	5	1
1987	82	32	71	28	50	19	53	21	2	1
1988	88	25	134	38	82	23	48	14	1	0
1989	151	33	117	26	118	26	67	15	2	0
1990	149	23	186	28	157	24	160	24	9	1
1991	155	23	239	35	130	19	151	22	6	1
1992	130	19	284	41	136	19	147	21	4	1
1993	158	23	209	31	127	19	181	27	6	1
1994	154	23	177	27	145	22	179	27	11	2
1995	135	24	165	30	100	18	146	26	6	1
1996	121	26	164	36	87	19	78	17	7	2
1997	91	21	154	35	83	19	98	23	8	2
1998	131	32	100	24	92	22	86	21	6	2
1999	73	19	114	30	105	27	82	21	10	3
2000	37	15	89	36	63	26	51	21	4	2
2001	41	18	64	29	55	25	57	26	6	3
2002	52	26	47	24	60	30	34	17	4	2
2003	62	26	45	19	54	23	72	30	4	2
2004	69	24	68	23	59	20	93	32	3	1
TOTAL	2,132	24	2,829	31	1,979	22	1,974	22	109	1

Source: New York State Division of Criminal Justice Services, Indictment Statistical System, August 2005.

Note: These data include JO indictment and Supreme Court Informations (SCIs). SCIs are cases in which a defendant pleaded guilty prior to grand jury indictment. SCIs are more common in some boroughs than others due to different cultures of prosecution. As a representative from the Manhattan DA's office explained it, SCIs are more common in Queens, where the DA has a policy of not plea bargaining once an indictment is filed. In Manhattan, where the approach to plea bargaining is more open, SCIs are rather rare.

Table 2.4

New York City Juvenile Offender (JO) Indictments by Gender 1984–2004

	Male	Female	Unknown	Total	% Male	% Female
1984	359	14	0	373	96.2	3.8
1985	392	10	0	402	97.5	2.5
1986	333	24	0	357	93.3	6.7
1987	251	7	0	258	97.3	2.7
1988	337	16	0	353	95.5	4.5
1989	428	23	4	455	94.1	5.1
1990	602	58	1	661	91.1	8.8
1991	637	44	0	681	93.5	6.5
1992	639	61	1	701	91.2	8.7
1993	620	60	1	681	91.0	8.8
1994	612	49	5	666	91.9	7.4
1995	503	48	1	552	91.1	8.7
1996	416	41	0	457	91.0	9.0
1997	390	44	0	434	89.9	10.1
1998	370	42	3	415	89.2	10.1
1999	336	48	0	384	87.5	12.5
2000	220	24	0	244	90.2	9.8
2001	205	17	1	223	91.9	7.6
2002	186	11	0	197	94.4	5.6
2003	212	24	1	237	89.5	10.1
2004	268	24	0	292	91.8	8.2
TOTAL	8316	689	18	9023	92.2	7.6

Source: New York State Division of Criminal Justice Services, Indictment Statistical System, August 2005

Race

Just as the early data on JOs suggested, black and Hispanic youth are considerably more likely to be indicted as Juvenile Offenders than white youth, with black and/or Hispanic youth accounting for between 86% and 97% of all JO indictments in Manhattan every year between 1984 and 1995 (see Figure 2.1, Table 2.5). Due to reporting problems with the New York City Division of Criminal Justice Services (DCJS) data set on JO indictments by race/ethnicity citywide, only Manhattan data were reliable. In addition, it should be noted that for some years between 1995 and 2002 the total percentage of black and/or Latino youth dropped, but that during these years there is a problematic percentage of "other/unknown" listed.

Figure 2.1

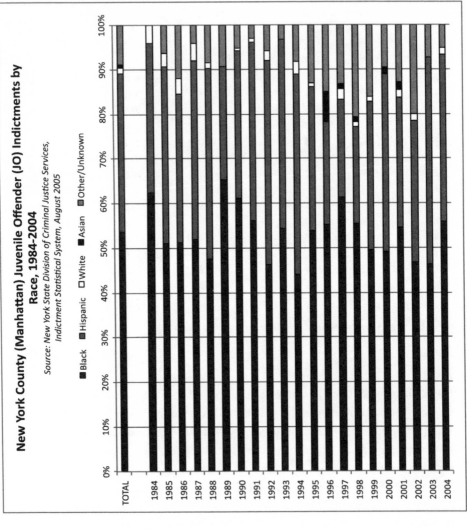

New York County (Manhattan) Juvenile Offender (JO) Indictments by
Race, 1984-2004

Source: New York State Division of Criminal Justice Services,
Indictment Statistical System, August 2005

■ Black ■ Hispanic □ White ■ Asian ■ Other/Unknown

Table 2.5

New York County (Manhattan) Juvenile Offender (JO) Indictments by Race, 1984-1995

| | PERCENTAGES OF TOTAL NEW YORK COUNTY JO INDICTMENTS | | | | | | |
	% WHITE	% BLACK	% HISPANIC	% ASIAN	% OTHER	% UNKNOWN	% TOTAL BLACK & HISPANIC
1984	4	63	33	0	0	0	96
1985	3	51	40	0	4	2	91
1986	4	51	33	0	8	4	85
1987	4	52	40	0	0	4	92
1988	1	48	43	0	5	4	90
1989	0	65	25	0	5	4	91
1990	1	61	33	0	4	1	94
1991	1	56	40	0	1	2	96
1992	2	46	46	0	1	5	92
1993	0	54	43	0	1	2	97
1994	3	44	45	0	6	3	89
1995	1	54	32	0	5	8	86
1996	0	55	23	7	1	14 *	78
1997	2	61	22	1	1	12 *	83
1998	1	55	22	1	0	21 *	77
1999	1	50	33	0	0	16 *	83
2000	0	49	40	2	0	10 *	89
2001	2	55	29	2	0	13 *	84
2002	2	47	32	0	0	20 *	78
2003	0	46	46	0	0	7	93
2004	2	56	37	0	0	5	93
TOTAL	2	54	35	1	2	7	89

Source: New York State Division of Criminal Justice Services, Indictment Statistical System, August 2005.

The Case of Robbery

Robbery is the most common Juvenile Offender crime. In the first three years of the Juvenile Offender Law, 76% of arrest charges were for robbery.[46] Between 1984 and 2004, second-degree robbery accounted for more than half of all JO indictments in New York City every year except three (42.5% in 1988, 46.8% in 2002, and 49% in 2004; see Table 2.7). First-degree robbery accounted for the second-highest percentage of indictments citywide (ranging from 14.9% in 2000 to 27.9% in 2002). Taken together, the vast majority of all JO indictments in New York City have been for robbery, first or second degree, across all years—accounting for no less than 66% of all cases in any given year.

Table 2.6

Juvenile Offender (JO) Indictments by Offense Charge, New York City, 1984–2004

Indictment Charge	Assault 1	Manslaughter 1	Murder 2	Rape 1	Criminal Sex Act 1	Aggravated Sexual Abuse 1	Kidnapping 1	Burglary 2	Burglary 1	TOTAL BURGLARY	Arson 2	Arson 1	Robbery 2	Robbery 1	TOTAL ROBBERY	Criminal Possession of a Weapon 3	Criminal Possession of a Weapon 2
1984	7	0	29	9	9	1	0	2	6	8	1	0	96	211	307	n/a	n/a
1985	12	3	31	30	8	0	1	1	6	7	2	1	90	214	304	n/a	n/a
1986	13	2	28	22	9	0	0	0	6	6	1	0	76	198	274	n/a	n/a
1987	12	0	31	21	4	0	0	1	3	4	0	0	44	140	184	n/a	n/a
1988	12	0	62	28	4	0	2	2	4	6	0	1	83	149	232	n/a	n/a
1989	11	2	65	32	9	0	0	0	6	6	1	0	91	235	326	n/a	n/a
1990	19	3	97	18	18	0	5	2	4	6	2	0	120	368	488	n/a	n/a
1991	18	3	96	9	6	6	0	0	3	3	1	1	127	403	530	n/a	n/a
1992	24	3	84	24	9	0	0	1	9	10	2	0	102	441	543	n/a	n/a
1993	24	3	92	16	4	0	0	0	4	4	0	1	133	401	534	n/a	n/a
1994	17	3	78	16	11	1	0	0	9	9	1	0	137	386	523	n/a	n/a
1995	21	0	50	14	11	0	1	1	10	11	3	0	112	328	440	n/a	n/a
1996	23	2	37	14	5	0	1	7	11	18	2	0	90	264	354	n/a	n/a
1997	44	0	30	12	7	0	0	0	2	2	5	0	88	239	327	n/a	n/a
1998	30	1	17	12	8	0	1	0	7	7	2	0	65	271	336	0	0
1999	38	3	28	7	10	0	0	2	9	11	1	0	72	211	283	0	3
2000	25	0	14	8	6	0	0	0	3	3	8	0	36	137	173	3	2
2001	35	1	11	7	7	0	0	2	3	5	1	0	42	113	155	1	0
2002	21	0	4	5	2	0	1	2	3	5	3	0	56	94	150	7	3
2003	26	1	7	6	9	0	0	1	2	3	1	0	51	125	176	1	0
2004	40	0	11	4	7	2	0	0	5	5	1	0	75	142	217	0	3
Total 84-04	472	30	902	314	163	10	12	24	115	139	38	4	1,786	5,070	6,856	12	11

Source: New York State Division of Criminal Justice Services, Indictment Statistical System, August 2005

Table 2.7

Robbery as Percentage of Total Juvenile Offender (JO), New York City, 1984–2004

| | Percentage of Total JO Indictments | | |
	First Degree Robbery	Second Degree Robbery	**Total Robbery**
1984	25.7%	56.6%	**82.3%**
1985	22.4%	53.4%	**75.8%**
1986	21.4%	55.8%	**77.2%**
1987	17.1%	54.3%	**71.3%**
1988	23.6%	42.5%	**66.1%**
1989	20.1%	51.9%	**72.0%**
1990	18.2%	55.8%	**74.1%**
1991	18.8%	59.5%	**78.3%**
1992	14.6%	63.0%	**77.6%**
1993	19.6%	59.1%	**78.6%**
1994	20.7%	58.3%	**79.0%**
1995	20.3%	59.4%	**79.7%**
1996	19.7%	57.8%	**77.5%**
1997	20.6%	56.0%	**76.6%**
1998	15.7%	65.5%	**81.2%**
1999	18.8%	54.9%	**73.7%**
2000	14.9%	56.6%	**71.5%**
2001	18.8%	50.7%	**69.5%**
2002	27.9%	46.8%	**74.6%**
2003	22.2%	54.3%	**76.5%**
2004	25.9%	49.0%	**74.8%**

Source: New York State Division of Criminal Justice Services, Indictment Statistical System, August 2005.

The Curious Case of Burglary

Indictments for first- or second-degree burglary make up a surprisingly low percentage of JO indictments (see Tables 2.6, 2.8). Looking at this data one might assume that 14- and 15-year-olds in New York City weren't committing many criminal acts that qualified as first- or second-degree burglary.

Merril Sobie's 1981 study of the Juvenile Offender Law also found surprisingly low rates of burglary indictments in the first year after its passage. According to the available arrest data, 99% of all burglary charges against 14- and 15-year-olds citywide during that first year had been for *third*-degree burglary, with only 1% being for first- and second-degree burglary. The low rates of first- and second-degree burglary charges, Sobie concluded, pointed to discretionary police and prosecutorial practices, given that burglary was the only JO offense that was not a violent person offense. Police and/or prosecutors just did not see burglary as a "JO worthy" offense, and therefore chose to substitute a non-JO offense such

Table 2.8
Burglary as Percentage of Total Juvenile Offender (JO), New York City, 1984–2004

	Percentage of Total JO Indictments		
	First Degree Burglary	Second Degree Burglary	Total Burglary
1984	1.6%	0.5%	2.1%
1985	1.5%	0.2%	1.7%
1986	1.7%	0.0%	1.7%
1987	1.2%	0.4%	1.6%
1988	1.1%	0.6%	1.7%
1989	1.3%	0.0%	1.3%
1990	0.6%	0.3%	0.9%
1991	0.4%	0.0%	0.4%
1992	1.3%	0.1%	1.4%
1993	0.6%	0.0%	0.6%
1994	1.4%	0.0%	1.4%
1995	1.8%	0.2%	2.0%
1996	2.4%	1.5%	3.9%
1997	0.5%	0.0%	0.5%
1998	1.7%	0.0%	1.7%
1999	2.3%	0.5%	2.8%
2000	1.2%	0.0%	1.2%
2001	1.3%	0.9%	2.2%
2002	1.5%	1.0%	2.5%
2003	0.9%	0.4%	1.3%
2004	1.7%	0.0%	1.7%

Source: New York State Division of Criminal Justice Services, Indictment Statistical System, August 2005.

as third-degree burglary or breaking and entering, which would send the case to the Family Court.[47]

I was also struck by the lack of youths charged with burglary in the Youth Part. Conversations with court personnel and defense attorneys pointed to practices similar to those identified by Sobie during the first year of the Juvenile Offender Law's implementation. First- and second-degree burglary were rarely indicted against 14- and 15-year-olds as a JO-level offense because there was a sense that as nonviolent offenses they simply weren't worthy of prosecution in the criminal court. A representative from the DA's office agreed that such discretionary practice may be taking place, though he insisted that it was not bureau policy. Even if there is no formal policy at the level of prosecution, informal decision-making as well as police discretion must help explain the low number of JO burglary indictments.

I provide these details here as a reminder of the important role of discretion at all levels of criminal case processing. Even within the manda-tory rules of transfer under a statutory exclusion law like New York's Ju-venile Offender Law, discretion is a powerful force. Discretion takes place throughout criminal justice systems, and even so-called "mandatory" transfer laws can be applied with discretion, particularly on the part of prosecutors.[48] The low incidence of JO burglary indictments demonstrates just one of the many ways in which criminal court actors employ discre-tion in order to apply or not apply transfer law as they deem legitimate.

Removal

The Juvenile Offender Law as written in 1978 provided for the "removal" of certain cases from the criminal court to the Family Court. However, the law set up several criteria that had to be met before removal could take place. In the case of serious charges such as murder, first-degree rape, sodomy, or robbery, removal was only allowable if the defendant was a secondary participant in the charged offense, if there were "mitigating cir-cumstances that bear directly upon the manner in which the crime was committed," and if there were "possible deficiencies in the proof of the crime."[49] Removal in such cases also required the consent of the prosecu-tion. Even for less serious offenses, removal required the consideration of a number of factors. Thus, removal was not applicable in many cases and provided a limited alternative to criminal prosecution.[50]

Under the Juvenile Offender Law, so-called "transfer down" or "re-moval" decisions were left to the determination of the criminal court. This was in stark contrast to transfer laws in place in every other state at the time, which left the determination to "transfer up" to the discretion of the juvenile courts.[51] Although an in-depth analysis of removal provi-sions within the Juvenile Offender Law is beyond the scope of this book, it is worth noting that in the years just after its passage removals were much more common than they are now. In the first six months, 44% of all JO cases were removed to Family Court.[52] Between 2001 and 2005, no more than 6.5% of indicted JO cases citywide were removed each year (see Table 2.9).[53]

The decline in post-indictment removal is most likely explained by the institutionalization of discretionary practices, as prosecutors, judges, and defense attorneys developed standards for handling JO cases. A rep-resentative from the DA's office, for example, explained that as a rule his office liked to indict only those cases they thought they could win; thus, many so-called transfers to Family Court took place prior to grand jury

Table 2.9

Percentage of Juvenile Offender (JO) Cases Removed to Family Court, Citywide, 2001–2005

	Brooklyn	Bronx	Manhattan	Queens	Citywide*
2001	4.5%	0.0%	0.0%	0.0%	1.4%
2002	0.0%	0.0%	0.0%	0.0%	0.0%
2003	2.4%	0.0%	0.0%	5.6%	2.2%
2004	2.9%	1.2%	0.0%	0.0%	1.0%
2005	1.1%	14.3%	0.0%	0.0%	6.5%

* Not including Staten Island

Source: Gewirtz (2005–2006).

indictment. In other words, those cases that are susceptible to post-indictment removal procedures may simply be funneled through prosecutorial discretion into Family Court prior to indictment. Such cases are "referred" by prosecution to the Family Court, but are not legally "removed" from the criminal court to the Family Court. The lack of removal in Manhattan in particular was also the direct result of the culture of the Youth Part. Many defense attorneys simply felt that because of the individual attention and emphasis on diversion that prevailed in the Youth Part, their clients had the potential for a better outcome than if the case was handled in the Family Court. Thus removal was rarely sought in the Youth Part, even for cases that may have been eligible.

According to available data, the typical JO has largely remained the same—a black and/or Hispanic male charged with first- or second-degree robbery, prosecuted in New York City, whose case will not be removed to the Family Court. It was these urban boys, black and Hispanic, most of them poor, that I saw come in and out of the Manhattan Youth Part on calendar days. These were the kids for whom the Manhattan Youth Part sought to create alternatives to the harsh impact of mandatory transfer law. It was these kids the Youth Part tried to give a second chance—a chance to avoid the stigma of a lifetime felony record and a sentence of incarceration, a chance to avoid the full impact of the Juvenile Offender Law. It was for them that this experiment in justice was undertaken.

Rehabilitation, Youth Part Style

When his name was called in the Youth Part, Simon, a black youth, strode from the audience where he had been waiting with his aunt and took a seat next to his lawyer. He moved with the confidence of a seasoned veteran of the court. The judge announced that Simon was ready for sentence and asked him to stand up.

"How long have you been with us, now?" Judge Corriero asked.

"A long time," Simon replied easily, looking up at the judge.

CHAPTER THREE

"Since April, Your Honor," offered Simon's white female attorney. Simon had first come before the court eight months earlier on a second-degree robbery charge, but he had done well in the alternative to incarceration (ATI) program he had been set up with, and had pleaded guilty. Now, after months of monitoring by the ATI program and by the court, he was ready to be sentenced as a "Youthful Offender," with five years' probation. The judge first asked Simon if he had learned anything.

"Not to do stupid things or hang around stupid people," the boy answered.

"Okay. That sounds good," replied the judge nodding, smiling slightly. After a short pause the judge's tone of voice changed from the conversational one he had been using with Simon to a more formal, official, judicial tone.

"The sentence of the court," the judge stated formally, "is a sentence of probation for a period of five years. The defendant is declared a Youthful Offender."

Simon, over the prior eight months, had demonstrated that he was worthy of getting a second chance to avoid a lifelong felony record and of receiving Youthful Offender (YO) treatment. As long as he continued to stay out of trouble and didn't violate the terms of his probation for the next five years, his felonious transgression would not have to be declared on job applications or elsewhere. His criminal records would be sealed, and he would have the chance to create a life unhindered by the stigma of being a felon. If Simon failed to complete his five years' probation, he could be sentenced to incarceration for two to six years. In "earning YO" during his time with the Manhattan Youth Part, Simon had, essentially, *earned back* his juvenile status. He was no longer a youth being sentenced as an adult, but rather a kid who had been charged as an adult who was, in the end, sentenced as a "youth."

A sentence of "YO + 5" was the gold-medal prize of the Youth Part's experiment in justice under Judge Corriero. Much of what went on in the court during his term as judge was the process of monitoring eligible defendants as they attempted to "earn" YO treatment and the second chance it provided. Not all defendants before the court were legally eligible for this treatment, and being legally eligible alone did not guarantee that a kid would have the opportunity to earn it as Simon did. Some who were given the opportunity ultimately failed. "Earning YO" was a complicated process in which both formal legal procedures and informal extralegal factors were drawn upon in the court's attempt to divert as many youths as possible from full adult felony convictions.

New York's Youthful Offender Law

The trick of the law that allows for some Juvenile Offenders (JOs) and some non-JOs to be sentenced as YOs is based in legislation passed in New York State in 1943, decades before the legislature passed the Juvenile Offender Law in 1978. As noted earlier, New York had historically set the age of criminal court jurisdiction at 16. In 1943, however, the state passed legislation that allowed criminal defendants 16 to 19 years of age not charged with a crime punishable by death or life imprisonment and with no prior felony convictions to be sentenced as a "Youthful Offenders" at the discretion of the presiding judge.[1] Records of those so designated would remain sealed, and rather than being charged with a specific crime the defendant was to be charged as a "Youthful Offender" and given a sentence of probation or a limited term of incarceration.[2]

When the JO law was first passed in 1978 state law required that certain 13- to 16-year-olds be tried as adults for serious crimes at the same time that it allowed for some 16- to 19-year-olds to be sentenced as YOs for several of these same offenses. This meant that, immediately after the passage of the JO Law, an 18-year-old charged with first-degree robbery as a first-time offense could receive YO treatment while a 14-year-old in the same circumstances could not. Revisions to the Juvenile Offender Law in 1979 quickly corrected this unconstitutional oversight and made YO status available to JOs as well.[3]

The counterintuitive coexistence of these two laws is yet another of the many contradictions at work in the criminal prosecution of youth in New York. More importantly, it illustrates well the competing notions common to legal responses to adolescent transgression: the idea that some kids should be punished harshly for committing serious crimes, and the idea that adolescents are different from adults and therefore worthy of sentencing alternatives and attempts at rehabilitation. New York State law provides confusing legal mechanisms to accommodate both sides of this debate.[4] It is exactly this set of coexisting counterintuitive and confounding laws that allowed for the discretionary work of the Youth Part.

When the Youth Part was created, Judge Corriero, coordinating with other court actors, set about creating a series of procedures for getting as many kids as possible, both JOs and non-JOs, on a path to Youthful Offender treatment. The first step was determining if a kid was legally eligible for YO. According to current New York State Criminal Procedure Law, a person "charged with a crime alleged to have been committed when he was at least sixteen years old and less than nineteen years old or a person charged with being a juvenile offender" is eligible to be found a YO unless the charge to be replaced is for an A-I or A-II felony such as murder in the first or second degree, rape in the first degree, sodomy in the first degree, or aggravated sexual abuse. Further, a defendant is not legally eligible for YO treatment if found guilty of "an armed felony." An armed felony, under state law, is any offense that involves use of a loaded weapon or "display of what *appears* to be a pistol, revolver, rifle, shotgun, machine gun or other firearm" (emphasis added).[5] The presence of a gun or something that appears to be a gun, then, often precludes YO.[6] These specifics are important because it was not uncommon for cases involving fake guns or starter pistols to come before the court. Defendants are not eligible for YO treatment if they have a prior felony conviction, a prior YO adjudication, or previous conviction for a designated felony in the Family Court.[7]

The most important aspect of the Youthful Offender Law for the work of the Youth Part is the judicial discretion it allows in the application of YO treatment to eligible youth: "If in the opinion of the court the interest of justice would be served by relieving the eligible youth from the onus of a criminal record and by not imposing an indeterminate term of imprisonment of more than four years, the court, may, in its discretion, find the eligible youth is a youthful offender."[8]

In her 1982 dissertation detailing New York's Youthful Offender Law, criminal justice scholar Marilyn Chandler suggests that such discretionary powers were given to criminal court judges in order to facilitate rehabilitation-centered case processing for 16- to 19-year-olds found to be worthy of such an approach. At the time of the law's passage in 1943, the state legislature was reluctant to raise the age of jurisdiction of what was then called the Children's Court, but it was also inclined to support an alternative sentencing option for some 16- to 19-year-olds not considered serious violent and repeat offenders. In her analysis of the laws' implementation, Chandler writes that "youthful offender status is a discretionary sentencing option, with an explicit intent to aid the rehabilitation of the young adult offender."[9] Without the broad discretion allowed by the YO statute, much of the work of the Manhattan Youth Part would not have been possible.

Earning "YO + 5"

"Earning YO" in the court was a complicated and often lengthy process, only the beginning of which was determining a defendant's legal eligibility. A number of informal mechanisms were also employed within the court to assess the potential of an eligible youth to be successful in earning YO. For most kids, this process started on their first visit to the court. During this first encounter the court would begin to collect "evidence"—both formal and informal—to determine whether or not a kid was a likely candidate for YO treatment.

A defendant's individual role in the alleged crime was an important factor in assessing potential for YO treatment given that most of the kids in the Youth Part had codefendants.[10] While three young people involved in perpetrating a robbery are all charged with the same offense, individual involvement in the commission of the crime can vary significantly. New York State law is clear on issues of accomplice liability, stating that anyone who "solicits, requests, commands, importunes, or intentionally aids" someone in the commission of a criminal offense is criminally liable for the same offense.[11] So, while simply being present at the commission of a crime is not a crime, playing any role (e.g., acting as a lookout, blocking a victim's path, holding stolen property) makes one fully guilty of the crime under the law.

The Youth Part, however, recognized the real-life differences between threatening someone with a knife and acting as lookout for the knife-wielder. The court attempted to ascertain the actual involvement of each individual defendant in any alleged co-offended crime. The judge explained it this way: "The idea of who is responsible and to what degree they are responsible—this is the real crux of what we are trying to do—how much culpability do you place on an individual kid's shoulders."

In addition, the court was always interested in the larger context of a defendant's life. When a new case was before the court, the judge, with the consent of defense counsel, would most always order two reports: a pre-pleading investigation (PPI) and a 390 examination. A PPI is conducted by the probation department and reports on a kid's prior court involvement in either criminal or Family Court, school attendance, living situation, foster care placements, and the like. The 390 examinations are mental health evaluations. The judge was not required legally to order these reports, but he always did because they provided valuable information on a defendant and his life circumstances.

During a kid's first appearance, the court would also begin to gather extralegal information informally. The judge would talk with the parents or guardians if they were present or ask a kid where he went to school. The judge would attempt to learn something about the young person before him by observing his mannerisms, the way he spoke, his presentation of self. According to Judge Corriero, he wanted to hear a kid's voice, to see "if there is potential there." A defendant's first encounter with the court was also seen as an opportunity to impress upon the kid, and any family members present, the seriousness of the charges, the potential sentence the youth was facing, and the reality of being tried in the criminal court. Although each case before the court had its own unique features, Walter's first day and Lazaro's early experiences in court were quite typical.

WALTER

On his first day in court, Walter, a black kid who was OUT at the time, came from the audience and took a seat in the chair next to his white male attorney when his case was called. A black man stood up for him in the audience. The judge examined the paperwork in front of him.

"This is the first time this case is on before me?" the judge asked.

"Yes," replied Walter's attorney.

"How old are you, young man?" the judge asked Walter, adding, "Stand up." Walter stood up.

"How old are you?" the judge asked again.

"Fourteen," Walter answered.

"What school do you go to?" the judge asked. Walter gave the name of his school.

"Are you his father?" the judge asked the black man standing at the audience railing.

"Yes, sir."

"May I ask what you do for a living?" the judge asked him.

"I work for a home service. I'm a community associate."

"Do you know what your son is charged with?" the judge asked the father.

"Yes, sir," replied Walter's father. The court clerk interrupted to ask if she could arraign the defendant.

"Please," the judge replied.

"Walter Russell, the Grand Jury of the county of New York has filed with the court indictment #_____, charging you with the crimes of robbery in the first degree and robbery in the second degree. How do you plead to those charges, guilty or not guilty?"

"Not guilty," Walter answered.

"The people are filing and serving copies of the indictment and the voluntary disclosure form," stated the assistant district attorney, handing forms to the judge and to the defense attorney.

"Do you go to school every day?" the judge asked Walter.

"Yes."

"You go to school *every day*?" the judge asked again.

"Yes."

"Is that the first high school that you were in?" the judge asked.

"Yeah . . . yes," answered Walter. The judge reviewed the documents before him for a moment and then said to Walter's father, "Your son is charged with placing a knife to somebody's body or throat and stealing their iPod. Is that right, counsel?"

"A PlayStation, I thought it was," answered Walter's lawyer.

"PlayStation," said the judge, "Has he been in trouble in the Family Court before?"

"My information is, no, Your Honor," said the lawyer. The judge put the question directly to Walter: "Never been in Family Court?"

"No."

"What was the bail that was set for this young man?" the judge asked. "Why was he released without bail on such a serious crime? He can go to jail for as much as ten years. Why was he released without bail?"

"A couple of things," responded Walter's lawyer. "One, obviously, he had family contacts. His father was right there in the courtroom when the case was called. He had been waiting in the court for . . ."

The judge cut the lawyer off and asked Walter, "So, you didn't spend any time in jail?"

"No," replied Walter.

"How strong is the evidence in this case?" asked the judge.

"The evidence wasn't so strong," Walter's attorney said. "The property at issue was found on another person who wasn't charged on the same sheet as this." The judge looked at the paperwork and said the date of the alleged incident aloud. "What day of the week was that?" he asked to no one in particular.

"That was a Thursday, judge," the court clerk offered.

"That's a school day," said the judge, again looking at the indictment. "He's out at eleven o'clock at night." The judge looked at Walter's father, addressing his next question to him: "What is he doing out at eleven o'clock at night on a school day?"

"He was having a basketball tournament and he was coming from a tournament," the father offered as an explanation.

"At eleven o'clock at night isn't the basketball tournament over?" questioned the judge.

"They have late games," Walter's father said.

"Does he live with you?" the judge asked.

"Yes, sir."

"How many other children do you have?"

"Four."

"I don't want him out of the house beyond six o'clock from here on in. That's the first thing. Look at me," the judge said to Walter. "Do you understand me?" he asked in a calm, serious, authoritative voice.

"Yes," replied Walter.

"You are in the house at six o'clock," the judge said firmly, "and you are to be involved in the Youth Advocacy Project" [an ATI].

"Whatever you wish," said Walter's lawyer, adding that another program had also expressed interest in Walter as well.

"I want him involved with the Youth Advocacy Project," the judge said. He then addressed Walter again with a tone of firm authority: "You better be where you are supposed to be, keeping your curfew. And you are supposed to be in school when school *starts*. Do you understand me?"

"Yes," said Walter.

"You step out of line with me and I'll set appropriate bail in this case," the judge said, tapping his index finger on his desk.

"Yes," said Walter.

"The defendant is continued on ROR [Released on Own Recognizance]," said the judge, adding, "He should be involved in the Youth Advocacy Project. Counsel and father will stay here for that to be arranged. Should we order a PPI and a 390 examination for your client?"

"Yes, Your Honor, that would be fine," said Walter's lawyer, who then asked if he could approach. After a sidebar discussion, the judge asked the father about the basketball league that Walter was involved with. The judge wanted to know that Walter was on a real team in a real league.

"What time does the team play?" the judge asked Walter.

"After six, sometimes," Walter replied.

"If you are playing basketball . . ." the judge said, "he can play basketball, but he'd better come home directly after that. Do you understand me?"

"Yes," answered Walter once again.

"That's only if you are in a league, not that you are going out to play basketball. Do we understand each other?"

"Yes."

Just then the representative from the ATI program walked into the courtroom. The judge told her, "I want you to interview this young man and his father to see if he's acceptable to your program." She nodded. Walter was given an adjourn date one month away, the amount of time generally needed for the PPI and the 390 reports to be completed, and for the program to have completed its intake and assessment and to develop a case management plan for Walter.

LAZARO

A 14-year-old Hispanic JO who had been arrested on a criminal weapons possession charge, Lazaro was IN the first time I saw him in court. He had originally been released on a low bail that had been set at arraignment, but Judge Corriero had remanded Lazaro on his first appearance in court. Lazaro had no Family Court record, and his mother, who required the services of the court's Spanish interpreter, was present for all his court dates. A month after Lazaro's first appearance, the court was still gathering information on his case. The judge used Lazaro's second court appearance to try to determine something about his character, to see if he could be responsible enough to be given a chance to earn YO. After learning that Lazaro had read the first of the Harry Potter books, the judge started a discussion with Lazaro about the book to make a point.

"How long have you been in jail now?" the judge asked Lazaro after the court officers had escorted him to his seat and taken the handcuffs off.

"A month."

"Well, I just got the PPI this morning. I haven't read it yet. I'd like to read it, as well as the 390 report," the judge said to the attorneys. "My suggestion is that we put it over for conference." Then the judge asked Lazaro how he was doing in the school at the detention facility.

"What's your best subject?" the judge asked.

"We just started yesterday," said Lazaro.

"You didn't go to school over the summer?"

Lazaro's white female attorney interjected, "They didn't have summer school."

"And when you went to school, what was your favorite subject?" the judge asked Lazaro.

"English," answered Lazaro.

"And what was your worst subject?"

"Math."

"What about history, do you know anything about history?"

"No, sir."

"What was the last book that you read?"

"Harry Potter."

"Which one?"

"The first one."

"What happened at the end with the book?" the judge asked.

"I don't really remember."

"Do you remember when they are getting awards for who had the best house? Do you remember why Harry Potter's house got the most points at the end?"

"I know that his mom and his dad died."

"And who is the redhead fellow that got the points in Harry Potter? Who was it? Do you remember?" Lazaro couldn't remember.

"Ron," offered the ATI representative, coming to Lazaro's aid.

"Right," said the judge. "And you know why he got the most points? Because, who was it, it was Dumbledore, right? He said something like, 'It takes great courage to stand up to your enemies . . .'"

"Yes," said Lazaro remembering that part of the book.

"'But even more to stand up to your friends,'" the judge said seriously. "Do you understand what I'm saying to you?"

"Yes."

"You want to be a tough guy? You want to be a gangster?" the judge asked in an accusatory tone.

"No," Lazaro answered quickly.

"You can't do that in your world," the judge continued. "You are gonna have to walk alone."

"Yes, sir."

"And if you want me to take responsibility for you for the next five years, you better fully understand what's at stake here. Do you understand?"

"Yes, sir."

Like Walter, some defendants were released on their own recognizance (ROR'd) at their bail hearings and were OUT when they first came before the Youth Part. Some, like Lazaro, were remanded in the early part of the process. Others may have had a bail set low enough for families to afford and were also OUT when they came before the judge. Those not offered, or not able to make, bail were held either at Rikers Island or at a secure juvenile detention facility, depending upon their age.[12]

Judge Corriero had the discretion to set new bail terms for any defendant if he so chose, and he regularly did so. This meant that a kid who had originally been ROR'd or had made a low bail could be remanded by the judge on his first visit to the part. That is what happened to Jamar. A non-JO, Jamar had been arrested on a first-degree robbery charge in which he and several others were accused of punching someone and taking a PlayStation. Jamar had no Family Court history, and his mother and his pastor had put up his original bail. He had spent no time on Rikers Island. On his first appearance in the Youth Part, the judge felt the original bail to be inadequate and set new bail at $25,000 cash, an amount most likely impossible for the family to meet. Two court officers (COs) moved in to where Jamar was sitting, asked him to stand, handcuffed him, and led him out the back, to the shock of Jamar, his mother, and his pastor.

Such actions by the judge often appeared harsh, and seemed to be in contradiction to his basic child-saving philosophy. The issue of bail is complex, however, and Corriero's motivations were often multilayered: "When it comes to bail you have to recognize the irony of this whole thing of trying kids as adults. Say a 14-year-old gets out on bail. If he were charged in the Family Court there would only be two choices—remand him or not." The judge's motivation to remand a defendant often stemmed from concern for the long term outcome of the case:

My experience is that the kids who spend time here who are bailed out on serious matters are—good chance they are gonna be rearrested before this case is resolved because the impact of being arrested does not exist. The consequence of their behavior is non-existent. And so it's almost in a way counterproductive in the sense that my hands will be tied if this kid goes out and commits another crime while this case is pending. Then how can I justify giving him YO or a non-jail sentence?

Long-term plea bargaining goals were often a consideration for bail decisions as well. In a case where the judge might have been willing to give the kid a chance to earn YO, but knew that the DA's office would be pushing for a plea to the charge with no YO, the judge would set a high bail so that the kid did some time IN. Then down the line the judge could say to the prosecutor, "Well, he's been in for two months." The judge explained it this way:

> So let's say I have a case and right away I see that in order to give this kid Youthful Offender treatment, there has to be a combination of some jail time and probation. So let's say that I see that it is gonna take four months, and where is the district attorney on this case, are they gonna object to Youthful Offender treatment for this kid who may have been involved in the Family Court, and yet I still want to work with the kid. So all these things go into the basket, if you will, of what is the ultimate sentence. So if what comes together is a split sentence and I see a kid is out—how am I gonna get him there?

Sometimes, staying IN was part of a negotiated plan worked out among the defense, the prosecution, and the judge. Often the DA's office would oppose YO initially, and although the judge could grant YO over the objection of the People, he preferred to work toward consensus.[13] For example, the DA might agree that a certain high-risk defendant could be released into a program and monitored by the court after he had done three months, or six months, even a year, IN. Such negotiations were worked out in case conferences in the judge's chambers with the prosecutor and defense counsel. The judge explained it this way: "All these things ultimately work towards bringing everyone to a consensus about how to deal with a kid and perhaps get more kids out of the system, or out of the system without a record, than they would otherwise."

Such attempts to reach consensus were a large component of the culture of the Manhattan Youth Part, a culture not all defense attorneys or prosecutors were used to or trusting of at first. The judge said of defense attorneys and ADAs, "Some learn the culture of the Youth Part and they pick it up right away, and others don't and it is a rude awakening. Or there is a lack of trust. And I understand that, and I was a defense lawyer and a prosecutor and I try to be conscious of this." Such "operating realities of cooperation," as political scientists Edward Clynch and David Neubauer call them, have been reported in numerous studies of courts in action, often resulting in "shared decision-making" processes—the most common, of course, being plea bargaining.[14]

Finding Spaces within the Law: The Art of Discretion and Delay

Generally, in the process of earning YO, a defendant would first plead not guilty and the case would keep being put over while the kid worked with an ATI program. After enough time in the program had passed for the defendant to have been deemed worthy of YO, and all parties had agreed on a disposition that satisfied the prosecution, the defense, and the court, the defendant would plead guilty. The case would then be put over several more times until the kid had "earned YO" and was given a sentence of five years' probation and legally labeled a "Youthful Offender." This whole process could easily take six months, a year, sometimes two years, especially if a kid struggled to meet program requirements or had to be temporarily remanded along the way. Some kids reached success quickly; others took considerable time. Most kids spent several months working their way toward YO. Nothing in the law requires such a long journey to YO. In fact, under the law, the judge could have sentenced a defendant to YO very quickly, without ever requiring that he be involved with an ATI program or have his behavior monitored over time. The Manhattan Youth Part, under Judge Corriero, was known for the length of time that its cases took, compared with other New York City boroughs. Comparing the numbers for Manhattan to other boroughs is enlightening. For calendar year 2003, for example, as shown in Table 3.1, the median number of days from first court appearance through to sentencing (whatever it may be) for JOs in Manhattan was 574, compared with 275 in Brooklyn, 273 in the Bronx, and 78 in Queens.[15]

Judge Corriero was aware of this discrepancy and was not overly concerned by it. Such delay was almost always intentional in his court and was within the allowable exercise of his discretion. As the judge explained, "I use imagination to find spaces within the law. I think it was the first Judge Cardozo who said he finds the interstices in the law. So it is not novel

Table 3.1

Median Number of Days from First Supreme Court Appearance through Sentence for Juvenile Offenders (JO), 1999–2005

	Brooklyn	Bronx	Manhattan	Queens	Citywide*
1999	249.0	207.5	392.0	70.0	222.0
2000	134.5	252.0	364.0	76.0	241.5
2001	223.0	287.0	458.0	79.0	287.0
2002	171.5	213.5	542.0	34.0	183.0
2003	275.0	273.0	574.0	78.0	267.0
2004	184.5	270.0	476.0	32.5	157.0
2005	210.0	231.0	271.0	34.0	224.0

* Not including Staten Island

Source: Gewirtz (2002–2006), Criminal Justice Agnecy (2001)

to me." Indeed, Benjamin Cardozo did articulate a similar understanding about the creative nature of statutory interpretation: "[The judge] legislates only between the gaps, he fills the open spaces in the law . . . none the less, within the confines of the open spaces and those of precedent and tradition, choice moves with a freedom which stamps its action as creative. The law, which is the resulting product is not found, but made."[16]

As scholars of judicial discretion point out, the law as written is, by necessity, often general in nature and requires interpretation because written laws cannot account for the real-world contingencies encountered in the actual day-to-day administration of justice.[17] The manner in which criminal statutes—such as New York's Juvenile Offender or Youthful Offender laws—become enacted during the mundane work of a court depends upon a number of nonstatutory factors, such as the goals of various court actors (defense counsel, prosecution, social welfare agents, judges, even defendants and family members), the constraint imposed on judicial discretion by administrative guidelines, and the nature of the legal culture that emerges within a given court, as well as the individual creativity (or lack thereof) of a court's presiding judge. Judge Corriero articulated his own understanding of his right to exercise discretion within the broad parameters allowed by law when he explained his justification for the practice of purposefully delaying case processing in his court:

The idea is that if the law is silent, then I have a right to fill in the gap, theoretically, within the spirit of the law, but that involves an interpretation on my part. Let me give you an example: There is no rule that says I can't adjourn a case for a year until I sentence him.

Administrators, of course, want me to get these cases through, but there is no rule, there is no rule. There might be some question of unreasonable delay, but there is nothing to prevent me from doing it. In that sense, that's a space in the law. There is nothing to prevent me from developing, through my imagination, if you will, a way of putting a kid in a better position to earn Youthful Offender treatment than they would otherwise get.

By using his discretion to postpone disposition of a case to allow time for evidence to accumulate about a kid's ability to be rehabilitated, the judge felt he was in a much better position to make an informed and realistic determination on the best possible disposition for a kid: "I ask, How do you determine a kid's prospects for rehabilitation? Solely on the basis of prior behavior? No. I think we should see what a kid has learned from the interaction [with the court] and by postponing sentence. [Then] I am in a better position to determine the prospect for rehabilitation and that's how we justify that."

After a kid had been monitored for several months by an ATI program and the court, the judge was no longer limited to making a sentencing decision based solely on a defendant's alleged behavior prior to indictment. Slowing down the process also afforded the ATI programs time to identify issues and provide services for distressed kids and their families. Delay, beyond the normal bureaucratic variety, was a purposeful exercise of discretion used to affect sentencing outcomes and allow kids to avoid felony convictions. Many defense attorneys went along with this intentional delay because it often worked toward better outcomes for their clients. As one defense attorney put it, "He's carved out a space for judicial discretion. Which the YO statute allows for. And I collaborate with him, if it is best for my client." A representative of the DA's office voiced similar attitudes of acquiescence to Judge Corriero's way of doing things:

He has developed a way of handling these cases that is probably working out reasonably well—as well as anything else, or better— and he has control of it. He basically puts those kids through their paces, and if it works, [then good]. And in many ways we go along with it. Occasionally we might complain a bit, but it is not frequent. He keeps those cases for a long time; even after they plead guilty, they go on and on and you have to "earn" whatever he is going to give you, and that is a good approach. So we basically rely a lot on that wisdom of the judge.

Both Aaron Kupchik and Malcolm Feeley, author of *The Process Is the Punishment: Handling Cases in a Lower Criminal Court*, found in their respective courtroom research that strategic delay was an institutionalized practice used by court actors for the purpose of improving dispositional outcomes.[18] Such unofficial collaboration among members of a court workgroup is quite common in the daily administration of criminal justice.[19] I asked Judge Corriero once, "So the irony here is that delay in the legal system, which is usually criticized, may actually work, in the end, to help some of these kids?" His response was a simple "yes" and a smile. When asked if he ever got complaints from other court actors, he said, "We've been very fortunate that our judgment hasn't been overly called into question by granting so many of these kids YO." This statement reflects the judge's own awareness of the limits, both formal and informal, on his judicial agency. While he had considerable power over case processing and procedure, his discretion was not without constraint. He could only operate "creatively" within the parameters established by statute, and there was always the threat of appeal and possible reversal of his decisions and the accompanying diminishing confidence in his abilities to judge fairly. These, along with the dictates of precedent and ever-present political considerations set significant boundaries on his exercise of discretion.[20]

More importantly, Judge Corriero's judicial agency was also constrained by the emergence of a set of known standards within the court for handling similar cases.[21] Consistency builds trust among courtroom actors, where defense attorneys, prosecutors, defendants, parents, and others come to know what they can expect from the judge and from the process. By establishing a consistent pattern of case processing, the court can better maintain smooth daily operations. Stepping too far outside established parameters can jeopardize this spirit of unofficial collaboration. All of these factors worked to establish reasonable limits on the exercise of judicial discretion within the part. Judge Corriero articulated his awareness of these multiple constraints: "The Youth Part is an institution that is kind of struggling to go upstream while the current is running downstream.... You cannot take for granted the existence of the Youth Part so it was very important for me to try and harmonize the different power structures, the different interests. So that is an essential requirement—to balance the different claims that are going on."

The judge was not required by law to place youths in programs and monitor their progress, or to spend time getting to know them individually, listening to their stories, allowing them time and space to prove themselves rehabilitatable, giving them second, sometimes third and fourth chances. Such diversionary tactics actually run counter to the intent of the Juvenile Offender Law, which implied that kids charged with JO offenses were beyond the scope of traditional models of youth rehabilitation, that they were the kids for whom little could, or should, be done. In developing diversionary mechanisms in opposition to this attitude, Judge Corriero exercised not only judicial agency, but a certain degree of activism. The judge has written, "I stand by the belief that no adolescent should be incarcerated unless every consideration has been given to an alternative."[22] This philosophy guided the work of the Youth Part. Tactics of discretion and delay, of course, are not unique to this judge or this courtroom, but their manifestation in the Manhattan Youth Part was particular to the specific culture that prevailed within the court and the overt desire of the judge and others to create alternatives to the harsh intent of the Juvenile Offender Law. Thus, through the establishment of what sociologists Jeffrey Ulmer and John Kramer have called "formal and informal case processing norms,"[23] the Manhattan Youth Part developed a system, a culture, for the administration of law that reflected its own negotiated version of substantive justice.[24] Because of this, the judge sometimes garnered criticism—either that he coddled young offenders or that he exerted way too much control over them.

ATI Programs and Court Monitoring of Progress

Alternative-to-incarceration programs were invaluable for the work and culture of the court, and it was mostly through them that defendants earned YO. ATIs helped the court monitor defendants and connect kids and their families with needed social-welfare services. The exact mandates and program designs of the various ATIs differ. Some are publicly funded, while some are funded only with private monies. Some are mandated to work with certain populations or age groups. The Youth Advocacy Project (YAP), part of the Center for Community Alternatives (CCA), for example, provides six- to twelve-month programs specifically for JOs. The Center for Alternative Sentencing and Employment Services (CASES) offers a six-month program for youths aged 16 to 19. The Andrew Glover Youth Program (AGYP), a privately funded, community-based program, provides a variety of services for kids of all ages residing in the Lower East Side and East Harlem. While these and other ATI programs are each structured in their own way, all served three major functions for Youth Part defendants: monitoring, reporting to the court, and providing services or referrals for services. Monitoring of youths included enforcing curfews through call-in mechanisms, making home visits, conducting school visits to check on attendance and performance, random drug testing, and verifying that clients were attending all in-house or outsourced programming. ATI programs generally assign a case manager to each kid to assess his individual needs and sometimes that of his family. After assessment, kids are linked with needed services provided either in-house or outsourced. These services include evaluations to determine the presence of mental illness and/or learning disabilities, GED preparation, IQ testing, individual and group counseling, substance abuse counseling, job preparedness training, educational assessment and placements, family therapy, anger management classes, mentoring, tutoring, internships, life skills training, HIV/AIDS prevention education, recreational activities, and residential placement for homeless youth and others who cannot, for whatever reason, return home. The ATIs provided the court with written weekly reports on a youth's attendance and progress in the various programs, reported the results of random drug tests, and communicated with the court between defendants' court appearances if needed.

The judge, his staff, and many defense attorneys who frequented the court were familiar with the various ATIs and other program services available for kids. The judge often made specific recommendations for service providers for an individual kid: "[I]t is very important to link a kid with the right program because what happens if they fail in the program? Then my back is against the wall—but it may be a program that wasn't suited for them." ATIs can't solve all problems in a young person's life in a short six months or even a year, but they can at least begin to identify and address issues that may have led to their clients' alleged offending in the first place. Many ATIs purposefully connect clients with outside agencies so that kids can continue to receive services and programming even after their limited time in an ATI was over.

Program representatives I interviewed expressed a reality-based understanding of the impact they could make in a kid's life in the short time they were involved. As one representative put it: "I don't contend that I engage a defendant or a client and tomorrow the magic wand is waved.

It takes time. These kids have been living under certain premises and living certain lifestyles, and then all of a sudden they have to do something else." ATI personnel described several recurrent themes among their clients—lack of a father figure, parents with drug and/or alcohol problems or mental health issues, lack of parental supervision, peer pressure, gangs, distressed communities, persistent poverty, and inadequate educational resources.

The judge explained the court's dependence on the ATI programs: "ATI programs are an essential component of what we do. We rely on them—they are extensions of the court in the Youth Part. No kid comes through this part who isn't connected to an ATI program, whether you plead guilty or not." The ATIs, defense attorneys, and the court worked in tandem to monitor the progress of a kid over the months they were with the court. If things were going smoothly with a kid in an ATI, the judge would schedule a court date about once a month. If there were indications that problems might arise, he would schedule court dates more frequently. If things were going exceptionally well, he might put the case on for two months out. If a problem arose between court dates, programs would notify the court and the case would be added to an upcoming calendar day. Generally, the judge knew the contents of ATI reports before a kid stepped before him on a calendar day, especially if there were problems.

If a kid was OUT and in a program and all was going well, his appearance in the court might only take a few minutes. The case would be called, the ATI representative would report that all is going well or that they were still working on a particular referral or some other detail. If nothing more was needed, the next court date would be scheduled and the next case called. For kids who had been doing well in programs, their few minutes before the court were often used by the judge to praise their progress. The ATI representative would tell the court, "He is doing very well," or would share with the judge an award the kid got in the program or some other achievement. The judge would say, "Keep up the good work," and schedule the next court date. If a kid was doing particularly well, the judge would extend his curfew or give permission for a family trip out of state as a reward for good performance.

Not surprisingly, not all cases of kids trying to earn YO went smoothly. Sometimes, if a defendant was not meeting all the requirements set by the program or by the court, the judge would decide to remand him for a while as a reminder of the potential consequences of not completing the program. Such was the case with Lorenzo, a black youth.

When Lorenzo's case was called one calendar day, his lawyer asked to approach and after a long sidebar the judge told Lorenzo to stand up.

"You haven't done what I expected," the judge stated. "You've acted irresponsibly. I gave you a chance, just to show up, and you didn't show up [to the program]. You haven't acted responsibly in the community. The defendant is remanded."

Lorenzo was handcuffed and escorted out of the courtroom by COs. The judge put the case over for the following week, which was also the first day of classes for the city's public schools. On that date, Lorenzo was released back to the program so that he could enter school, and three weeks later the program reported to the judge that he was "doing well, has attended all sessions, testing negative." On that calendar day the judge told Lorenzo to "keep up the good work."

Javier's Journey to Y.O.

Javier's story is a useful case study for many of the issues surrounding the process of earning YO and demonstrates the type of relationship that many defendants developed with the court over their months of interaction. In this account we see the judge getting to know Javier, the process of connecting Javier with services, the second chance he is given after a temporary remand, and the issues surrounding school and employment.

JAVIER

Javier, a tall, lanky Hispanic non-JO, had been with the court for a few months and had been working with one of the ATI programs. Javier knew the ropes and walked easily through the low gates when his name was called. His hair was almost to his shoulders.

"You are letting your hair grow?" the judge asked as Javier arrived.

"Yes," said Javier.

"Why is that—new look?" the judge inquired.

"No reason," said Javier noncommittally.

"Didn't you have long hair when you were young, judge?" Javier's white male attorney joked.

"I wasn't criticizing," the judge said, smiling. "I wish I could do it. I understand he's doing well."

"Everything is going good," Javier said.

"How about working?" the judge inquired.

"He's got an application," Javier's attorney said.

"Did we follow through on Big Brother?" asked the judge.

"We are awaiting word," Javier's attorney answered.

"How old are you now?" the judge asked Javier.

"Seventeen."

"We ought to get this young man ready for sentence, shouldn't we? Where is the program representative? Did they show up?" the judge asked, looking around the court.

"Not here," Javier said.

"I would like to sentence the defendant if he's doing well," the judge said. "Why don't we wait and see if the program people are coming." Javier's attorney explained that he needed to be in another part and was not able to wait around so the judge put the case over for a month.

A month later, when Javier's case was called, the program representative was there.

"How's he doing in the program?" the judge asked her.

"He's been attending, he's been attending," she said.

"Who is here with him today?" the judge asked.

"His mother," Javier's mother answered from the audience.

"If I can approach?" asked the program representative.

"Yeah," said the judge and the representative, defense attorney, and ADA approached the bench.

After their sidebar discussion, the judge addressed Javier, "You've been using drugs?"

"No," said Javier.

"What time did you go to bed last night?" the judge asked, his voice shaded with frustration and impatience.

"One-thirty," said Javier.

"What were you doing?" the judge asked, frowning.

"Watching TV," replied Javier.

"What about school?" the judge asked, knowing that it was a school night.

"I had court," said Javier in a matter-of-fact tone.

"You think it is okay to come in here unfocused?" the judge said, his voice showing more frustration. "STAND UP YOUNG MAN!" the judge said.

Javier stood up.

"I DON'T LIKE YOUR BEHAVIOR IN THE PROGRAM. I DON'T LIKE WHAT'S GOING ON. I DON'T LIKE THE FACT YOU ARE WALKING

AROUND WITH A KNIFE WHEN YOU ARE OUT ON A GUNPOINT ROBBERY, WHERE I'VE GIVEN YOU A SECOND CHANCE, YOU UNDERSTAND ME? I'M NOT GOING TO TOLERATE THIS. THIS DEFENDANT IS REMANDED AND IT'S NOT JUST FOR TODAY. HE'S REMANDED AND I WILL SEE HIM ON WEDNESDAY."

A CO handcuffed Javier and led him out the back door. The judge, his voice softening, said to Javier's mother, "Let me explain to you why, so you fully understand. Walking around with a knife, he's crossing personal boundaries with people who are trying to work and help him. He's got an attitude. It seems to me, there is a lot of things going on with him, and it can't be tolerated. He's only out of jail because I put him in this program. I don't expect him to get worse, and I don't expect him to disrespect anybody that I connect him with. And until he learns that, he's going to have to stay where he is or I am not taking a chance with him, and I'm just going to sentence him on the original sentence recommended by the district attorney, alright? Do you have any questions you want to ask me?" the judge asked.

"When is his next court date, Wednesday?" Javier's mother asked.

A week later, Javier was ROR'd by the judge and returned to the program; a month later, the same ATI representative gave Javier a positive report. The judge told Javier to "keep up the good work" and adjourned the case for another month. A month later, Javier came before the court again, this time with his long hair braided into narrow cornrows.

"I have a report from the program," the judge said, and then asked Javier, "Have you finished summer school?"

"No, I'm still in the process of summer school," Javier replied.

"How is he doing at home?" the judge asked Javier's mother, who, as always, was in the audience. "He's doing good," she said, "he stays home."

"He doesn't have to stay home," the judge said.

"No, actually he stays home," said Javier's mother.

"Does he do something when he's home, something positive?" the judge asked.

"He helps me around the house, picks me up from work at times," she said easily.

"When are you expecting to get your report card?" the judge asked Javier. Javier said he would get it in about a month, and the judge gave Javier a court date after that time, saying, "We'll put this on for sentence. If you stay out of trouble, continue to do what you are supposed to do, I'll sentence you to probation and Youthful Offender treatment." There was no trace in the judge's voice or demeanor of the frustration or disappointment he had demonstrated two months prior.

"The defendant would like to inform you that he has a job," said the attorney who was filling in for Javier's regular attorney.

"What are you doing?" the judge asked, and Javier explained that he was working in a restaurant. The judge asked if he worked in the kitchen, and Javier said, "No, I'm on the line," and went on to explain the details of what he did at work. The judge listened to Javier's explanation with interest and then said, "Good, keep up the good work."

On Javier's next scheduled date, about five weeks later, the first thing the judge said as Javier walked up to take his seat was, "You better be do doing well." Once again the program representative asked to approach, and after a short sidebar conversation the judge said, "I want to see your report card, and where have you been working?"

"Same place," said Javier, "But the thing is, I was talking to my mom about it. I had a discussion with by boss of how I was last year—to go back to weekends because school started."

"So you're going to be able to work on weekends?" the judge asked.

"Yes, I'm going to talk to my boss today," answered Javier.

"And you want to work?" the judge inquired.

"Yes, but it is just interrupting with my school."

"This is a good job that you have?" asked the judge.

"Yes."

"You're not going to get in trouble anymore?" asked the judge.

"No," said Javier.

"So what you have to do is make sure the people at the program understand your problems and check in with them," the judge said. This statement implied that the program was having some issues with Javier, though the representative did not announce them in court and they were not severe enough to jeopardize Javier's status.

Two and a half months later, the program reported that all was going well with Javier and the judge put the case over for one more month saying, "We'll put it on for sentence, if all goes well."

A year later, Javier was still with the court. He was doing well after a few more bumps in the road, during which time the judge had continued to delay sentencing. Eventually Javier made steady progress, and the case was finally put on for sentence. Javier was doing well in school and had a part-time job. After more than a year and a half with the court, he was finally going to earn YO and five years' probation.[25]

Cesar and Timo: Not Earning YO

Not all kids who came before the court earned YO and five years' probation. Some, of course, simply weren't eligible. For these defendants, the options were very limited. Most of them would take a negotiated plea, opting to plead guilty for an agreed amount of time incarcerated, rather than go to trial.[26] Some defendants who are given the chance to earn YO will ultimately fail. Cesar never had the chance to earn YO, while Timo had the chance but failed to earn it.

CESAR

Cesar was not eligible for YO. A 15-year-old Hispanic JO charged with a first-degree robbery in which he pointed a gun and threatened to kill someone, his options were limited. Under the law, the use of a real gun precludes YO unless a case can be made for mitigating factors, and the law is very strict about what qualifies as evidence of mitigation. As the court attorney explained:

> Unless the judge finds mitigation—and it is not mitigation that you had a terrible childhood, that you were beaten, your parents were drug users or in jail, it's not that kind of mitigation. It's not that kind of mitigation that makes you almost sympathetic toward the defendant. It is mitigation in the manner in which the crime was committed—which is very difficult, very difficult. It is almost impossible in those kinds of situations to find that kind of mitigation for the gun wielder.

There was no mitigation in Cesar's case. The ADA was recommending a sentence of two to six years and no YO (the maximum sentence allowable was three and a third to ten years).

When Cesar was brought before the court on his adjourn date (he had been remanded since his arrest), the judge said, "I have all your information, I've been trying to find a sentence that I think is fair in this case. I don't know all the answers; I find this case to be extremely difficult. I see a young man before me who doesn't appear to be capable of the charges against him. But I am limited by the nature of the crime. The DA is recommending two to six with no YO. He pointed a gun and threatened to kill someone. It was a real gun, and he did this by himself. I have very little choice. I wish I could wave a magic wand."

Cesar pleaded guilty. During his allocution, Cesar said that he had been with two others but that they hadn't been caught. When the judge asked Cesar why he had done it, he said, "I had to prove myself." Cesar's mother, sitting in the audience, sobbed through most of his allocution. After the COs handcuffed Cesar and led him out, the judge stared hard at the back wall of the courtroom for a few minutes, as he was prone to do after a particularly difficult interaction. There was nothing else to be done for Cesar. Two months later, the judge sentenced Cesar, with his mother and sister in the audience, to one and a half to four and a half years with no YO. The judge explained to Cesar that he was going to have a record, saying, "It is a hard thing to go through life with a record."

TIMO

A Hispanic JO, Timo had been OUT and in a program for about four months, long enough for him to have studied for and taken a GED exam, but the court was still keeping a close eye on him. As Timo approached the desk one Friday, the white female attorney who was filling in for Timo's usual lawyer said, "As far as I know he is doing well in [the program]."

"Is that right?" the judge asked Timo. "I am not going to hear any bad reports? You are making all your appointments?"

"Yes," replied Timo.

"How is school coming along?" the judge asked him.

"I am doing okay. I just finished taking the GED," Timo explained.

"What time did you go to bed last night?" the judge inquired, seeing something about the kid's affect that seemed off.

"I didn't go to sleep."

"Why not?"

"Because something happened to my sister and I couldn't sleep," Timo explained.

"What happened to your sister?" asked the judge.

"She had a miscarriage," Timo said softly.

"You were up with her?" the judge asked in a soft tone.

"Yes," said Timo.

"Is she alright now?" the judge asked in a sincere tone.

"She's okay," said Timo. After a short pause the judge asked, in a steady, patient tone, "Are you sure that's the only reason you didn't go to sleep?"

"That's the only reason, sir," Timo replied.

"Okay, see you on the adjourn date." The judge announced a date five weeks in the future and then stopped himself. "Actually, I want to see you sooner than that," he said and set a date two weeks away. "I want to make sure your report is where it is supposed to be."

Two weeks later, when Timo came before the court, the judge asked for a report from the ATI program.

"Unfortunately, Timo has been going through a personal issue that has been brought to our attention," she reported. "I will not present Timo's personal information to Your Honor. If he wishes to share that with you, which I have encouraged him to do, then he can. Hopefully, this will be able to, not excuse his actions, but give some sort of understanding as to what's been going on."

"What actions are we talking about?" the judge asked.

"He has not made a great effort in calling in for curfew and he moved out of his home with his mother and in with his girlfriend," the representative explained.

"Where is his mother?" the judge asked.

"He is here by himself," the representative answered.

The judge directed his next question to the program representative: "He moved in to his girlfriend's house without asking your permission or mine?"

"Yes."

"He took it upon himself to do that?" the judge asked, his voice tightening.

"I explained it to him . . ." the representative started to say.

"While he's out on a robbery?" the judge interjected with notable frustration in his voice.

"He has since moved back home and he understands," the representative offered. "He had a little derailment and I really . . ." She then turned toward Timo and said, "Timo, I want you, really, to explain to the judge what's going on."

Timo attempted to explain: "For the past two weeks, I have been going through arguments with my mother and then I moved in with my girl because . . . right now . . . my . . . my girl . . . is one month pregnant, so I was staying with her."

"You are acting responsibly?" the judge asked, frustrated and slightly angry.

"He was trying to act responsible," the representative said, coming to Timo's defense.

"You say he got his girlfriend pregnant?" the judge asked the representative, as if to say, "This is acting responsibly?"

"He understands that's not the best thing to do," she said. "He thought that being responsible meant moving in with her and helping to take care of her. I told him that he will not have anybody to take care of if he is sitting in jail and does not take care of his own responsibilities first."

"This is . . ." the judge started. "I have to unwind this. Why are you arguing with your mother?" he asked Timo.

"Because me and my moms . . ." Timo started to explain.

"Your MOTHER, not your 'moms,'" the judge said, correcting Timo.

"Me and my mother . . . whatever I do, she don't agree with it."

"Understand that getting your girlfriend pregnant is something I wouldn't agree with," the judge interjected impatiently, and then added, in a calmer tone, "Go ahead, continue."

"It's like my mother, she likes to argue for every little thing I do. I don't like to argue with my mom and disrespect my mom."

The judge's frustration seemed to grow as he said, "I don't think you are doing ANYTHING that I expected you to do. I let you out on a VERY serious case. I don't expect nonsense like this to interfere with you dealing with the program."

Again the ATI representative intervened: "If it makes any consolation, up until the past two weeks, Timo has been doing excellent since his release. It's just recently he found out his girlfriend was pregnant. He has been going through an issue."

"You should have thought about the issue of getting her pregnant. That's the issue, not after she's pregnant," the judge responded, sounding somewhat exasperated.

Timo's attorney chimed in, saying, "Judge, as she said, he has done very well up until the last two weeks and there was a major case conference yesterday involving his mother. I am making a referral to our therapeutic social worker."

While the attorney was speaking, the judge reviewed the paperwork for the case on the desk before him.

"This is a real gun used in this case," the judge said, "whether it was on him or not." Although Timo was most likely not the gun-wielder, the very presence of a gun on any codefendant makes the charges against all that much more serious. The judge took a moment to look again at the papers in front of him and then, in a stern voice announced, "The defendant is remanded."

Timo turned his head to one side, and though he made no real facial expression, the muscles in his jaw tightened.

"The defendant is remanded until Wednesday," the judge said.

As the COs escorted him past the judge's bench, Timo didn't look at the judge and the judge didn't look at him. Instead, the judge turned his head a bit to one side, and I could see the muscles in his jaw clenching as well.

As Timo was led out the door, the judge turned to the court reporter and said, in a softer tone, "The record should be clear: he's not being remanded because he got his girlfriend pregnant, but because he didn't do what we asked of him."

Timo's case had not been resolved by the end of my fieldwork, but he was eventually re-released into a program, subsequently failed to meet the program requirements, and was again remanded. Nearly a year after he had first been released into a program, Timo remained incarcerated at a DJJ facility. The ADA on the case was asking for a sentence of two to six years and was opposing YO for Timo. There had been a gun involved in the original case, after all. The options available for Timo were now quite limited—Timo had been unable to earn YO.

Data on Youthful Offender Treatment

Claims often leveled at Judge Corriero—that he was overly lenient or relied too heavily on giving kids YO—are not borne out by the data. Data on JOs who are given YO in New York City show that, between 1995 and 2005, JOs in Manhattan did not receive YO status at higher rates than JOs citywide, and that for class A felonies, Manhattan JOs were actually much less likely to receive a YO sentence.[27] I was not able to obtain data on the percentage of non-JOs in the Manhattan Youth Part that received YO treatment, but given that similar court strategies are used with JOs and non-JOs, we would expect similar percentages. A study, by the nonprofit

Criminal Justice Agency, of JOs processed in New York City between January 1997 and December 2000 reports that only 74% of cases in Manhattan received YO, compared to 77% in Brooklyn, 84% in the Bronx, and 85% in Queens.[28]

More general claims of leniency on Corriero's part are also not borne out by the data. In Manhattan, 76% of JOs were detained at arraignment (24% were released) compared with 78% citywide. In addition, among those detained at some time, the median number of days held in Manhattan was 201, compared with only 112 citywide (116 in Brooklyn, 68 in the Bronx, 66 in Staten Island, and 57 in Queens).[29] Moreover, as mentioned above, the Manhattan Youth Part took longer to resolve cases, and kids tended to appear in court more times before sentencing than in other boroughs. These findings support the general understanding of many who worked in or around the Manhattan Youth Part: The judge's concern for the kids in his part, his sympathy for their circumstances, and his dedication to diversion did not necessarily translate into leniency. In fact, in many ways, Judge Corriero was harder on his kids—requiring long periods of close court and ATI supervision in order to earn YO. As a representative from the DA's office said about the Youth Part practices, "[Corriero] can be tougher in a sense because he has a great insight into those cases. I think Corriero has a heart of gold, but I think can be tough. He basically puts these kids through their paces."

Individualized Justice in a Criminal Court

One of the main tenets of the early juvenile justice movement was the emphasis on the need for *individualized justice*—the idea that the punishments meted out or treatment and social welfare interventions prescribed for young offenders were to be based on the circumstances, history, and life conditions of each individual child. In contrast, criminal law had traditionally been more focused on the nature of the offense than the offender. Since the retributive turn and due-process revolution of the 1970s, the popularity of rehabilitation-based individualized responses to youth offending has waned considerably, even within the juvenile courts. In her juvenile court ethnography *Inside a Juvenile Court: The Tarnished Ideal of Individualized Justice*, M. A. Bortner found that while the concept of individualized justice was touted as an organizing philosophy, it was rarely enacted in the court. She instead found a strong depersonalization of juveniles and parents, with both largely reduced to stereotyped roles and "not treated as individuals."[1]

Individualized justice, however, was the order of the day in the Manhattan Youth Part. The approach Judge Corriero used in the court was specific to each individual defendant, to his family and his history, and reflected the specifics of each kid's case. Over the months that defendants came before the court, the judge and the ATI program personnel got to know the kids and the issues in their family lives as well as the nature of any drug dependencies, psychological problems, learning disabilities, or other issues that may have been instrumental to the alleged offending. The judge had an ongoing relationship with each kid, especially those eligible for YO treatment, and their interactions on calendar days reflected the nature of that relationship.[2] The Youth Part was required to operate within a much more strict legal structure than early juvenile courts, but the guiding philosophy of those earlier institutions was fully embodied within courtroom interactions, attitudes, and language. It was a criminal court, yet in its day-to-day handling of cases, it harkened back to the early Progressive Era *parens patriae*–style juvenile courts with their emphasis on individualized justice and rehabilitative goals. In her writings on the Manhattan Youth Part, sociologist Caroline DeBrovner also points to the individual relationship of trust that Judge Corriero tried to establish with defendants and the humanitarian approach he took in dealing with the Youth Part kids. She likens the judge's way of interacting to a "therapeutic jurisprudence" based on factors of humanity, consistency, reciprocal trust-building, and the cultivation of different future behaviors for the kids.[3]

The nature of the relationships that the judge developed over the months with most of the kids was quite paternalistic. He always looked for an opportunity to connect with a kid or to use a situation to teach a lesson. Much like a caring father would, he praised, lectured, admonished, reproached, got frustrated with and disappointed by his teenagers. He showed concern and pride and patience, but also reprimanded and delivered swift and sometimes serious punishment.

As the judge took on the role of a surrogate father, the ATI program personnel in many ways assumed the role of surrogate mothers. ATI programs monitor and surveil, but they also mentor, counsel, nurture, help problem-solve, and assist kids and their families. On calendar days, ATI personnel would often advocate for their clients, sometimes coming to their defense. Although not unwilling to give a negative report to the court, they would often seem reluctant to share bad news, or they would pad bad news with good, saying, for example, "He has tested positive for marijuana, but he hasn't missed any sessions and he always calls in for curfew." When a report was particularly negative, ATI representatives would sometimes report "just the facts" without elaboration, such as, "He hasn't been to the program in two weeks; we tried to call but the phone was disconnected," and wait for the judge to ask before providing any more negative information. They would also often go out of their way to alert the court to a defendant's accomplishments, such as passing the regents exam, or they would offer a statement like, "He is doing much better, Your Honor."

In interviews, many ATI representatives articulated strong empathy for their young charges. When talking about the rather frequent use of marijuana among her clients, one representative said, "Some of them, just, that's what they do when they hang out with their friends, and you know, some of them, their lives aren't that great anyway." Another ATI worker, when discussing the anger-management issues many kids faced, said, "Yeah, a lot of these kids are angry. A lot of them have reasons to be angry." Another ATI worker explained how empathy often resulted in her taking a position of advocacy for a kid in the court:

> You know these kids aren't going to be perfect. But that's why sometimes I might stand up and beg, or try to convince the judge to not lock them up in some way, because in their own way they are

progressing, they have come a step up from where they were before they were arrested. So they might not be the perfect angels that we would hope them to be, but no one is and I don't know if they ever will be. We try to find progress. We forget that we are working with teenagers. I remember what I was like as a teenager, and that is hard enough, and then they have all this other stuff going on.

The calendar-day interactions detailed below show the many ways that maternalism, paternalism, and individualized justice were enacted within the court as kids worked their way to earning YO. These accounts also illustrate the variety of discursive strategies the judge utilized in his encounters with the kids and the often nurturing and advocating role taken by ATI personnel. These accounts are organized by defendant rather than by particular themes or the discursive techniques employed. There are a number of reasons for this. First, often more than one discursive technique was employed with each defendant, sometimes within a single calendar call. Second, although many of the strategies utilized by the judge —praising, cautioning, counseling, admonishing, lecturing, trust-building —were used consistently across defendants, such strategies were regularly tailored to the specific circumstances and personality of individual defendants. The judge's patience, or impatience, his selective use of a particular cautionary tale, the specific type of lesson he may have tried to drive home, the exact "deal" he made with a defendant, reflected the knowledge the judge had of each particular kid and the details of his case. How the judge lectured Jeffrey differently than he did Wesley demonstrates how the discursive strategies used in the court were highly individualized.

Further, each defendant in the Manhattan Youth Part—indeed, each of the court actors—had a personal style, a particular pattern of speech, a unique courtroom persona. Although all names used for defendants are pseudonyms and many identifying descriptors have been left out to protect their privacy, I prefer to leave the accounts of courtroom interactions intact in order to allow each of the kids to exist, on the page, as an individual, not just a member of a generic group of "defendants." Since they were not treated as such within the part, I would not want to do so here.

These accounts show the court's daily dedication to diversion, the empathy, the *parens patriae*–infused treatment, and the array of discursive and dramatic tactics used to teach lessons, build trust, admonish and punish errant behavior. By applying a model of justice wherein kids were allowed to develop relationships over time with the court, by giving these kids "second chances" when allowable under the law, by emphasizing ATI program–based models of rehabilitation, and by allowing opportunities to "earn YO," the court in essence succeeded, in many ways, to re-enact the basic concepts of *parens patriae*—updated and restructured to work within the constraints and limited "spaces" allowable under criminal statute.

Parens Patriae in Action

Roger and David—Teaching Lessons, Giving Fatherly Advice

ROGER

Roger, a 15-year-old black JO, had been OUT and in an ATI program for a while. The judge had extended Roger's curfew because he had been doing well and was trying to get a summer job. On the court date recounted below, however, it was reported that Roger had tested positive for marijuana, an infraction of the terms of his agreement with the court. Here, the ATI representative stood up for Roger and the judge used the minor infraction not as an excuse to punish Roger, but as an opportunity for a "teachable moment," a chance to reiterate the potential consequences of future infractions. In this interaction, the judge attempts to understand the circumstances around Roger's marijuana smoking, to try and understand, and help Roger understand, why he had smoked it.

"How are you, Roger?" the judge asked when Roger walked up.

"There has been a minor slip, judge," Roger's white male attorney said.

"What is that?" the judge asked.

"There was a positive test for marijuana," the attorney answered.

"Is this the first time he's tested positive?" the judge asked the white female ATI representative, without any anger in his voice.

"Yes," she said. The judge then turned to Roger and asked, "What was the occasion of that?"

"It was a mistake," Roger said.

"We all make mistakes," the judge said, "but what was the *reason* for the mistake?"

"I wasn't thinking at the moment."

"You mean when your friend passed you a joint?"

"Yes."

"You weren't thinking. Were you in a dream?" the judge asked, still with no hint of anger or frustration in his voice.

"I feel that I'm not trying to get out of line. There's no excuse."

"You wanted to smoke marijuana. That's understandable. But what was the occasion? Were you having a party, or were you hanging out on the corner? What?"

"There was no occasion."

"So, you were just standing around smoking marijuana?"

"I was just hanging out."

"Hanging out, smoking marijuana?"

"Um-hum."

"Do you know what the problem is with that?" the judge asked. "I make no judgments as to the medicinal value. The problem is that you are out on a robbery case and we placed you in a program. If you continue to smoke marijuana, I'm going to have no choice but to put you in jail. Do you understand that?"

"Yes," said Roger.

"What's going to happen the next time your friends are hanging out and they want to pass you a joint?" the judge asked.

"Nothing, because I'll be going back in," explained Roger.

"So, you've been warned. Do you understand me?"

"Yes."

"Otherwise, how is he doing?" the judge asked, turning to the ATI representative.

"He comes to every appointment, individual, group," she offered.

"How is he doing at home?" the judge asked Roger's mother, who was standing in the audience.

"He's doing good," she responded.

"He listens to you?" the judge asked her.

"I have no problems, maybe just an attitude," she said.

"What kind of attitude? He talks back?" the judge inquired.

"He talks back," Roger's mother said. "Other than that, he's going to the programs and doing what he's supposed to."

The judge looked back to Roger and said, "You have to respect your mother. Do you understand me?"

"Yes."

Six weeks later, when Roger was again before the court, the ATI representative reported that he was doing well and had continued to test negative for marijuana. When the judge asked his mother how he was doing at home, she replied, "Since you spoke with him I've had no problems."

Another month later, Roger was still testing negative and doing well at home. The judge used Roger's time before the court to engage him in a discussion of his schooling and to praise his progress. The judge allowed time for Roger to speak about his positive progress in school and used self-deprecating humor to praise Roger's hard work.

"How are you, Roger?" The judge asked.

"Fine. And yourself?" Roger answered.

"I'm not bad, but I am struggling to be good," said the judge who had had several difficult cases that morning. Roger's mother also reported that he was doing well at home.

"He is doing excellent," the ATI representative reported. "He is doing excellent with our program at the center, he is an active participant. He attends all sessions."

"Good, I'm proud of you," the judge said to Roger. "How are you doing in school?"

"I like it."

"You passing everything?" the judge inquired with an interested tone.

"Yes, they said I should finish in February."

"What's your best subject?"

"I am starting to get good at fractions," Roger replied, a hint of surprise in his voice.

"Give me an example," the judge said with enthusiasm.

"Like, I'm taught how to reduce them. Before I never used to know how to do fractions like that. But my teacher takes time to break it down and help me," the boy said.

"Good," the judge said, adding with a smile, "I still don't understand fractions." Several people in the courtroom chuckled. Roger laughed.

"Keep up the good work," the judge said, adding, "we will see how he does on the next adjourn date and we will get closer to sentencing him to probation and Youthful Offender treatment."

Over the weeks Judge Corriero had worked to build a kind of personal relationship with Roger, a relationship built on mutual trust.[4]

DAVID

David was a black JO who had been working with an ATI program and was only doing so well. The judge provided fatherly advice to David about what not to wear to a job interview, explained to him why testing positive for marijuana was problematic, and used David's interest in boxing for a quick lesson on anger management.

"How is he doing?" the judge asked David's mother, who was standing at the audience railing.

"He is . . ." David's mother started to answer.

"I got a desk appearance ticket," David told the judge.

"For what?" the judge asked.

"A clip of marijuana."

"What's a clip? The judge asked.

"It's a roach," David's white male attorney explained.

"You mean a roach. The lingo. Now, a clip is a small one—as opposed to your generation's lingo of a roach?" the judge asked the attorney.

"I think so," David's attorney answered.

"I was cutting class in school," David also confessed.

"Why are all these things happening?" the judge asked calmly.

"The class I felt was a little too hard," David said.

"It will only get harder if you don't go," the judge said.

"I know, and the marijuana—I was with a kid and he was flipping a knife and the cops rolled up on him and they checked me."

"And you had a roach clip in your pocket?" the judge asked.

"Yes."

"Because you smoke marijuana regularly?" the judge asked.

"Not regularly. Just at that time."

"This creates a problem, right?" the judge asked.

"Yes."

"Keep smoking marijuana, how am I going to explain to the district attorney that I should let you stay—what could I say to the district attorney? They say, 'Judge, you know, you placed him in this program and he is still violating the law. Marijuana is a drug.'"

"Ever since then, I haven't touched it. I wouldn't touch it," David insisted.

"I have your word?"

"You have my word."

"If you break your word?"

"Do what you please," David said.

"What do you think?" the judge asked the program representative.

"I think David has a lot of self-esteem issues," she said. "He needs to figure out what his goals are and how to fulfill them."

"How old are you now?" the judge asked David.

"Sixteen."

"We are concerned," continued the program representative. "We are greatly concerned because we are trying to work towards getting him back to the community. He seems to be doing a lot to keep himself out of it."

"You are not thinking clearly," the judge said to David. "You have one goal. Your goal is to get back into the community. Get a job. Straighten your life out and live well. You understand that?"

"Yes."

David got it together over the next few months, and on one calendar day the judge counseled him about preparing to look for a job:

"David, how are you?" the judge asked when David's case was called on a calendar day in the summer.

"Good. How are you doing?" David answered.

"What are you doing? Are you working?" the judge asked.

"I'm about to work."

"What kind of job?"

"I'm trying to get a job at McDonalds."

"What do you think you will do there?"

"Probably clean, mop," David said.

"You are willing to do that?" the judge asked.

"Yes, sir," answered David.

"Are there any openings in McDonalds?" the judge inquired.

"Around my way, yeah."

"How are you going to go for the interview?"

"A tie."

"A shirt and tie, long pants, right?"

"Yes, sir."

"And a belt?" the judge asked.

"Of course," David answered.

"Around the waist, not below the waist," the judge counseled. Then turning to the ATI representative, who was waiting patiently for her turn to speak, he asked, "How is he doing?"

"He has missed three times for curfew. He explained that he was at a picnic with his mother. He's attended his individual sessions. His last urine sample was negative. We are referring him to [a program] for anger management and also extracurricular activities. He says he likes to box."

"That's good anger management," the judge said to David. "You have to control your anger to be a good boxer. What happens when you lose your temper when you box?"

"You get out of the ring," David said.

"You get dropped," said the judge. "Why? Because you become wild, right? You lose your focus, right?"

"Mm-hmm."

"And somebody can whack you on the jaw, right?"

"Yeah."

"The fact that I say it's okay for you to box doesn't mean you can do it outside of the ring. Do you understand what I am saying?"

"Yes, sir."

"Your Honor," David's attorney interjected, "he wanted to ask, if he gets a job in this evening, can he have an extension on his curfew?"

"Absolutely," the judge said. "If you are working, I don't have a problem."

Wesley and Salvador—Admonishment and Performance

Exchanges between the judge and kids were not only for the benefit of individual defendants. Those in the audience observed the various inter-actions between court actors and youths, and over time, kids and family members learned what to expect from the process and from the judge. Judge Corriero was always very attuned to the potential impact, good and bad, that his interactions could have on those in the audience, and at times it seemed clear that he told a particular story or admonished a kid in a certain way intentionally to have maximum impact on his audience as well as on the individual defendant in front of him.[5]

WESLEY

Wesley was a black youth who was IN on two separate indictments, one for a first-degree robbery and one for a second-degree robbery. The alleged crimes had taken place about two weeks apart. Wesley was a JO when arrested, though he was 16 at the time of the following account. A plea deal had been worked out in which Wesley would receive a sen-tence of incarceration and still get YO treatment, placement with an ATI having been deemed inappropriate in Wesley's case. Here we see the judge using Wesley's allocution as an opportunity to advise and counsel him about not getting into trouble and on how to create a bet-ter future for himself. We also see how the judge's exchange with Wesley is orchestrated for the benefit of those in the audience. Wesley's allocution was a good opportunity to send the clear message to any kid in the audience just what was at stake and how lucky they were if they were avoiding a sentence of incarceration.

The judge asked Wesley's Legal Aid attorney, "I understand the district attorney is offering a sentence that would include Youth Offender treatment for both of these cases with an understanding that he would be sentenced to one and a third to four years?"

"That is correct," said Wesley's white female attorney.

"I think that is a fair disposition," said the judge.

"We do too," said the attorney.

"So we have a meeting of the minds?" the judge asked.

"Yes," said the attorney, "At this point, Mr. Beckett is interested in entering a plea to both incidents.

"Stand up, young man," the judge said to Wesley. "How old are you now?"

"Sixteen years old," said the youth.

"You understand that by pleading guilty you give up some very important rights?"

"Yes."

"You give up your right to a jury trial—do you understand that?"

"Yes."

"And you give up your right to face and confront the witnesses against you. Do you understand that?"

"Yes."

"You give up your right to remain silent. That means you have to tell me the truth about what happened. You understand that?"

"Yes." The judge then read the date, time, and location of the first incident and said, "It's charged that you and another individual surrounded a person and you threatened them, told them that you had a gun, and stole property from them. Is that true?"

"Yes."

"Why did you do that?"

"Because I needed the money."

"You needed the money? What does that mean? When you need money again, what are you going to do?"

"I'm not going to do that."

"Why?"

"Because I'll try to get a job."

"What if you can't get a job?"

"I have some parents."

"What if your parents can't give you money?"

"I'm not going to have it."

"Where are you now, Horizon or Crossroads?"

"Horizon."

"You like being locked up?"

"No, I do not."

"What do you not like about it?"

"Everything."

"Give me an example."

"The food."

"Food. Freedom," the judge stated. "The next time you think about doing something like this, think about the fact that you're going to lose both of them, lose the ability to eat the way you would like to eat. You're going to have to smell the kinds of smells that you have to smell. You're going to have to be surrounded by people who want to hurt you. You have to walk around in chains. Is that the way you want to live the rest of your life?"

"No."

"You're being offered now an opportunity not to have a record. If you want to do whatever you want to do in life and not be hindered in any way by this, not be held back by this, even though these are two serious matters. You understand that?"

"Yes."

"So you better educate yourself while you're in the institution. You better learn something that you like to do and stick with it. Did you graduate school?"

"Not yet."

"You didn't go to school regularly when you were out, did you?" Wesley shook his head "no."

"You're a bright young man. I know that. And if you can read and learn, there's no reason why you can't get a job and do the right thing in life. And if you want to give up on yourself and think this is the way, the easy way to get money, you'll find yourself back before me and you'll spend the rest of your life in institutions. That's just the way it is." The judge then continued with the allocution, "It is also charged that [on another date] you forcibly stole property, and during the course of that one of the people you were with, if not you, displayed a pistol. Is that true?"

"Yes."

"Did you have a gun?"

"No, not me."

"Someone else that was with you?"

Wesley nodded. Then the clerk took Wesley's guilty plea: "Wesley Beckett, do you now withdraw your previously entered plea of not guilty, and do you now plead guilty to the crimes of robbery in the second degree to cover and satisfy indictment #_____? And do you plead guilty to robbery in the first degree to cover and satisfy indictment #_____? Are those your pleas?"

"Yes," Wesley answered.

"I think we can sentence this young man today," said the judge. "Does he want to be sentenced today?"

"Yes," said Wesley.

"Anything further the People would like to say before sentencing?" the judge asked the ADA.

"No, Your Honor," said the ADA.

"Anything further?" The judge asked Wesley's attorney.

"No," she said.

"Is there anything you want to say to me before I sentence you?" the judge asked Wesley.

"Thank you for giving me the chance," the young man said.

"The way you thank me is by leading the best life you can lead and not hurting anybody in this life. You understand?"

"Yes."

"The sentence of the court is as promised, the sentence of one and one third to four years, and the defendant is declared a Youthful Offender on each of those cases, and the term is to run concurrent. So the total sentence is one and a third years to four years," the judge announced.

SALVADOR

Salvador was a Hispanic JO who was IN. He had been in trouble with the Family Court, which had placed him in a residential program (considered one of the best available). Salvador still managed to end up in the Youth Part. The DA's office was pushing for a plea to the charge and time, though they were not opposing YO. Prosecution felt that Salvador had already been given chances, which the youth had wasted. The options available for Salvador were limited, but the court and Salvador's dedicated attorney worked hard to find a workable solution to his situation—placement into another residential program. Without the attention to the details of the case, and without the expertise of all the experienced folks who worked on it, this would not have been possible. It was not required that the court or attorneys go to the lengths that they did in Salvador's case. It was the culture of the Youth Part, however, to pay attention to the details surrounding a kid, to respond to the individual defendant, not just the offense, while carefully weighing public safety concerns.

Salvador's white female attorney asked to approach, and after a long sidebar discussion the judge asked Salvador, "Why is it that I should give you this opportunity to go into the program?"

"Well, Your Honor, I know what I did was wrong," Salvador said.

"Well, let me tell you what worries me. You're in the Family Court for what was originally charged as a robbery. And, according to my understanding, what happened is that you and your codefendant were surrounding and intimidating somebody. You weren't getting along with your mother. You were an angry young man. You were given the opportunity to go to [the residential program], which is a terrific place. Obviously, you weren't ready to take advantage of what happened. . . . You see, from my reading of the papers—if I didn't see you or talk to you, I've read your probation report—I would be very worried about leaving you in a community setting. I have an obligation to the community, as well as to you. Sometimes, the options that are available, the choice that is available to me, are not the ones I'm very happy about. But I have to make them. Now, I'm worried you simply want to get out earlier than your crime warrants. You don't fully appreciate what's at stake —what's at stake for you and your family. What did you want to tell me, to make me feel that I'm serving the community by giving you this additional choice?"

"I just wanted to tell you I feel like, better, more from this program than going to a lock-down facility," Salvador said.

"When you went to [the residential program], did you have a marijuana problem?"

"I still have it," Salvador said. "They ain't really help me with it."

"Why do you think you have this marijuana problem?"

"I don't know. I just don't know."

"You know the program is not the solution; you have to find a solution within yourself."

"Yes."

"There's not going to be any magic that happens in these programs. You are going to have to work . . ."

"Yes."

"... to deal with your problems, and then when you're finished with the program, you're going back home. And I'm worried that you're going to forget what it was that brought you here in the first place, and then go out and rob somebody else or hurt somebody."

"I'm not."

"And then, in a way, I'm responsible for that, because if I look at your record—I look at the paper—it's very hard for me to give you this choice."

"But Your Honor, I'm not going to forget this experience," Salvador pleaded. "I made a mistake, I know. I learned my mistake."

"Well, what I would suggest," the judge said to Salvador's attorney, "is that if he were to remain in right now, the district attorney is opposed to me—the only way he can get to this program is for me to release him without bail. And eventually, in order to serve a nonjail sentence, he has to be granted Youthful Offender treatment. That makes that very difficult, given the nature of his crime. So, I'd suggest that he remain in for approximately what I would have sentenced him to, on an indeterminate sentence—let's say one and a third to four. That he remain in for a year and then I will place him in this program. But, if he doesn't cooperate, if he leaves the program, or does anything in violation of their rules, I would sentence him to three to nine years in prison.

"So, it's important for you to appreciate that this is a serious matter," the judge said to Salvador. "There is no room for you not to cooperate with the residential program. They're not easy—they have rules that sometimes don't appear to make sense. Also it's not an easy thing to be in a drug-rehabilitation program. Usually they require eighteen months. You fully understand that?"

"Yes."

A month later Salvador's case was again before the court.

Salvador's attorney said, "I don't know if [the assigned ADA] sent a note, but in my talks with him, he refused what was the court's offer of a compromise solution. In other words, he refuses to allow Salvador to go into a drug treatment program after being incarcerated for a year. I don't know if his note indicates anything different."

"Your Honor," the ADA said, "the note indicated his recommendation —a plea to the charge. Although he consents to YO, his recommendation is for one and a third to four years. He does not believe probation is appropriate for this defendant."

"Judge," said Salvador's attorney with a note of frustration in her voice, "when I spoke briefly to the assigned assistant, he said, 'Well, this young man had the benefit of [a residential program] and didn't do well, so he won't do well in any other program.' I said that I believe that this is a longer conversation. I have not heard back from him. I've made several attempts to talk to him."

The judge suggested that they conference the case again. "What I would like you to do is articulate your argument as to why [this program] would be more appropriate than the recommendation of the district attorney, given the fact that the defendant did have the benefit of placement in [the residential program]. So, if you could give your rationalization for that."

"I can tell you again," the attorney said.

"You can tell everyone," the judge said, smiling.

"I'd be happy to do that," said the attorney. "Tell me when." The judge picked a date for a case conference.

"Do you have any questions, young man?" the judge asked Salvador.

"No."

"What have you got to say for your lawyer's argument that you should go into [the program] as opposed to getting a sentence of one and a third to three? Do you have anything to say about that? Sit up straight, first of all. How old are you now?"

"Sixteen."

"You want to be a gangster?" the judge asked in a confrontational tone.

"No."

"You want to be a tough guy? Did you graduate from high school?"

"No."

"Did you go to school every day? No! Your lawyer wants me to give you another chance. I have to hear from you. When I look at you, I see a kid who acts and walks and talks like a tough guy!"

"I don't want to be no tough guy. I'm not trying to be no tough guy. I just feel that I deserve another chance."

"Why do you deserve it?" the judge pushed.

"Because from my behavior, how I was before, and now I think—a big change happened."

"The change didn't happen when you were in [the residential program]."

"They didn't really help. Because they just had a little program in there to try and help me. But the rest of the time, it was just a placement."

Salvador's attorney interjected, "I talked with the people from [the first residential program]. What they said to me [was] that he had a drug problem, that the drug problem continued through his stay, that it was not addressed, and that he was discharged, nevertheless, to outpatient, whatever."

"What drugs were you using?" The judge asked Salvador.

"Marijuana."

"How much?"

"I don't know. I can't say."

Two months later, Salvador was again before the judge.

"You understand that if I give you this chance, there's no room— there's NO room for you not to do everything that you're supposed to do. You understand me?" the judge asked sternly.

"Yes, sir."

"Because you've had chances like this in the past. You've had opportunities to deal with your problem and you haven't resolved it. Now, I cannot tolerate, I cannot permit you to take advantage of the offer that we're giving you and then to fall down on the job. You understand what I'm saying?"

"Yes, I understand."

"You understand if you foul up with me I put you in jail for two to six years?"

"Yes."

"I understand the district attorney is opposed to me giving you this opportunity because from their point of view you had opportunities in the past. So have you thought this through?"

"Yes."

"Are you really ready to deal with this issue?"

"Yes."

"The district attorney is recommending one and a third to four—am I correct—as a sentence?"

"That is correct, Your Honor," said the ADA.

"Now how long have you been in?"

"Like eleven months," said Salvador.

"We'll put this on the calendar one more month," the judge said to Salvador's attorney. Then, to Salvador he said, "In the interim, you will reach out to where I think you suggested there's a possible program, and if you're acceptable to them, I'll release you to their custody. If you don't do everything you're supposed to do, if you don't, I'll give you a sentence that is more than the People are recommending, and you'll have a felony record for the rest of your life. Do you understand me?"

"Yes," said Salvador.

The judge took Salvador's plea, in which he admitted to participating in a robbery wherein a fake gun was used.

"Why did you do this?" the judge asked.

"I really don't know."

"What do you mean you don't know?"

"I just . . ."

"What was your reason for doing this?" the judge pushed.

"Get money," said Salvador

"What did you do with the money?"

"I wasted it on marijuana."

"Is that the way you want to lead your life? Every time you need marijuana go out and rob people for it?"

"No."

"You're 15?" the judge asked.

"Sixteen."

"In the 16 years since you were born, do you realize the trouble you've put on your mother's shoulders?"

"Yes."

"Does she deserve this?"

"No."

"THIS BETTER BE THE END!" the judge yelled. "You understand me?"

"Yes."

"You BETTER not just be yessing me," the judge yelled again, "because I'm going to be all over you, because I'm doing this over the objection of the district attorney. Do you understand what that means? It means that they don't agree with my judgment with respect to you."

"Judge," said Salvador's attorney, "I would just like the court to be clear that Salvador understands that if he were to accept the prosecution's offer it's very likely that he would be out of custody sooner."

"That's true," said the judge.

"And that he has chosen to stay in a drug treatment program in hopes that he can turn his life around," the attorney added.

"That's one of the reasons that leads me to believe that he's sincere," responded the judge. "But this is not going to be easy. You understand me?"

Salvador nodded.

A month later, Salvador's attorney told the court that the drug treatment program that they were trying to get Salvador into was not willing to accept him. The judge said he would speak to the program directly to see what the problem was. Meanwhile, Salvador remained remanded in the juvenile detention facility.

Jeffrey and Ramiro—Patience and Understanding

Jeffrey's and Ramiro's cases both called for extended patience by the court, as building reciprocal trust and developing a new outlook from the kids happened only incrementally.

JEFFREY

Jeffrey was small in stature, shy and soft-spoken. It was hard to imagine that this young Hispanic boy could ever have been involved in a robbery. The judge's numerous interactions with Jeffrey over his nearly two years with the court were characterized by the court's extraordinary patience. In those two years, Jeffrey never got into any more trouble, but he also had a really hard time doing well in the program. With Jeffrey the judge addressed a number of different issues, trying hard to draw him out, trying to understand the struggles that Jeffrey was having, and working to cultivate new behaviors for the boy. Jeffrey's attorney and the program representative regularly came to Jeffrey's defense. Jeffrey had been in an ATI program for a while when the following exchange took place in court:

The judge looked over the copy of Jeffrey's report card, which was attached to the ATI program's report.

"Not doing well at all," the judge said.

"Not that great," admitted the white female program representative.

"Why is that?" the judge asked Jeffrey. "Still on the phone two, three hours with your girlfriend?"

"Not really," answered Jeffrey in a soft voice.

"Why is it that you are not doing well?"

"I haven't been doing my homework," Jeffrey admitted easily.

"What do you do when you are home?"

"I just watch TV and talk on the phone," said Jeffrey.

"He stays home alone?" the judge asked Jeffrey's mother, who was standing with an older gentleman in the audience.

"I get him up at six, tell him to get ready for school," she said in a thick Spanish accent.

"Then you have to go to work?" the judge inquired.

"Yes, because I have to go at 8:30."

"What time do you come home?" the judge asked.

"Four o'clock," she said.

"And this is his grandfather?" the judge asked.

"Yes."

"Does he live with you?"

"No."

"There is no excuse for this young man doing what he is doing," the judge said to no one in particular, with a hint of frustration in his voice. "If he is going to go home and be on the phone and be watching TV, I'd rather he be at [the program] in all his spare time, reading a book, doing his homework."

"So you want him to report Monday through Friday?" the ATI representative asked.

"Absolutely," the judge said emphatically. The program representative explained to the judge that Jeffrey had brought some of his drawings to show the judge. A court officer handed up the collection of papers. The judge looked through each of the drawings, examining them closely. Jeffrey had depicted himself in some of the drawings.

"Do you smile?" the judge asked Jeffrey.

"Yes," he said shyly, a slight smile on his lips.

"How come you didn't do a portrait of you smiling?" the judge asked.

"I didn't want to," said Jeffrey softly. The judge took a few more moments to look over the drawings.

"This is really terrific," the judge said. "How do you feel when you are home all by yourself? Do you listen to music?"

"Yes."

"You like music?"

"Yes."

"How does it make you feel?"

"Some music, I could relate to. I just feel . . ." Jeffrey's voice trailed off.

"Do you have friends, close friends?" the judge asked.

"Yes."

"Boys or girls?"

"Boys."

"And you get along well with your friends?"

"Yes."

"Are you sad about something?"

"No."

"Are you scared about something?"

"No."

"Okay," the judge said. The ATI representative offered that Jeffrey had an appointment in two weeks at a mental health center "His mother really wants him to get counseling," she said.

"Why?" the judge asked.

"She feels that he needs individual counseling, maybe someone to talk to."

"Why?" the judge asked Jeffrey's mother directly.

"Because every day," she said, "I tell him 'you have to get up. You have to go to school,' and that worries me."

The judge looked back to Jeffrey and asked, "Are you smoking marijuana?"

"No."

"He's not," chimed in the ATI representative. "Urine analyses are all negative."

The judge paused for a moment and then said, "I'm running out of questions. I need answers. I am running out of questions."

Jeffrey's white male attorney said, "I think there is a psychological component to Jeffrey's situation that hasn't been explored. He definitely has very strong motivational problems."

"He has great talents," the judge said, pointing to the drawing still sitting in front of him.

"He has great talents," the attorney agreed. "He is intelligent. He is able to comply with the curfew. He is good at doing passive compliance. The problem is he has a lot of difficulty getting himself out the door in the morning and to school on time, and doing his homework and things that require effort. It's not that he's doing bad things. It's just that . . ."

"How do you feel physically?" the judge asked.

"Fine," the boy said.

"Sometimes he doesn't want to eat," Jeffrey's mother offered from the audience.

"You love your mother?" the judge asked Jeffrey, who nodded.

"That's very, very good. That's what young boys should do, take care of their mothers. All right. Keep up the good work. I want you to do better in school. I want you in the program. I want you to talk to people. You understand me?"

"Yes, Your Honor."

"Tell them what's on your mind. There is no reason why you can't be terrific at whatever you want to do. I can't even write my name, and look at this wonderful work that you can do. You're talented."

A month later the judge was still being patient with Jeffrey.

"How is he doing at home?" the judge asked Jeffrey's father, who was in the audience this time.

"Good," he replied.

"How is his homework coming, better?" the judge asked the program representative.

"I wish I could give you a positive answer for that," she said. "Unfortunately, no."

"Why do you think that is?" the judge asked patiently.

"I believe he is not applying himself to his fullest potential in school," the representative answered. The judge looked at Jeffery and asked, "Why do you think that is?"

"Because I . . ." Jeffrey was at a loss for words.

"Are you distracted at school?" the judge inquired.

"I have a lack of motivation."

The judge responded softly and slowly, "How about jail, would that motivate you?"

"No," Jeffrey said in a whisper.

"Why do you have a lack of motivation?" the judge inquired.

"I don't know."

"He is in the process of being evaluated," the ATI representative offered.

The judge addressed Jeffrey again, "You don't like studying?" The boy shook his head no.

"Nobody likes studying," the judge said. "You like to read?"

"I do," said Jeffrey. The ATI representative came to bat for Jeffrey: "Despite not doing well at school, he is doing well at the program. He is on time. He was in the photography group. We also enrolled him in a portfolio class, if he doesn't have to go to summer school."

"So you are failing?" the judge asked Jeffrey, who nodded.

"How many grades are you failing?" the judge asked.

"All of them," admitted Jeffrey.

"All of them?" the judge asked with surprise in his voice. This time Jeffrey's attorney jumped to the boy's defense, "I mean, I think part of the issue was that he kind of missed the first half of the school year because he was incarcerated, he was behind. I think you know . . ."

"What about the tutoring he is getting, the individual tutoring?" the judge asked the program representative. "I thought he was there every day?"

"You told him to come every day," the representative said.

"Has he come every day?" the judge asked her.

"No, he has not. He reported on three days."

"Why did you do that?" the judge asked Jeffrey, still not losing his patience or raising his voice. Jeffrey shrugged and said, "I went to home instead of going to the program, I got real lazy."

"You are lazy?" the judge asked.

"Yes."

"So, because you are lazy, you don't follow my rules?"

"No."

Still not losing patience or raising his voice, the judge said, "Do I have to put you in jail to make sure that you understand what I mean?"

"No," Jeffrey replied quickly, yet softly.

"Well, it seems that I do because you don't follow my rules."

"I don't think so, Your Honor. I think I could fix myself."

"If I put this on for one more week, will you make every appointment at the program?" the judge asked.

"Yes," said Jeffrey.

"Even if you get lazy?"

"Yes."

"Even if you are not motivated to go?

"Yes."

"And if you don't go?" the judge asked.

"Then I get locked up," replied Jeffrey.

"So, we understand each other?"

"Yes."

"See you next Friday."

Over the next few weeks, Jeffrey's attendance in the program improved and he started individual counseling. But his progress was still slow.

"Is Jeffrey doing what I expect of him?" the judge asked when Jeffrey came before him a couple of months later.

"He has been coming in for group and individual," the ATI representative reported. "It's not 100% attendance. The issue that we have now is summer school."

"How is he doing at home?" the judge asked Jeffrey's father, who was standing in the audience. "He listens to you?"

"He's doing things well," Jeffrey's father reported, "but we try to get him to do things in the program."

"And he doesn't want to cooperate?"

"I want him to cooperate, but you, because it's for his own good, but . . ."

"How about the counseling?" the judge asked. "Is he going for counseling?"

"He has been attending every Monday," the program representative said. "There might be an issue with the medication that he's on. It might be causing depression."

"What kind of medication?"

"It's a growth hormone," the representative said.

"He has been taking it for a while," offered Jeffrey's attorney. "It's been medically prescribed. Judge, I think there is an issue that Jeffrey has with his motivation. I don't know if it's depression. And I am glad that he's now receiving therapy. However, I was wondering if you would consider allowing me to retain a social worker to work directly with him through me."

"Absolutely," the judge said. "I'll sign it. Jeffrey, what have you got to say for yourself?"

"I'm doing good. I'm not doing perfect, but I'm going to try and do my best."

"Are you unhappy?" the judge asked.

"No, I'm not, I'm not unhappy."

"So, you are happy?"

"Yeah."

"You still have a girlfriend?" the judge asked.

"Yeah," said Jeffrey, smiling.

"That puts a smile on your face. Are you getting along with your girlfriend?"

"Yeah."

"You talk to her?"

"Yeah."

"Do you have a good relationship with her?"

"Yeah."

"Do we understand each other?"

"Yes."

"How old is your girlfriend?"

"Fifteen."

"She's able to talk to you and have a good relationship with you?"

"Yes."

"Why can't you do that with other people? The judge asked.

"I could do that," said Jeffrey.

"Except that you like her and that's why it's easier for you to do that?" the judge asked, smiling.

"How is he doing at home?" the judge asked Jeffrey's father. "Does he go out late?"

"No."

"Do you know of his girlfriend?"

"Yes."

"Is she a good influence?"

"Yes."

Then, looking at Jeffrey, the judge said, "You have to be smart. You better not do anything inappropriate. Do you understand what I am saying?"

"Yes, sir."

"I'll see you on the adjourn date."

Two months later, Jeffrey's mother and grandmother were with him when he came to court.

"Did you get a new haircut?" the judge asked as Jeffrey walked up from the audience.

"Yes."

"How's school coming?" the judge asked.

"Fine, Your Honor."

"You still painting and drawing?"

"Yes."

"What are you painting and drawing?"

"In school I'm not painting."

"Don't they have any kind of art?" the judge asked.

"I was in the art program but they had—see, I wasn't attending the class before. They switched me to a class that has like, like no credentials. See, I could draw better. They put me in a class where they're learning how to draw."

"And why is that?" the judge asked. "In other words, they put you in a class where you're not being challenged."

"Yeah."

"Why is that? Because he wasn't going to class before? You see what happened now? You like to create things, right?"

"Yes."

"Now you lost that opportunity because you didn't go."

"Yes."

"Jeffrey has been improving in our program," the ATI representative reported. "He has not missed any groups. He's only missed two out of five sessions. He has been calling in for his curfew every night. He's been testing negative. He has also been cooperating with the [mental health center]. He's been going to his appointments."

"Now," the judge asked Jeffrey, "if you got into the other class, the advanced class, would you go now?"

"Yes, Your Honor."

"You sure?"

"Yes."

"Why don't we do this," the judge said to the program representative. "Why don't we contact the school and see if we can get him transferred? If they have a problem, let them call me or his lawyer." The representative nodded yes.

"The family want to ask any questions?" the judge asked, looking up at Jeffrey's mother in the audience.

"No."

"How's he doing at home?"

"He's doing well."

"Is he happy at home?"

"Yes, but he's barely eating. He doesn't like to eat. He's not eating breakfast."

"Why not?" asked the judge.

"I don't know. Sometimes he says he doesn't want it. I'm worried about him because he has to go to school and that's necessary for his health."

"Absolutely," the judge concurred. The judge then asked Jeffrey what he liked to eat for breakfast (cereal and frozen waffles) and suggested that Jeffrey eat breakfast because he did look like he had lost some weight.

"I want you to eat breakfast every morning, you understand me?" the judge said. "We'll see if we can get you back into that other class. And we'll put him on for sentence." The judge then looked up to Jeffrey's mother and said, "You let me know if he doesn't eat his breakfast."

"I want to let you know," Jeffrey's mother said, "that if you don't see me that the father may be here because I have to punch a time card and his father doesn't have to punch a time card. His father may be here, not me."

"That's no problem," the judge reassured her. "I know you well."

"Thank you," said Jeffery's mother.

A month later, Jeffrey's case was on for sentencing; he was finally going to get YO + 5 years' probation. He had been with the court for over a year at this point, but had made steady, albeit slow, progress and hadn't gotten into any kind of trouble. The ATI program was still working to find him a more suitable educational placement. This was still in progress, and if the judge sentenced Jeffrey then he would no longer be monitored or assisted by the ATI program and would move over to supervision by the probation department. The ATI representative explained:

"We are in a state where we are trying to get him into a new school. He is going to school now. It's just him going to his classes, and I think he is just struggling; he is not in an appropriate setting. We have a school conference next week to meet with the guidance counselor. His parents will meet with his therapist next week on some personal issues that have come about as to why he might be feeling the way he is feeling now. He is in the program; he calls in every night for curfew. He also tested negative."

"Never been in trouble since he has been detained?" the judge asked.

"No," said Jeffrey.

The judge decided to put the case over for a long date to try and get everything in order before sentencing Jeffrey to probation.

On the next adjourn date Jeffrey was still doing well, but the educational arrangements were still being worked out. The judge put the case over yet again, saying, "I wouldn't dream of putting this in the hands of probation."

Delay, potentially excessive delay, was being used strategically to find the best possible educational placement for Jeffrey. This went on for several more months until Jeffrey was finally given YO treatment. While Jeffrey's extended time with the court may be viewed by some as excessive or as a waste of court resources, the time taken was what was needed to try to address the myriad of issues in his life. Those who encountered Jeffrey in court understood him to be a troubled kid, not a violent predator. It was unfortunate that Jeffrey had to become court-involved in order to tap the resources needed to resolve his issues, but this was rather common in the court. More than once I heard stories of parents asking why they couldn't have gotten such assistance for their child prior to his arrest. A long-time Youth Part defense attorney told me that on occasion she gets asked by parents how to get another of their children arrested so that they too may benefit from the services that can come along with court intervention.

RAMIRO

Ramiro, a Hispanic JO, had been working with an ATI program for a while when the following exchange took place on a calendar day. He had been doing well, meeting the requirements of the program, but was struggling in school. The program was working on finding him a more appropriate educational placement. In this interaction, the judge counseled Ramiro on how to be patient with educational bureaucracies, and how to make the most out of a not-so-great situation.

"How are you?" the judge asked.

"Fine," answered Ramiro.

"Good," the judge said, then turned to ATI representative, nodding for her to start her report.

"He is doing well in our program," she said. "He has attended all his groups except one that was an excused absence to go to a funeral. We're trying to get his credits transferred from Passages;[6] he is supposed to be in eleventh grade. Right now he is in the tenth grade at [school]."

"How do you feel about that?" the judge asked Ramiro.

"I don't want to be there."

"Why?"

"I feel like . . ." Ramiro's voice trailed off.

"You are too big?" the judge asked.

"Yeah."

"Everyone else is smaller than you," the judge said, nodding to indicate that he understood the situation. He then turned to the program representative and asked when new educational arrangements would be made.

"We're working on that right now; it takes a little time to get the credits transferred. I told Ramiro that he needed to do his homework so there wouldn't be any problem moving him from the tenth to the eleventh grade."

"You think you know everything already?" the judge asked Ramiro, smiling.

"I don't think I know everything."

"I know you don't," the judge said in a soft tone to indicate that he wasn't upset.

"I know most of the stuff," Ramiro said.

"Well, that's okay," the judge said in an encouraging tone, "because if you are going over it again that means you are going to learn it more —so you can probably do much better because they put you in a class where you know everything already. Look at it that way. Don't be embarrassed. Do the kids bother you?"

"No."

"They probably look up to you."

"Maybe."

"Just be patient, and don't create a situation where you have to go back [to jail]. Nothing is, nothing can be that difficult that would warrant you going back. Right?"

"Right."

"It's a horrible place, isn't it?"

"Yes."

"So, you put up with being with little kids and you put up with all of this until we get this straightened out." Ramiro nodded in agreement.

With Ramiro, the judge conveyed the message that they were working together, that they both needed to be patient with "the system" and help each other out. The judge invested Ramiro with the responsibility of focusing on long-term goals rather than short-term annoyances.[7] In so doing, the judge sent the message that Ramiro was capable and could be trusted with that responsibility.

Marvin, Tameron, and Jalen—Humor in the Court

Most interactions in the court were serious, but light-hearted moments also took place in which the judge and defendants would chat or joke with one another. These humorous moments served to ease tension and to humanize both the judge and the kids. Such informal interactions allowed the judge and the kids to develop, if only for a moment, a "nonlegal" relationship. The following accounts of Marvin, Tameron, and Jalen each depict such moments in the court.

MARVIN

Marvin was a black JO who had been doing well in his program. When his case was called on this particular summer day, Marvin walked up wearing long denim shorts and a long red t-shirt.

"Why are you wearing red?" the judge asked with concern and surprise in his voice. Red is the color of the Bloods street gang.

"Because it matches my sandals," Marvin said innocently. The judge stood up and leaned over his bench so that he could see Marvin's sandals. They were indeed red.

"Good answer," the judge said, smiling, and everyone in the court had a good laugh.

TAMERON

Tameron was a black JO who had been doing well in the ATI program. The representative told the judge that Tameron was interested in having his curfew extended.

"Why?" the judge asked.

"Because I want to go to the movies," Tameron said.

"What kinds of movies?" the judge asked.

"Scary movies," Tameron told him.

"Have you seen *The Grudge*?" the judge asked him. "It is very scary, very." You could see by the judge's expression that his memory of the film was still with him. Several of the young people in the audience found this entertaining—that Judge Corriero was frightened by a scary movie, that he had even watched a scary movie.

Tameron said he had not seen the film, but that he wanted to. The judge extended Tameron's curfew to 8:30.

JALEN

Jalen was a black JO who had been with the court for a while. He was now 16 and was doing well in his program. Jalen had a Walkman in his hands when he approached the defense table. The judge asked him who he liked to listen to.

"I like Cam'ron and Mace," Jalen answered.

"Do you like Wu Tang Clan?" the judge asked.

"No, not really," said Jalen. This made the judge laugh, and he said, "Some of them have been in and out of here, you know?"

Then the judge asked Jalen, "Snoop Dogg's new song, 'Drop It Like It's Hot,' what does that mean?"

"I don't know," said Jalen.

"Someday someone will tell me what that means," the judge said, smiling. There were chuckles all around the courtroom, especially among the young defendants waiting their turn in the audience.

These light-hearted moments were as important as any others in the court. They conveyed to Marvin, Tameron, Jalen, and others in the court that they, and the judge, were people—people who could joke or share a laugh occasionally, even amid the somber work of the court. Such moments helped build relationships of mutual trust and respect.

Zayne, Rafael, and Jackson—Coping with Tough Realities

Zayne's, Rafael's, and Jackson's cases show how the court was cognizant of, and attempted to deal with, the often difficult realities Youth Part kids faced in regard to violence and trauma in their young lives. Some kids carried grief and fear due to the violent death of a loved one. Others were facing daily threats of violence against them on the street or in jail. Recognition of these challenges allowed the court to work with kids to resolve any potential disruptions with ATI programming. These three accounts are also poignant reminders of some of the types of burdens kids in the Youth Part often carried with them.

ZAYNE

Zayne was an older, non-JO black youth who was OUT. He walked in and sat down in the audience halfway through a calendar day. The judge saw him come in and said, across the court, "Zayne, you were supposed to be here yesterday." Zayne nodded, but said nothing. The judge, realizing that Zayne's Legal Aid attorney was not in court, called to one of the other attorneys from the same office.

"Henry, can you take Zayne's case?" the judge asked. "Ms. Bryant is his attorney and she's not here, can you take it?"

"Yes," said the attorney, who then walked out into the hallway to meet with Zayne. At the end of the day, after all the other cases were done, Zayne's case was added to the calendar and his name was called.

"Where were you yesterday?" the judge asked.

"The hospital," was all Zayne said.

"Everything okay?" the judge inquired with sincere concern. Zayne remained stoic.

"His brother was shot, Your Honor," offered the attorney solemnly. "He is in the ICU."

"I'm sorry," the judge said to Zayne. "What happened?"

"He started up trouble," Zayne said stoically. The judge told Zayne that he was very sorry and that he hoped his brother would be okay. Zayne had been scheduled to be sentenced, and the judge asked if he wanted to go ahead. Zayne said he did. The judge gave Zayne the agreed-upon sentence: YO + 5. Then the judge said to Zayne, "I know you have some problems, but I hope you stay out of trouble on probation." Zayne nodded. After Zayne left the courtroom the judge stared hard at the back wall of the courtroom for a few moments. The judge felt and expressed genuine sympathy for Zayne when he discovered the reason why he had not shown up for court. Had he not built a relationship with Zayne over time, the judge may have reacted differently to Zayne's absence from court the day before and issued a bench warrant for his arrest. Instead, he gave Zayne the benefit of the doubt and offered him a chance to explain.

RAFAEL

Rafael was a slender non-JO Hispanic youth who was being held at Rikers Island on a first-degree robbery charge. He had prior misdemeanor charges and an open burglary charge in another court. He was only in the Youth Part because one of his codefendants was a JO. The DA's original offer on the case was a three-and-a-half-year prison sentence plus five years post-release supervision with no YO treatment. A few weeks later, the prosecution was offering a plea to a second-degree robbery with three and a half to five years, but was still opposing YO. Rafael's case was a hard one. The PPI and 390 reports revealed that the youth had serious issues. A representative from a community-based ATI program had had prior involvement with the family. The ATI representative advocated and testified as to Rafael's "redeemability," in spite of the fact that on paper he did not appear to be amenable to treatment. The judge relied on the trust that had been built up over the years between the court and the ATI personnel. He patiently navigated legal bureaucracies to try to work out an appropriate arrangement for Rafael.

"How are you young man?" the judge asked Rafael after the court officers removed the handcuffs.

"Good," answered the youth.

"What's happening with the burglary case? Is that resolved?"

"No, Judge," said the ATI's male Hispanic court advocate. "I believe that was the question."

"Was this a real gun that was used in the robbery?" the judge asked.

The ADA asked for a moment to look through her files.

"Judge," interjected Rafael's attorney, "while the People are looking, my understanding is that when the three young men were arrested, recovered nearby was an imitation pistol."

"Your client is not alleged to be the gun wielder?" the judge asked.

"No, he's not alleged to be the gun wielder, in any event," the attorney said.

"Your Honor, that's correct," the ADA chimed in, "an imitation pistol was recovered."

"Any offer by the people?" the judge asked.

"The top charge is rob one," said the prosecutor, "so there is an offer of rob two, with three and a half to five years. No YO."

"My suggestion is this," the judge said, looking at the ATI advocate, "I understand that you're interested in getting this young man appropriate treatment to deal with his issues."

"Yes, judge," said the advocate, adding, "I'm not looking to bring this young man home at this time. There's been a lot of issues, and after discussion with his mom, who is very open and honest with me, I discussed it with him as well. I also spoke this morning—just to say that I'm at a stage to see whether in the immediate future we can work this out—this young man can be released with a condition of the court into [a residential program]. It has a juvenile program where he can go to school and hopefully change a lot of his behavior and give him a second chance."

"Is he acceptable to that program?" the judge asked.

"I believe—I spoke to a boss from the program and we'll put an interview on for this Friday."

"Why don't we put it on the following Friday?" the judge said. "Why don't we conference it on the Thursday before which would be . . ."

"The sixth," Rafael's attorney said.

"We could do it on the sixth," the judge said. "You just want to speak to the DA first? I don't want a situation where I don't have the actual DA here."

"I believe that Rafael has the trespass case pending next Friday," said the ATI representative.

"So do the following Friday," said the judge.

"I'm in arraignments," Rafael's attorney said. "Can we do the conference on the sixth? Maybe we can quickly get everything done."

"We'll try for that," the judge said. He then looked up at Rafael's mother, who was standing in the audience with another teenage boy.

"Who's this young man with you?" the judge asked.

"That's my other son."

"Older than your son here?"

"Yes."

The judge asked Rafael's mother if she was working.

"I'm a housewife," she replied.

The judge looked at Rafael and asked, "You care about your mother?"

"Yes."

"How much do you care about your mother?"

"A lot."

"Enough to stay out of trouble?"

"Yes."

"When did this realization come to you?" the judge asked in a somewhat irritated tone. "When did all of a sudden you realize that you cared so much about your mother that you wouldn't get involved in any kind of criminal behavior?"

"When I walked through the Rikers Island doors," Rafael responded.

"You were never in Rikers Island before?" the judge asked.

"No."

"What do you think of it?"

"No good."

"What's not good about it?"

"Being there."

"Didn't anybody ever tell you that you could be in Rikers Island?"

"No."

"Judge," the ATI advocate said, "he has problems at Rikers. He has a problem with a Blood, an older Blood, and the action that was taken; he's been in a box. He hasn't been able to make a phone call. They've taken away his commissary privileges. Mom hasn't been allowed to see him because of something that happened."

"Have you worked with this family before?" the judge asked the advocate.

"Yes."

"And his brother here?"

"Actually, the brother was young when I was involved with the sister, who went through our program and got through five years' probation and has been fine. I wish that this young man would've been directed to me before."

"What do you think of him?" the judge asked.

"I've known him since he was very young, possibly eight," the advocate said. "I believe in the last two years is when he lost his way. Like I said, I wish he would've been brought to me before, but I think coming out as a young teenager, in that community, and obviously with the wrong people, is the problem. When I see him, it's more as a follower than that he is a bad guy. But again, the same penalties apply to the followers as it is to anybody else. But I think it can be solved, judge."

The judge listened carefully to the advocate's comments and then said, "Let's try to get those other cases resolved so there's nothing else in the way; see if we can work those cases out."

Trying to find an alternative to a sentence of incarceration for Rafael proved difficult. The first step was to clear the nonviolent cases that he had pending in other courts. A month later, the ATI advocate told the court that the program that had interviewed him had deemed Rafael unacceptable. The representative speculated that it was because he didn't "look good on paper." The judge said that he would contact the program to see if he could persuade them to take Rafael. The representative also pledged to keep looking for other suitable residential programs. Meanwhile, Rafael remained IN at Rikers Island.

Jackson, a 14-year-old black JO, had been doing well in an ATI program for a while.

"Jackson, how are you?" the judge asked when the youth walked up. "Fine," he said.

The ATI representative reported that Jackson had "been very compliant with curfew, he's been attending all life skill courses; he's doing pretty well in school."

The judge looked over the written report in front of him and asked, "Why did he get assigned anger management classes?"

"He requested it, Your Honor," the ATI representative answered.

"Why?" the judge asked Jackson.

"Because I get mad," he answered.

"Well, you know, getting mad is not the problem—we all get mad. It's what you do with your anger that is important."

"Yes."

"So maybe they can help you with that, right?"

"Yes."

Then the ATI representative, advocating for Jackson, asked if his 6:00 curfew could be extended.

The judge asked Jackson, "What time should we make it?"

"Seven-thirty?" asked Jackson.

"Okay, I can trust you until 7:30?"

"Yes."

"Okay, keep up the good work."

Two months later, on Jackson's next court date, the judge engaged him in a discussion of anger management classes.

"What have you learned?"

"How to control my temper and just walk away," he replied.

The judge told him to "keep up the good work" and set his next court date for two months out. On that court date, Jackson was still doing well. A month later, however, the situation had changed. When Jackson and his lawyer took their place before the judge, the attorney told him that Jackson was not doing great. The ATI representative explained that there was a situation at school in which Jackson had been subjected to threats, and that his mother was keeping him from going to school because she believed it was too dangerous for him.

"Your Honor," Jackson's attorney interjected, "two of Jackson's older siblings have been killed and Jackson's mother is very frightened about this situation." The judge asked where Jackson's mother was, and Jackson's attorney explained that she was agoraphobic and had never been able to come to court. The ATI representative explained that they were trying to get Jackson into a different school setting—maybe something more vocational. She added: "Otherwise he is doing well in the program, although he did admit that he would test positive for marijuana." The judge put the case over for six weeks, telling the ATI representative to try to work out the school situation by then.

"I'm not gonna force him to go to that school, maybe [the program] can bring in some tutors or home instruction until they can get all things worked out."

Because Jackson had been coming to the court regularly and had developed relationships with his attorney, the ATI personnel, and the judge, the fact that he had been missing school—a clear violation of release— could be understood within the larger context of the reality of Jackson's life. Because the judge had witnessed Jackson do well over the months, even requesting services for himself, the judge was able to evaluate the infraction in light of all the good work that Jackson had been doing, and within the family circumstances with which Jackson was trying to cope, rather than just punishing him for breaking the rules.

Judge Corriero and ATI personnel got to know each of these kids and many of the facts of their individual lives and family circumstances. Because the judge felt like he knew something about them, he could better tailor his interactions with them in order to achieve the goals of the court —rehabilitation and no felony records for as many deserving youths as possible. For some kids, it took patience and encouragement to set them on the road to YO, some needed coaxing, some needed a stern lecture, and still others needed the threat of incarceration. Of course, not all would make it through the process and earn YO, but those who did encountered an individualized style of justice attentive to their unique circumstances and needs—a style of justice that understood them to be kids, often troubled kids, many of whom might be redeemable, if we just took the time.

A Comparison with Kupchik's Court Research
Qualitative research on the case processing of adolescents in criminal courts has been quite sparse, so the ability to compare the rich findings

of Aaron Kupchik's in-depth research in another of New York City's youth parts with my own provides a rare occasion to understand the varied mechanisms court actors employ to manage the tensions inherent in the criminal prosecution of adolescents.[8] Operating under the same criminal statutes, the two specialized courts exhibited many similarities but had evolved distinct strategies and courtroom cultures for responding to the kids that came before them. The ability of two similarly structured courts operating under the same statutes to evolve different modes of operation speaks to the significant influence of judicial discretion and the importance of courtroom workgroup culture in understanding any and all court settings.[9] Kupchik's 2006 book, *Judging Juveniles: Prosecuting Adolescents in Adult and Juvenile Courts*, is an excellent mixed-method study comparing criminal prosecution of juveniles in New York with juvenile court adjudication in New Jersey. However, here I primarily use two articles by Kupchik—one published in the journal *Social Problems* in 2003, the other in the journal *Punishment and Society* in 2004—for comparison because they focus more closely on the ethnographic data he collected while conducting his research in the courts.

Like the Manhattan Youth Part, the court in New York where Kupchik did his research "straddles the boundary between juvenile and criminal justice" and utilized specialized tactics—admonishing discourse, sentencing alternatives, and delayed sentencing—to reconcile the tensions of trying youths as adults.[10] Further, both judges openly declared their personal dedication to the basic rehabilitative ideal of the juvenile court, and both expressed a general belief in the reduced culpability of young offenders. Further, Youthful Offender treatment was utilized within both courts as a method for reducing the severity of sentences for many "deserving" kids.

The process by which each court enacted these goals was different, however, resulting in two distinct styles of case processing. First, differences in personal style between the two judges resulted in different court cultures. For example, Kupchik reports that the judge in his study always referred to all court actors, including defendants, by their last name (Ms. Jones, Mr. Wilson, etc.).[11] Judge Corriero often addressed attorneys and court personnel by their first names, and he almost always referred to the kids by their first names. As the accounts above show, he almost always greeted the kids by first name ("How are you, Roger?") in a purposefully conversational style. He tended to use last names (Mr. Gonzalez, Ms. Tate) when addressing court or agency personnel or attorneys he did not know, and he always used last names when addressing defendants' parents, grandparents, or guardians.

Second, in Kupchik's account, the judge rarely, if ever, smiled in the courtroom. In contrast, Judge Corriero often smiled, even joking and laughing sometimes with court personnel and even with kids: "I try to bring out the best in all the lawyers, to relax everybody. To try to use humor in a constructive way," he told me. There was purposeful intent by Judge Corriero to create a relaxed environment, to speak and act in a way that attempted to ease tensions and create a less adversarial atmosphere in the courtroom.

Third, Kupchik reports that the judge in his study *demanded* reports and "assumes priority for his case" over other demands on court actors' time.[12] Again, as seen in the exchange during Rafael's appearance above, Corriero worked in a more collegial manner, placing himself in a position of what Edward Clynch and David Neubauer would call "first among equals."[13] Judge Corriero was often willing to reschedule cases around attorney's schedules or move a case to the top of the list on a calendar day if an attorney needed to be elsewhere on the same day.

While these differences in style may seem minor, they resulted in two distinct styles of operation in the two courts. Such differences can have a significant impact on case processing, as well as on the dispositional outcomes, and should not be disregarded as incidental. The guiding philosophies of the two judges and the differing cultures of prosecution in the two jurisdictions, along with the types of informal cultures that existed in each, help explain the differences in case processing in two courts operating under the same set of laws.[14] The personal style of each judge, who by the nature of his position functioned as the workgroup leader, influenced the informal culture of each part in significant ways.[15]

Kupchik reported a hybrid model of justice at work in the court he studied.[16] He observed, prior to a defendant's sentencing, a style of justice more akin to that of a criminal court, with attention on the offense and an emphasis on formal case processing. At sentencing, in contrast, Kupchik reported seeing a style of justice more akin to a juvenile court, with attention paid to the offender and the nature of his life circumstances. Kupchik refers to this as a "sequential justice model." In the early phase (the one more like the criminal court), the interaction was formal and adversarial; defendants were "not allowed" to speak, and the language of all court actors was largely formal and ceremonial. At this phase the courtroom workgroup was restricted to the prosecution, the defense, and the judge. In the later phase (the one more like the juvenile court), interactions became more informal and collegial, and ATI personnel became more involved and active courtroom workgroup members.[17] It was during this phase that the judge interacted directly with defendants, and in which defendants were finally allowed to speak. Here, the judge "talks to defendants in ways that communicate both responsibility and youthfulness," attaching a "rhetorical punitiveness to a relatively lenient sentence."[18] The judge might engage a youth in a discussion of the "why" of his criminal act, or lecture him in what Kupchik referred to as "admonishing discourse."

In contrast to the "bifurcated model" Kupchik describes, the culture of the Manhattan Youth Part under Judge Corriero represented a juvenile justice–based model during all phases of case processing—from first appearance through to final case disposition. This was evidenced in the non-adversarial, collegial atmosphere that existed in the court most all the time. While always attentive to the formal requirements of the law and the due-process protections of defendants, Judge Corriero created a much less formal environment than that described by Kupchik. Further, ATI personnel were most often involved with a case from the defendant's first appearance in court.

More importantly, in contrast to Kupchik's judge, Judge Corriero almost always engaged directly with defendants upon their first, or at least second, time before him, asking about school or about the last book a defendant had read.[19] At his first interaction with a defendant, Judge Corriero would attempt to learn about the kid, his family, and the nature of his life circumstances by speaking directly with kids and their families, and any OUT defendant was immediately connected with an ATI. This style of case processing represents a mode of justice more in line with the individualized, *parens patriae* style of the juvenile court. Whereas Kupchik reports that the juvenile justice model emerged within his court only after it had been determined that a defendant was deserving of leniency, the Manhattan Youth Part, under Judge Corriero, employed such a model from the very beginning of nearly all case processing. The rare exceptions were those very few cases that would undoubtedly go to trial, or those in which sentencing alternatives were simply out of the question, such as when a defendant was charged with murder or was a chronic violent offender. In these instances, the court maintained a much more formal climate in which Judge Corriero might only briefly engage a defendant directly, if at all. Few such "hard" cases were brought before the court.

Where Kupchik's research revealed a bifurcated model of justice at work in the court he observed, the Manhattan Youth Part evolved a culture wherein the classic juvenile justice model was reimagined—revised, if you will—to fit within the constraints imposed by the criminal law, a process Simon Singer, Jeffrey Fagan, and Akiva Liberman call the "specialized reproduction of juvenile justice" in a criminal justice setting: "The specialized treatment of juveniles in a youth court reproduces the progressive vision of juvenile justice within the jurisprudential framework and operational boundaries of the criminal court."[20]

Additionally, in comparing Kupchik's study to my own, I found that Judge Corriero employed the types of "admonishing" techniques Kupchik reports much less often, opting, when possible, to try and establish a relationship of trust and mutual respect with kids—a type of paternal bonding—rather than merely employing authoritative admonishing techniques. We can find instances of similar admonishing discursive tactics used by both judges in both settings. For example, both accounts quote the judge asking a defendant a very similar question: "You want to be a tough guy? You want to be a gangster?" asked by Judge Corriero, and "You're some kind of tough guy, Mr. [last name]?" asked by Kupchik's judge.[21] Regardless of these similarities, the discursive style used by Judge Corriero, on those occasions when he engaged in admonishing discourse, was considerably less demeaning in character than that reported by Kupchik. He also reports that his judge often employed "judgmental discourse," such as saying to a kid, "You're stupid if you want to be in a gang."[22] Judge Corriero's style of discourse with defendants, while sometimes containing occasional moments of judgment, was generally much more paternalistic than authoritarian. A simple example can be found in the different practices regarding the identification of codefendants during allocution. In Kupchik's account, the judge names specific codefendants in open court and asks the defendant questions about their actions.[23] Judge Corriero, in contrast, never required the naming of codefendants out loud in court. This wasn't by accident. Corriero told me that he understood the possible embarrassment, ostracization, and/or real danger a youth may face if he names a codefendant in open court. Since such information was generally contained in written statements and other official court documents, there was no need for such details to be spoken aloud in open court.

The overall atmosphere of the Manhattan Youth Part represented a courtroom culture that had many commonalities with the court studied by Kupchik, but was also quite unique. Although working within the same statutory structure, often utilizing similar diversionary mechanisms, as well as the creative use of discretion and delay, in the service of "child-saving," the culture of the two courts was indeed different. In one court, we see the emergence of a bifurcated model, while in the other we see the reconceptualization of the juvenile justice model within the boundaries of a criminal court—a model more continuously rooted in the philosophy of individualized justice.

Differences in case-processing styles aside, Kupchik's findings and my own both show how court actors acknowledged defendants' youthfulness regardless of their being labeled legally as adults, and both courts developed ways to modify case-processing strategies toward rehabilitative outcomes. Both courts were specialized criminal court parts set aside specifically for the purpose of handling Juvenile Offender cases, a fact that sets them apart from most nonspecialized courts charged with handling adult-juvenile cases. How, or even if, court actors in nonspecialized criminal courts accommodate or treat adult-juvenile defendants differently than adults is still uncertain. Much more ethnographic research is needed in this area before we can truly begin to understand the full range of case-processing strategies employed by court actors as they encounter the many challenges that arise from the inherent contradictions of prosecuting kids as adults.

Managing Contradictions

The kids in the Manhattan Youth Part were teenagers and as such did not pay rent or have full-time jobs, and most were dependent upon parents or guardians for food, shelter, clothing, transportation, and the like. As nonadults, they were expected to live by their parents' or guardians' rules and attend school and were, in fact, much less autonomous social actors than adults.[1] This is a fundamental fact about the prosecution of youths as adults: young offenders don't become older because they offend—they remain kids.[2] The simple legal denial of youthfulness, even when mandated by law, cannot erase the reality of defendants' social status as adolescents. This contradiction between kids' legal and social status was the most fundamental contradiction at work in the Youth Part—and, indeed, is the most fundamental contradiction at work in the criminal prosecution of adolescents, wherever it is carried out. Thus, as Kupchik has argued, criminal court actors must find ways to "filter" transfer laws to accommodate their own understandings of defendants' youthfulness.[3]

The contradictions between defendants' legal and social status created many challenges in the Youth Part. First, the kids' dependence upon adults often created difficulties during their attempts to earn YO. Second, issues arose about the appropriate role for parents in a court where kids are being prosecuted as adults. Parents, guardians, and families were an integral part of the work of the Manhattan Youth Part, but it wasn't a juvenile court, where parents and family have a long tradition of participation, and where familial rights and roles are firmly established. Although family members frequently interacted with the judge and were an important factor in case processing, their role could be precarious at times. Further, direct clashes sometimes arose between the different legal statuses occupied by some of the kids in the court. This issue manifested in two basic ways: First, it was not uncommon for a defendant to have one case in the Family Court and another in the criminal Youth Part, resulting in his simultaneous prosecution both as a juvenile *and* as an adult. Second, sometimes kids in the part, legally constructed as adults for the purpose of prosecution, were also legally defined as children in need of the care and custody of the state through their involvement with child protective services. These kids encountered a paradoxical legal status wherein they were marked by the law as children in need of special care or protection and at the same time that they were constructed by the law as adults deserving of criminal court prosecution. Through the accounts of Alonzo,

Walter, Isaac, Jorge, Kendrick, and Dario below, we see how these contradictions played out in court, as well as the strategies created within the Youth Part for responding to these paradoxical situations regarding kids' legal labeling.

Non-Adult Social Actors

The court understood well that its kids were largely dependent upon the adults in their lives to comply with court and ATI requirements. Kendrick and Randal both had situations arise during their case processing in which circumstances beyond their young control could have significantly impacted their attempts to earn YO. Kendrick, a 14-year-old black youth, was absent one Friday when his name was called, so the judge prepared to issue a bench warrant for him. Kendrick's attorney informed the court that he had just received a call from the boy from a pay phone saying that his mother wasn't letting him come to court. The attorney didn't say why the boy's mother wasn't letting him come. The judge instructed the attorney to tell the mother that he would hold her in contempt of court if she held up the boy. The judge held the warrant, and before the day was over Kendrick showed up in the court; the judge did not hold the matter against him and proceeded with his case as if nothing had happened. Kendrick had been dependent upon his mother to provide him train fare to get to court. Had the judge not been understanding, Kendrick's dependence upon an uncooperative adult might easily have left him remanded. However, because the court was cognizant of the reality of Kendrick's social status as a dependent child, his initial noncompliance was not seen as a mark against him. In fact, the court may well have been impressed by Kendrick's maturity and sense of responsibility in contacting his lawyer so quickly and eventually finding his way to court.

Randal, a 14-year-old Hispanic youth, found himself in a similar situation. He had first come before the court one summer day, charged with a robbery during which he and another youth allegedly injured a 15-year-old girl and stole her cell phone. During his first appearance, it was revealed that he had no prior arrests and was a good student who had been attending school regularly. He was assigned to an ATI program, and a month later it was reported that he was doing well in the program, though he had tested positive for marijuana. Two months later, however, things were not going well for Randal. He appeared in court after turning himself in on a bench warrant. He had missed an earlier scheduled court date and the ATI program had not seen him in a while. Randal was noncompliant in just about every manner possible. In court, his attorney explained that Randal's family had been evicted and had been moving to and from different shelters every two to three days for the past two to three weeks, which was why Randal had missed his appointments with the program and had been unable to call in for curfew, and also why he had missed his scheduled court date. The judge chose not to remand Randal, which would have been standard procedure for such noncompliance. A month later, the ATI program reported that although they had some problems keeping track of the family, things were getting better and Randal was doing okay.

Randal, at 14, was dependent upon the adults in his life to provide a stable home environment from which he could comply with the requirements of the ATI program. But his family had become homeless. The judge could easily have remanded Randal or denied him another chance in the ATI program. Rather, the court saw Randal as a good candidate for rehabilitation who was stuck in a bad set of circumstances beyond his control. The judge chose not to hold it against him. In both these cases, the reality of kids' dependence on adults, their lack of autonomy, directly impacted the work of the court. In order to deal adequately and accurately with their cases, the court could not ignore that reality; rather, the role of parents and families had to be taken into account in order to properly handle these "adult-juvenile" cases.

Standing For, Testifying, and Telling On: Families' Voices in Court

The inclusion of parents and/or guardians in juvenile court proceedings is generally believed to be appropriate and desirable. Parents are believed to have a special role—that of advocating for their child and assisting in decision-making within juvenile court settings.[4] The involvement of parents in juvenile courts has largely been neglected by researchers, though some ethnographic studies have demonstrated the role of family members within these settings.[5] Research on the role of family in criminal courts, and in the criminal prosecution of youth in particular, is nearly nonexistent. If it is acknowledged that parents can, and should, play an important role in juvenile court proceedings, the question arises: How important should parents or guardians be in the *criminal* prosecution of adolescents in criminal courts?

The Manhattan Youth Part chose to answer this question unequivocally: parents were extremely important. Because the court acknowledged the reality of the adolescence of its defendants, understanding them to be kids, family played a vital role in case processing similar to what might be expected within the traditional juvenile court system. Family members in the Youth Part were paid attention to, were given opportunities to address the court, and were an important part of the court's decision-making process from the beginning. Such attention was not required by law, but was yet another instance of the exercise of judicial discretion and the result of the creation of a unique culture within the part. In her analysis of Judge Corriero's style of interaction, DeBrovner observed that his "judicial interactive process treats [defendants] as children belonging to a family, and actively involves the families in court proceedings."[6] In contrast, Kupchik found limited participation among family members in the criminal court proceedings he observed.[7] In the bifurcated model he encountered, parental involvement only came into play at the sentencing phase of case processing. In the Manhattan Youth Part, however, family members were involved from day one. The family participation I observed in the Manhattan Youth Part was actually closer to what Kupchik observed in the juvenile court he studied. Writing about the role of nonlegal participants in the New Jersey juvenile court, Kupchik noted:

> Parents' and defendants' participation introduces peripheral issues that might be considered irrelevant in a *criminal* court. These issues provide the courtroom workgroup with personal, extralegal information about defendants, and arm the court with greater knowledge of the defendants and their personality beyond legal issues related to the alleged offenses [emphasis added].[8]

In the Manhattan Youth Part, such "peripheral issues" were not considered irrelevant prior to the sentencing phase and, in fact, became vital information upon which the court, in coordination with ATI programs, devised case-planning toward the goal of earning YO. Thus, family members assumed a meaningful, albeit precarious, role within the informal workings of the Youth Part. Repeatedly throughout my time in the court, I saw relatives claim a presence there, testifying and advocating for their children and even sometimes calling upon the court to assist them with parenting.

As previously discussed, when first getting to know a kid, the judge would speak with the parents, asking about what kind of work they did and how many other children they had at home. This was done in an attempt to understand the larger context of an individual defendant's life circumstances from the very beginning of his case. A kid could not be released into an ATI program unless there was a stable place for him to call home, and there was a better chance of success in the program if a parent or guardian was willing to cooperate with the program and with the court. Parents were also needed to assist adolescents in navigating various institutional systems—keeping appointments, getting back to court when due, filing paperwork, negotiating bureaucracies, and so on.[9] Thus, parents and family, when cooperative, were an invaluable resource for the court and for ATI programs, becoming important partners in the process of alternative sentencing and treatment.[10]

Family interactions with the court often came in the form of short answers to questions asked by the judge, such as, "How is he doing at home?" ("Good") or "Is he following your rules?" ("Yes, Your Honor"). Other times, it came in the form of short speeches or extended conversations with the judge. Family members often appeared nervous or unwilling to speak in the early weeks of coming to court, but as a case progressed over several months along the slow road to YO, most became more comfortable speaking aloud in court. There was a certain precariousness in many of these interactions. Family members did not have attorneys at their side, their role in the court was not well-defined legally, and the boundaries of acceptable speech and appropriate information for sharing were often uncertain. Defense attorneys sometimes frowned or flinched when a family member said something out loud in court that they would have preferred wasn't said, and I occasionally saw an attorney raise a hand to indicate that a family member should, please, just stop talking. Yet, at other times, attorneys seemed eager for a family member to speak, letting the court know that a mother or grandfather had useful information or wished to address the court. Family members sometimes testified as to how their child was doing at home, to the changes he had gone through, or to the difficulties he was working to overcome. Sometimes family members advocated for their child, requesting extra services or a later curfew. Now and again, some parents would "tell on" their kids if they thought the court should know about some errant behavior.

TESTIFYING: SALVADOR'S MOTHER AND SISTER

Salvador, the Hispanic youth with a Family Court history introduced in chapter four, had been given several chances by the Youth Part to succeed in an ATI program and was working on his last one. His dedicated attorney had worked out an option whereby Salvador would attend a residential drug treatment program. After the judge had talked with

Salvador, asking him why he should be given another chance, the judge spoke with Salvador's mother and sister in the audience, both of whom testified on his behalf.

"How do you feel about this?" the judge asked Salvador's mother.

"Me, Your Honor? I'll tell you, him being where he is now and when he gets out, I feel he has changed a lot. I see a lot of improvement in your giving him the chance. He would be a better person. I do see that."

Then the judge turned to Salvador's sister, who appeared to be about 18 years old, and asked her what she thought.

"I don't condone what my brothers have done," she said, "but I believe that Salvador has potential to change. He has potential to change. He's always talked positive. I never thought I was going to see the day my brother speaks the way he does. Sometimes, people that are bumped on the head a couple of times before they learn and see what they've done is wrong. I know most of the things he's done is because he has emotional problems. That's when the marijuana gets put in, and everything falls out of place. I feel if he does get this opportunity, he will change, he will become a good citizen to society."

ADVOCATING: ELLIS'S MOTHER

Ellis's mother advocated for her son the first time he was in court. Ellis, a black IN defendant, had been indicted on a charge of second-degree robbery. After the DA and the attorney told the judge about the case, Ellis's mother, who had been standing at the railing, appeared agitated. The judge asked her if she had any questions.

"Those other two are boyfriend and girlfriend," the mother said in a frustrated tone. "They stick together. I don't know why this whole thing is being put on MY child."

The judge said, "Your son has a great lawyer. If he wasn't responsible they will get to the bottom of it. And if he is guilty, then we have to find a way to make sure it never happens again. But it might take some time. I need you to keep an open mind. I know you love your son, but I want you to try and keep an open mind so that we can make sure this never happens again." The mother nodded quietly and appeared to calm down a bit.

ADVOCATING: SAMUEL'S MOTHER

Samuel was a black and Hispanic 17-year-old defendant who had been IN for nine months. On one of his visits to the court, Samuel's attorney reported to the court that they were trying to get the boy into a particular residential program. Samuel's mother raised her hand and said that she wanted her son to go into a different program from the one the lawyer had mentioned. The woman appeared nervous, couldn't remember the name of the program, and stumbled over her words. The judge waited patiently for her to remember and to find a piece of paper on which she had written down information. When she finally remembered the name of the program, the judge told the boy's attorney to look into the requested program and see if Samuel was acceptable.

ADVOCATING: ROGER'S MOTHER

Roger's mother brought her concerns and frustrations with the ATI program directly to the court. Roger was a black OUT defendant who was doing well in his ATI program. On a control date, Roger's attorney explained to the court that the program to which the youth had been referred for drug treatment and other services wasn't providing the right kinds of services for him. The ATI program representative reported that Roger was complying with all of their requirements, even though he and his family were not so happy with the outsourced services. As the lawyer, ATI representative, and judge were discussing this, Roger's mother raised her hand.

"Okay, Yes, ma'am," the judge said, acknowledging her.

"In reference to [the program]," Roger's mother started, "he's been doing everything they've required him to do. The only problem I'm having with him, he's been in there a month with them, and they've not provided him—I don't have the funds, so he's walking. It takes him 45 minutes to get there and 45 minutes to get back. I constantly am speaking with these people, and they're supposed to give him a MetroCard."

"Are they supposed to give him [one]?" the judge asked.

"Yes, he's supposed to have it," Roger's mother answered.

"If he doesn't get a MetroCard, he doesn't have to go there anymore," the judge said. "And you tell them that the judge is quite concerned that a month has expired and they are requiring him to be there."

"Every day," the mother said, "when I call them in reference to the problem, they tell me they're going to get in touch with me. I've spoken to the director and the supervisor in reference to the working papers. They won't even give him the working papers."

"Who's 'they'?" the judge asked.

She gave the name of the treatment program. "They're supposed to give him working papers and take care of all of that. He went for the physical before. [They] said he had to be examined, have a physical through their school. He had it. He had the TB test. They sent me over to the Bronx because it didn't come out right. When he took the chest x-ray, everything came back fine, where he was able to work. [They] still hasn't gave him working paper or anything, and then, what they have him doing for one to five o'clock? He's sitting inside a classroom with other kids with drug problems of cocaine, weed, or whatever. He's not doing nothing since. He's been in this school and has not brought home a piece of paper saying, 'Mom, look, they gave me work.'"

The judge asked the ATI representative about the options.

"I believed we referred him there because it was preventative," she said, "but I don't think . . ."

"Well it doesn't seem like there is anything being prevented," the judge responded.

"We see it's not beneficial to him," the representative said. "We're asking that, if he can—if we can go ahead and find him a new GED program."

"Yes," said the judge. "Make sure he gets working papers."

"One more question," said Roger's mother. "They had said he would have to do summer school. Where is he going to do summer school?"

"Well," the judge responded, "I know [the ATI program] can follow up with the necessary arrangements."

Sometimes parents "told on" their children in court. Their motivations for doing so were multiple and complex—genuine concern for the well-being of their child, frustration over a lack of control, possibly revenge. Some parents seemed to utilize whatever influence the judge may have had over their child to supplement their own parenting. In this way the court, in particular, Judge Corriero, was sometimes called upon to assume the role of surrogate or coparent. This was the case with Charles, Lazaro, and Ramiro.

TELLING ON: CHARLES'S GRANDMOTHER

Charles's grandmother didn't hesitate to tell on her grandson when the judge asked her how the black OUT youth was doing at home.

"He got to come in early," she said. "When I tell him to come in, I want him to come in." Given this information and the positive marijuana test reported by the ATI representative, the judge moved up Charles' curfew and let the boy know that he was running out of patience.

"Next time you test positive for marijuana," the judge said firmly, "the next time you miss a curfew, you are going straight to jail. Your curfew is going from 6:30 to 5:00 now. You're out later than five you are going to jail. I have a DA who wants to put you away for ten years. Do we understand each other?"

TELLING ON: LAZARO'S MOTHER

Lazaro's mother's plea to the court was a little more serious. Lazaro was a Hispanic JO who had been arrested for criminal possession of a weapon and had been released without bail at arraignment. Lazaro's mother stood in the audience when her son's name was called on his first time in the Youth Part. The judge asked if she spoke English, and when she said no, he asked the interpreter to assist her. Through the Spanish interpreter, the judge asked her, "Where are you from originally?"

"Dominican Republic," Lazaro's mother answered, through the interpreter.

"You know your son is charged with possessing a real gun?" the judge asked.

"Yes."

"You know he can go to jail for ten years?"

"Yes."

"Do you know that I can't even give him a sentence of probation because of the nature of the charge, that he has to be in jail? Do you understand that?"

"I didn't know," she responded. The judge reviewed the facts of the case and discussed the varying details with the defense and the prosecution. He then addressed Lazaro directly.

"Were you born here?" the judge asked him.

"Yeah."

"YES. No 'yeah' in this courtroom."

"Yes," said Lazaro.

"Your mother came here from the Dominican Republic?"

"Yes."

"Is your father with you?"

"No."

"Why do you think she came here?" the judge asked. Lazaro didn't answer.

"Why did you come from the Dominican Republic?" the judge asked Lazaro's mother directly.

"To make a better living," she said.

"To make a better life for her son," the judge said. "And this is how you repay her? Tough guy." He then spoke to Lazaro's mother again.

"Your son give you any trouble at home?" he asked.

"Yes," she replied.

"He gives you trouble?" the judge asked again.

"Yes."

"He doesn't listen to you?"

"No.

"Do you want me to put him in jail today?" the judge asked.

"Sí," Lazaro's mother said softly. The judge looked back at Lazaro. There was a moment of silence in the court.

"Because you are a tough guy," the judge said. "You put your mother in this situation. You need not worry, mother. I was going to put him in jail anyway. The evidence against him seems to be relatively strong. I don't think the bail is adequate. He'll have to stay with me for a while until we figure out what we're going to do with him."

The judge reset Lazaro's bail, had him remanded, ordered a PPI and a 390 examination, and asked an ATI representative to interview him to see if he was acceptable to the program. Although the judge would most likely have remanded Lazaro regardless of what his mother said, her statement was powerful confirmation for the court that much work needed to be done to turn Lazaro's case around.

TELLING ON, SORT OF: RAMIRO'S MOTHER

Ramiro's mother had other concerns one day when her son was in court. Ramiro, introduced in chapter four, was a Hispanic JO who had been doing well in his ATI program, though he was struggling with school. The judge took time to talk with the youth about it, and then his lawyer requested that Ramiro's curfew be extended. In the exchange that followed, Ramiro's mother didn't so much tell on Ramiro as rely on Judge Corriero to help her better parent her son. When Ramiro's attorney asked if it would be possible to change the boy's curfew, the judge asked, "What time is it now?"

"Six," Ramiro answered.

"That's pretty early," the judge said. "What would you like to see it?"

"Any time," answered Ramiro.

"Well, what time, like what?" the judge pushed.

Ramiro shrugged and said, "A time to hang out."

"Hang out? With whom?" the judge asked.

"My girl," said Ramiro.

"With your girl?" the judge said in a curious tone. "How long do you have this relationship with your girl?"

"Two years."

"Two years? While you were incarcerated, she—you still remained with your girl?"

"Yes."

"You care about her?"

"Yes."

"How did she feel when you went to jail?" the judge asked.

Ramiro's answer was interrupted by the Spanish interpreter.

"Excuse me, Your Honor, the mother would like it to be no more than 9:30 at night." The judge looked at Ramiro and said, "She is very generous, you should thank your mother for 9:30. I can trust you till 9:30?"

"Yes."

"Where does your girl go to school?" the judge asked. Ramiro said the name of the school.

"What grade is she in?"

"Twelfth."

"She is a little older than you?"

"Yeah."

"Is she smart?" the judge asked, and Ramiro nodded.

"She get into any kind of trouble herself?" the judge asked.

"No."

The judge got a serious look on his face and said, "As long as you are responsible."

"Yes," said Ramiro.

"You don't do anything that is going to create problems for her," the judge said in a cautionary tone. He then asked the program representative, "What kind of education is he getting in the program?" The representative understood the implication of the judge's question—whether or not sex education was a part of the curriculum.

"We can set him up," the representative said with a smile.

"Set him up," the judge said quickly, "set him up."

Again the Spanish interpreter interrupted, "Your Honor, the mother would like to say that she doesn't oppose the curfew but she wants the girlfriend's phone number, she doesn't even know who this woman is."

The judge looked at Ramiro with surprise and asked, "You haven't introduced this young lady to your mother?"

"I have," answered Ramiro sheepishly, "but she doesn't know which one." The judge raised one eyebrow.

"She doesn't know which one?" He paused for a moment and then added, "Well, that is important. Your mother should know where you are and what her telephone number is. You understand that?"

"Yes," said Ramiro.

"Thank you," said Ramiro's mother through the interpreter.

The inclusion of, and patience with, parents and other family members in the Youth Part was ongoing and common. They were an integral part of the work of the court. The court knew that the path to YO could be facilitated or hindered by the words, actions, and attitudes of kids' families. Thus, attention and respect was paid to parents and all family members in court. When I asked Judge Corriero about the way parents and family members were treated in the Youth Part, he said:

To me, you know, these are human beings who are very concerned about their children, and they have had their own problems in their own world. And they may not be articulate, they may not be educated, they may be angry at times, but they are still parents. And it is important for me to give them the opportunity to express themselves. It is important for me to get an idea of what they are capable of doing to help us. And the dynamic of it—I would hope in and of itself that would be part of the value of the Youth Part. You know, just the experience of giving people who feel hopeless and powerless an opportunity to express themselves and, when appropriate, to listen to them. It is to me part of the value of the experience of coming through the Youth Part, even though I may have to send their child to jail.

Here the judge not only articulated his awareness of the role that parents can play in the process of helping kids to earn (or not earn) YO, he also expressed his desire to treat parents and others with a respect they may not always encounter in large bureaucratic systems of social control, systems in which they often feel helpless and unheard.

Half a Boy and Half a Man

Because New York, like many states, uses a combination of age and offense criteria for deciding which juveniles must be prosecuted as adults, it is common for JO defendants to also have open cases in the Family Court. Thus, defendants could, and did, encounter situations where, in one setting, for one purpose, on one day, they were legally constructed as children deserving of the differential treatment of the Family Court, and in another setting, for another purpose, on another day, they were legally constructed as autonomous adults worthy of full adult legal prosecution in the criminal courts.

New York State law requires that 13-, 14-, and 15-year-olds be prosecuted as adults only for certain crimes. So, for example, if a 15-year-old were charged with a "non-adult" offense such as drug possession, the case would go to Family Court. If two weeks later the same 15-year-old were charged with an "adult" JO offense, such as second-degree robbery, that case would go to the criminal court system (see table 5.1). Thus, the same 15-year-old would be processed as an adult and as a juvenile, in two separate branches of the court system, at the same time.[11]

Simultaneous prosecutions in the Youth Part and Family Court could

Table 5.1

Court Jurisdiction under New York's Juvenile Offender Law for Selected Offenses

		Charged Offense			
		Drug Possession	Attempted Robbery	Robbery	Murder
Age	12	Family	Family	Family	Family
	13	Family	Family	Family	Criminal
	14	Family	Family	Criminal	Criminal
	15	Family	Family	Criminal	Criminal
	16	Criminal	Criminal	Criminal	Criminal

seriously complicate the resolution of cases in both jurisdictions. Sometimes Judge Corriero would delay the resolution of a case in his court until
he had time to see what the Family Court judge had decided, and sometimes Family Court judges delayed their dispositions until they learned
what Judge Corriero had decided. This resulted in a JO "Catch-22," with
each court waiting for the other to proceed before making its sentencing
decision. In order to navigate this difficult terrain, judges, defense counsel,
and ATI program personnel had to be fluent in the laws that governed
in, and the cultures that presided over, both the Family Court and the
Youth Part. Alonzo, Isaac, and Walter's experiences are emblematic of
how this legal contradiction played out in the day–to-day workings of the
Youth Part.

ALONZO

Alonzo was a 15-year-old black and Hispanic JO who had been
remanded by Judge Corriero.

"I understand he was placed in the Family Court?" the judge asked
the defense attorney as Alonzo was escorted to his seat by court officers
and his handcuffs removed.

"Your Honor, the Family Court has sentenced him," Alonzo's white
male attorney explained. "They want him to do a program. My information is that we are trying to juggle this court's demands with the Family
Court demands and trying to do a program that is acceptable to both of
the courts."

The judge put the case over for another two weeks to see if it could
be worked out. Meanwhile, Alonzo stayed in a juvenile detention facility.

WALTER

Walter, a 14-year-old black JO, had been enrolled in an ATI program for
about two months when he was arrested and charged with a "non-adult"
assault in the Family Court (only first-degree assault is an "adult" crime
at age 14 in New York). The Family Court did not remand Walter, and on
his next Youth Part court date, his lawyer argued rather convincingly
that the boy had been misidentified in the Family Court case. Uncertain
as to the best course of action and lacking needed information, the
judge told Walter to wait in the audience while the court tried to phone
the Family Court to learn more about Walter's new case in that court.
By the end of the day, the court had not been able to contact the appropriate people at Family Court. Judge Corriero, not yet knowing the full

details of the case, remanded Walter until he could learn more. A week later, and only after Judge Corriero was well informed about Walter's Family Court case, did he release the youth back into his ATI program.

ISAAC

Isaac, a 15-year-old black JO, had been remanded on a second-degree robbery case and also had a case open in Family Court (charge unknown). His criminal court case had been delayed so long that he had already spent a year in secure detention. Isaac's attorney had finally negotiated a deal in the Youth Part whereby Isaac would be released to an ATI program on the understanding that if he failed in the program he would get the maximum sentence allowable—two and a third to seven years and a lifetime felony record.

"He's going to be sentenced in Family Court on Monday," reported Isaac's white male attorney.

"On our case he's ROR'd [released on his own recognizance]," the judge said, adding, "Family Court will ROR him, I imagine."

"They were going to sentence him based on what this court did," the defense attorney said. "I'll alert the Family Court attorney."

The judge asked the ATI representative if she was going to be in the Family Court on Monday. She said she would be. "If he's released, he's to go immediately into your custody," the judge instructed.

Although Isaac was ROR'd by the Youth Part, he was not able to walk out of court because there was a Family Court hold on him. The next week, when his case came before the Youth Part, Isaac was still being held in a detention facility. The Family Court hadn't ROR'd Isaac, as Judge Corriero had anticipated, but instead sentenced him to a secure juvenile facility upstate.

Isaac's case in the Youth Part remained open, and the judge continued to monitor his progress during his Family Court placement upstate. A month later, juvenile detention facility personnel escorted Isaac to the Youth Part for his control date, and the judge scheduled yet another date a few months later—after Isaac was expected to be released from Family Court placement. At such time, the judge would reconsider releasing Isaac to the ATI as was originally planned in his criminal case processing.

Defendants with simultaneous cases like Alonzo, Walter, and Isaac face the bewildering reality that they are legally labeled one day as adult defendants, and another day as juvenile defendants. Each legal designation comes with its own distinct buildings, jurisdictions, personnel, case-processing requirements, and governing statutes. For example, bail is not an option in the Family Court, but is in the criminal court. In addition, the rights of parents are different in the two jurisdictions. For example, the Family Court Act requires that "a reasonable and substantial effort" be made to notify the juvenile's parent or legal guardian of the youth's first appearance in the Family Court. This is not true of the criminal courts. Each jurisdiction also comes with its own unique culture of case processing. It cannot be known if, when drafting the Juvenile Offender Law, the New York State legislature anticipated these illogical circumstances and the many challenges they would pose for young defendants and their families, as well as for judges, attorneys, and other court actors. I would hope not. The tangled contradictions created by this legal labeling *within* the criminal justice system is just another of the many unintended, and legally convoluted, consequences of New York's transfer legislation.

Adult Perpetrator, Child Victim, or Both?

Although not as common as having simultaneous cases in Family and criminal court, another contradiction of legal system labeling became apparent from my court observations. In its profile of the JOs it has served, the Legal Aid Society in New York estimates that 19% of its JO clients have suffered neglect, 33% have been or are in foster care, 11% have a family history of domestic violence, and 28% are in families with parental substance abuse involving "regular abuse indicating addiction."[12] Thus, many Youth Part kids came from seriously troubled homes and some of them suffered neglect and abuse. The task of acting as guardian for neglected and unwanted children is still very much within the mandate of the Family Court, but the Youth Part, a criminal court not mandated to handle such issues, nonetheless often had to confront these situations. Jorge, Kendrick, and Dario's cases were complicated by concerns about their possible abuse and/or neglect inside their homes. In their stories we see how the court tried to cope with situations in which an alleged "adult" perpetrator might also have been a "child victim" of parental neglect or abuse in need of child protective services.

JORGE

Jorge was a 16-year-old, non-JO, Hispanic youth who had been assigned to an ATI program. Jorge's mother rarely made it to court, and early on in his time with the ATI program there had been issues with his mother not cooperating. He was then placed in foster care. In Jorge's case, it was hard to determine the true source of his problems. Was Jorge himself failing in the program? Was he not being allowed to succeed by the adults around him? Was it a combination of both? For example, the ATI representative had reported that they were trying to get Jorge evaluated to see if he was in the appropriate educational setting, but his mother was very opposed to the testing and had not cooperated with the program.

About three months into Jorge's time with the program, the following exchange took place in court:

"Jorge," the judge asked when the boy took his seat, "are you doing everything I expect of you?"

"Yes," answered Jorge.

Jorge's white female attorney began to explain his circumstances to the court. "The family has broken apart because of his placement in foster care. Jorge is having a little bit of a hard time with that," she said.

"Where are you now?" the judge asked Jorge.

"I'm not sure of the exact address, but I'm on [street]," answered Jorge.

"You are in a foster care group home?" the judge asked.

"No, a foster home," Jorge said.

"When did this happen?" the judge asked.

"On the day after my last court date."

"And the family that you are with, how are you getting along with them?"

"I got two of my sisters with me," Jorge said.

"How is he doing in the program?" the judge asked the ATI representative.

"Since his last court date, Jorge has not been to our program or called in for curfew. I think his new foster mother doesn't know about our program. We did do a home visit this week and we gave her all the information—let her know about Jorge's curfew, that he needs to come once a week for individual and group. So I just think the foster mother did not know."

"Are you going to be able to do that?" the judge asked Jorge.

"Yes," replied Jorge.

The representative then explained that Jorge's new foster home was a good distance from the program, so there would be some details to work out around scheduling, school, and so on. The judge instructed the representative to have the program do its best to work it all out. He then said to Jorge, "You have to make the best of the situation, all right?"

Jorge nodded and said, "Mm-hmm."

"Especially if you have younger sisters."

"Mm-hmm," responded Jorge.

In Jorge's case it appeared likely that his struggles to comply with the program had been the result of upheavals created by being put into foster care.[13]

KENDRICK

Kendrick, an OUT 14-year-old black youth, had more complicated issues than just his mother not cooperating with the court. Over his months with the court the reality of his home situation was revealed.

Kendrick reported to the ATI program that he was abused in his mother's home—going so far as to tell program personnel that he would rather go to a detention facility than go home to her. The ATI program had contacted Administration for Children's Services (ACS), the city's child protective agency, which had evaluated the situation and found no reason to remove Kendrick from his mother's home. Until the situation could be worked out, the judge chose to remand Kendrick. He was later released and returned home, only to report more abuse to the ATI program. Again, ACS investigated and found no reason to remove him from the home. The court, Kendrick's attorney, and personnel from the ATI and ACS worked together to find an appropriate residential facility for Kendrick that would get him out of his mother's home and also satisfy the criminal court's supervision requirements. Eventually such arrangements were made, and on the day that all this was worked out in court the judge said, "I want to thank everyone for doing everything they have for this young man." He then looked directly at Kendrick and said, "I'm going to watch you very carefully. You're a bright young man with great potential."

On a later court date, representatives from the ATI and the residential program both reported that Kendrick was doing well. The judge asked him why he was doing so well.

"I made a promise," answered Kendrick.

"And I made a promise to you," responded the judge.

Several people from several institutions had gone out of their way to find a workable solution for Kendrick, who was both an alleged "adult" perpetrator deemed legally worthy of criminal prosecution, but also, apparently, a young victim of parental abuse worthy of the legal care and protection of the state—the same state that had labeled him an adult for his alleged transgressions.

DARIO

Dario was a tall and physically mature Hispanic youth. The first time I observed him in court he appeared disheveled, unshaven, and in less-than-clean clothes. Dario's father stood on one side of the courtroom's audience area, and Dario's sister, who was in her twenties, stood on the other.

"How is Dario doing?" the judge asked the ATI representative.

"As of Sunday he ran away from this father's home," the representative reported, "and he's been staying with his sister in [another borough]. We had an appointment for him for a residential at [a local facility], however, he didn't go. He has been going to the center for therapy sessions. He had been testing negative. He has a lot of missed curfews."

"Why did he leave?" the judge asked.

Dario's father answered from the audience, sounding frustrated and a little angry: "The last few months it's been difficult. He hasn't been complying with his curfew. . . . Things are very difficult at home. He cannot be controlled."

"Order a 390," the judge said. "He may have to . . ."

"Can I say something?" Dario interrupted.

"I would like to take him with me," Dario's sister interjected from the audience.

"I disagree with that," Dario's father said, his voice sounding angrier. "I have custody of this child." A court officer moved near the father and told him to "hold on" in an attempt to calm the man down.

"What do you have to say?" the judge said to Dario.

"The reason why I left on Sunday is because my father hit me. He was going to beat me up. I had to leave the house."

"That's not true!" Dario's father insisted.

Dario stated that he wanted to live with his sister.

"I figure if I lived with my sister that would be better. I feel my sister's is the best thing for me." The judge listened carefully and gave Dario the time he needed to say what he needed to say.

"What's your name?" the judge asked Dario's sister. She told him and then added, "I'm 21, I have three kids—they always have food, shelter. I have no problems with them. I feel if he comes with me he'll do better. I think if he goes to another place that's going to mess up his head." The judge asked the ATI representative for her opinion.

"I don't know what to do at this point," she admitted. "There's an open [abuse] case now as of Sunday, when the altercation happened with his father, so they're investigating that."

"May I speak?" asked Dario's father. The judge nodded and Dario's father made his case that Dario had been a disobedient son.

Dario spoke up in a pleading tone, "Since the last court date I'm doing everything I'm supposed to. I been doing good in school. I just had my regents exam and I think I did well. Living with my father I'm going back and forth to different homes. I have no space. No privacy to do anything. I can't study. I used to live with my sister. I feel I could progress there."

"How old are you?" the judge asked.

"Sixteen."

"It's not your choice to make," the judge said, stating the hard reality of Dario's situation—he was old enough to be tried as an adult in a criminal court but not old enough to determine his own living arrangements. The judge then asked if there was an open abuse case pending.

"They got in touch with me yesterday," Dario's father answered, "and someone told them I was abusive and neglectful. I smacked Dario on Sunday because he was being defiant and disrespectful."

"He PUNCHED me," Dario insisted.

"I did not!" responded Dario's father. "He's telling them all of this!"

After hearing Dario's father admit in open court that he had struck his son, the judge made a quick decision.

"The defendant is REMANDED," he commanded, "and the program will look into the viability of the sister's home. And also make sure that you get a residential program for him to enter."

A week later, Dario was in court with his sister and her husband. Dario was dressed in clean clothes and was clean shaven. His father was not in the courtroom.

"How is he doing in your house now?" the judge asked Dario's sister.

"Doing very well," she replied.

"He follows your rules?"

"Everything."

The judge then asked the program representative for her report.

"Since Monday he's been coming to the program and he's keeping curfew with the sister." Looking at Dario, the judge said, "Keep up the good work," and put the case over for a month.

Several months later, Dario completed the ATI program and was doing well. Eventually he received a sentence of YO + 5.

If it had not been cognizant of Dario's situation, or had not sought to look beyond the surface issues of his missed curfews and failed attendance record, the court may well have deemed Dario unworthy of a second chance to prove himself or to earn YO. He would have entered the secure detention system upstate and carried a felony record for the rest of his life.

Under the law, Jorge, Kendrick, and Dario were legally labeled by the criminal justice system as "adults" at the same time they were legally counterlabeled as dependent children in need of, and legally entitled to, protection by the state from abusive or neglectful parents. Actively aware of extralegal factors such as the often difficult life circumstances and dependent adolescent status of the kids that came before them, Youth Part court actors devised strategies to deal in practical ways with kids like Jorge, Dario, and Kendrick. Ironically, in such cases, the Manhattan Youth Part, a criminal court, ended up serving one of the fundamental functions of the Progressive Era reformers' ideal juvenile court— "child-saving," caring for abused and neglected children. The court attempted to deal with these kids in such a way that they could be held responsible for their alleged actions and be protected from abuse if and when necessary.

The dilemmas created by the internal contradictions of the legal system's own constructions and labeling are further evidence of the fundamental irrationality of the adult prosecution of adolescents. Such direct clashes between different institutional labels reveal the internal conflicts within the legal system itself—conflicts that, I would argue, severely strain the legitimacy of prosecuting children in criminal courts and point to the project's overall untenability. When I asked Judge Corriero whether or not prosecuting youths as adults made any sense legally, his response was: "It doesn't. It's an oxymoron. I can't explain it any other way. They are not adults. You can call them what you want, but they are not adults. And you know it's really mind boggling, a real conundrum that this was not thought out! And it's been ignored. . . . We've ignored it for so long, we've built structures around it, and now it has taken root."

The criminal prosecution of adolescents has indeed taken root, not just in New York but in every state in the union. Since the legislative changes pushed through in the 1990s, the criminal prosecution of youth has become standard, accepted, expected practice across the country. Along the way, legal absurdities and contradictory practices have become the institutionalized status quo. Some may argue that New York is exceptional in its internal legal illogic regarding Juvenile Offenders, and that the Manhattan Youth Part is even more extraordinary given its experiment in justice —so what larger lessons can really be gleaned from its stories? It is true that the specific challenges and solutions created in the Youth Part were particular to this specialized court, its judge, and the laws in place in the state. However, the contradictions inherent in the criminal prosecution of youth will obtain in any court, in whatever jurisdiction, charged to handle "adult-juvenile" cases. The laws that govern the practice in each state may well lead to different manifestations of these inherent contradictions and legal absurdities, but they will exist. And as Kupchik has argued, different courts and court actors will confront and respond to these contradictions in different ways.[14] The exact nature of the strategies devised by court actors to mediate through or around such conditions, will, of course, be informed by local laws and by the local culture of court actors and workgroups.

Much more ethnographic research on the criminal prosecution of adolescents in courtrooms around the country is needed so that more comparative work can be done to better understand the many ways that transfer laws create contradictory and unintended complications for case processing, as well as to uncover the different ways court actors develop strategies for managing (or not managing) these situations in the everyday practice of law. Only through more studies that capture transfer laws "in action" can we come to understand fully the ways in which the contradictions inherent in prosecuting youths as adults impact the kids caught up in these legal processes and the courts that handle their cases. In the meantime, I would offer the following for consideration and debate: If transfer laws create such convoluted and contradictory challenges for case processing, which in turn require court actors to develop special strategies that work to ignore, sidestep, circumvent, reinvent, or accommodate the intent of those laws, then might not the legitimacy of the routine prosecution of youths as if they were adults be suspect?

CHAPTER SIX

Judging the Court, Judging Transfer

My goal in this ethnography has been to document the law in action and shed light on how youths are constructed, or not constructed, as adults through the process of criminal prosecution. I tried to uncover how the criminal prosecution of adolescents was undertaken in one court in one jurisdiction and, in the process, discover what could be learned about trying youths as adults and about legal responses to adolescent transgression more generally. Invariably, whenever I discuss this research I am asked some version of the same basic question, though it is worded differently from person to person and place to place: "So, do these kids re-offend less than others?" or "What are the recidivism rates for these kids?" or the simply skeptical, "Does that really work?" These are important questions, whether one's interest is in helping disadvantaged, troubled kids (child-saving) or in protecting the public from violent and/or delinquent youth (social control).

Was the Manhattan Youth Part's experiment successful? An evaluation of the existing, albeit limited, evidence on Juvenile Offenders in New York City and in the Manhattan Youth Part sheds light on the potential success of the court's model of case processing. An examination of research on the deterrent effects of transfer laws on adolescent offending and reoffending questions the efficacy of transfer as a viable response to adolescent offending. Both of these lines of inquiry lead to a broader discussion of what the proper legal response to serious adolescent offending should be.

Judging the Youth Part

Does the Manhattan Youth Part's experiment in justice work? There are different ways to try to answer that question. Recidivism rates are one common measure by which criminal justice practices are judged. Available data on recidivism among kids who went through Corriero's court are limited, but the nonprofit Criminal Justice Agency (CJA) releases annual quantitative reports on the case processing of Juvenile Offenders in New York City that provide some insight. In 2005 and 2007, the CJA also produced two studies looking specifically at the rearrest rates for JOs in the city: The 2005 study compared case processing and rearrest data among JOs processed in Queens and Manhattan; the 2007 study compared the same data for JOs in all five boroughs.[1] One important caveat about using these studies to assess the Youth Part is that they look only at JOs, whereas in the Manhattan Youth Part there were, on average, three times as many non-JOs as JOs. Despite this limitation, the CJA reports still shed some important light on Manhattan Youth Part practices.

One important finding of these studies is just how much the practice of prosecuting JOs differs among the New York City boroughs. The first study focused on a comparison of Queens and Manhattan largely because of the striking differences in case-processing style in the two boroughs. The researchers found that, although case and offender characteristics were similar in both boroughs, "the experiences afforded to juvenile offenders prosecuted in Manhattan and Queens are so divergent that they actually seem to constitute different models of youth crime prosecution."[2]

Comparisons of case processing across all five boroughs support what court actors have long known about the Manhattan Youth Part's unique style of JO case processing:[3]

- *Youth Part Concentration*: In Manhattan nearly all JO cases were handled in the Youth Part, while in other boroughs many more JOs were handled in all-purpose parts. For example, between 2002 and 2006, 89% to 100% of JO cases in Manhattan were handled in the youth part, compared with a citywide average of only 51% to 79%. For some years in Queens, less than one-third of JO cases were handled in the borough's specialized youth part.[4]
- *Length of Court Interaction*: Kids in Manhattan spent significantly longer time with a youth part than kids in any of the other boroughs. For example, between 1997 and 2000, the average length of time for case processing (first appearance to case completion) of JO cases in Manhattan was 17.2 months, compared to just 9.4 citywide (8.2 in Brooklyn, 7.6 in the Bronx, 4.1 in Queens, and 3.7 on Staten Island).[5]
- *Reliance on Alternative to Incarceration Programs*: ATI programs were more heavily utilized in Manhattan than elsewhere: The 2007 CJA study concluded: "The opportunity for nearly every juvenile prosecuted in the Manhattan Supreme Court to be placed in an alternative-to-incarceration (ATI) program also accounts for much of the difference in length of case processing."[6]
- *Youthful Offender Treatment*: Contrary to what one might expect, YO treatment was slightly less likely to be given in Manhattan than in the other boroughs. Between 1997 and 2000, 74% of JO cases were given YO treatment in Manhattan, compared to 80% citywide (77% in Brooklyn, 84% in the Bronx, 85% in Queens, and 86% on Staten Island).[7]

The rearrest (within four years of risk) data presented by CJA for New York City's JOs are somewhat useful for evaluating Youth Part practices. They are also somewhat problematic. The authors of the report concede that rearrest data is problematic, in general, for a couple of reasons. They note, first, that not all reoffending leads to rearrest, and, second, that the study could not account for any rearrests occurring outside New York State. In addition, I suggest further general limitations of rearrest data. First, not all arrests account for an actual act of criminal offending. This is particularly salient in communities with high levels of surveillance where police "sweeps" are common. Over the course of this research, I heard many accounts of youths who were caught in sweeps or arrested for trespassing on the grounds of the housing complex in which they lived. Such "arrest first and ask questions later" practices, often deemed necessary by law enforcement in certain high-crime neighborhoods, lead to inflated arrest statistics. Second, many arrests ultimately result in a "decline to prosecute" decision from the DA's office or are never indicted by the grand jury. Indeed, the CJA study authors acknowledged that more than 25% of JO rearrests in their study did not result in prosecution.[8] All of these factors should caution against relying too heavily upon rearrest data alone for fully understanding JO recidivism in New York City.

Caveats aside, the rearrest data are interesting. The most basic finding of the CJA studies was that JO rearrest was high across the city. As the authors put it, "two-thirds of the juveniles had been re-arrested within four years at risk."[9] The quick conclusion to draw from these data would be that "nothing works" and that Manhattan Youth Part practices do nothing special.[10] Further examination of the data, however, reveals some interesting details:

- The most common charge citywide for first rearrest (15%) was "criminal possession of marihuana in the fifth degree, a B misdemeanor."[11] In Manhattan, 14% of first rearrests were for this charge.
- Citywide, 50% of JOs were rearrested for a violent felony, 46% in Manhattan, 57% in Brooklyn, 46% in the Bronx, 50% in Queens, and 41% in Staten Island.[12]
- Time to first rearrest came later for Manhattan JOs: The median number of days for Manhattan was 347, compared to 254 for Brooklyn, 279 for the Bronx, 250 for Queens, and 199 for Staten Island.[13]
- The CJA study reports that "Juveniles processed in Manhattan (17%) were significantly less likely than juveniles in the other boroughs

(25% or more) to be charged with murder, attempted murder or other felony assault charges."[14]

The authors sum up these findings by stating that, "taken together, the findings of the re-arrest models suggest that the way juvenile cases are processed in Manhattan Supreme Court with its emphasis on placement programs under court supervision may not only delay the initial re-arrest but also may reduce the likelihood of re-arrest for the most serious offenses."[15] The authors later state the policy implications of these findings: "The Manhattan model of youth prosecution may offer a window of opportunity for intervention to reduce recidivism."[16] These successes may be due to how closely kids are monitored by ATIs and the court in Manhattan; how long they are kept under court supervision; the active utilization of ATI and social welfare agency interventions to address individual and family issues; the style of individual justice and personal interaction that Judge Corriero developed with defendants; or a combination of all these factors.

One conclusion the CJA studies suggest, given the lower cost of ATIs in comparison to secure detention, is the need to advocate for more ATIs with more funding to provide more services and supervision longer than the usually mandated six months or one year. This makes even more sense if we acknowledge that it may be quite unrealistic to expect an ATI—no matter how well designed—to be able to identify and address a myriad of familial, social, educational, and psychological problems in the short time frame generally allocated. If heavy reliance on ATIs, as currently conceived, indeed delays reoffending behaviors or reduces the likelihood of serious violent reoffense, as the data suggest, might better-funded programs that engage youths for longer periods have even more success, leading to fewer rearrests?

Other studies point to the positive impact of ATIs in New York City. The Center for Alternative Sentencing and Employment Services (CASES), one of the ATIs active in the Manhattan Youth Part, documented its own successes by examining reconviction, rather than rearrest, rates for the youths it served. An assessment of the agency's program for 15- to 20-year-olds with felony charges (52% with charges for violent offenses) found that within two years of graduation from their program, "89% had no new criminal convictions" in any of the five boroughs.[17] Additionally, the study found that of those who were reconvicted, only 4% were for violent offenses.

The Andrew Glover Youth Program (AGYP), a community-based ATI active with the Manhattan Youth Part that provides services for JOs and non-JOs, documents their success rates by stating that "only 19% of all AGYP clients were re-arrested in New York State for three years after enrolling in the program. The three-year recidivism rate for successful graduates of AGYP was very low at 7%."[18] The Youth Advocacy Project, an ATI specializing in working with JOs, reports an average rearrest rate of only 20%.[19]

Now compare these ATI recidivism rates with those for secure detention: A study of youths released from state custody between 1991 and 1995 found that "75 percent were re-arrested, 62 percent were reconvicted, and 45 percent were re-incarcerated within three years."[20] Another study found that 89% of male youths who were in detention in New York went on to be rearrested by time they turned 28.[21] The Correctional Association of New York, a nonprofit organization dedicated to criminal justice reform in the state, reported in 2007 that "46% of the youth released from secure city facilities were readmitted to detention in the same year."[22] While serious difficulties arise in comparing many of these studies,[23] the data consistently suggest that ATIs are a cost-effective and valuable tool for reducing youthful offending.

Recent reports indicate an annual cost of $226,320 to house a youth in secure detention in New York City, and $210,000 for upstate placement.[24] Compare those costs with annual ATI costs, which range from $1,400 to $13,000 per person served.[25] Given the significant cost differentials between ATIs and incarceration, alternative programs could be considered highly successful even if they produced recidivism rates that were only on par with costly incarceration. Taken together, these data suggest that the experiment undertaken in the Manhattan Youth Part had a measured level of success. Further, the implication is that the consistent integration of ATI programs into the case processing of adolescents (in juvenile or criminal courts) is a viable and effective response to much youthful offending. Such diversion methods, as modeled by the Manhattan Youth Part, cost considerably less than an overreliance on incarceration and help reduce juvenile recidivism, thus increasing public safety and saving valuable tax dollars.

That said, if we focus too narrowly on recidivism outcomes and cost concerns, we may limit our understanding of other important functions of court processes. Are there other standards by which responses to youth offending might be judged? The concept of procedural justice provides us with another important method by which to evaluate the work of the part. Procedural justice refers to the subjective sense of fairness one feels when engaged in or observing legal processes. The focus is not solely on the outcome of the process (a proper verdict, a fair sentence), but on a subjective evaluation of the process itself. Do actors/observers feel that they were treated fairly, that the process was fair, legitimate, and impartial?[26] Belief in the fairness and legitimacy of legal processes results in greater compliance with the law, whereas a belief in the unfairness or illegitimacy of legal processes can result in defiance and law-breaking, or acceptance of law-breaking.[27] Issues of procedural justice are particularly relevant for younger defendants because it is during adolescence that people begin to form concrete attitudes toward societal institutions.[28] How youths evaluate the fairness of the legal proceedings they are caught up in can profoundly affect their attitudes and behaviors as they mature. It can also have a direct impact on their attitudes and behavior when dealing with ATI programs or probation and correctional personnel.

So how did the Manhattan Youth Part fare in terms of procedural justice? As described in this book's introduction, for several reasons I was unable to conduct interviews with defendants directly, so I can only offer my observations of them in court and secondhand accounts of their attitudes toward their experiences there. I asked several of the people involved with defendants about their own impressions of what the kids thought of the judge and the ways in which he interacted with them. Several defense attorneys and ATI personnel suggested that most defendants in the Youth Part respected and even liked the judge. They thought that the kids may have been willing to work so hard for him because they felt that he respected them and that they could trust him. One ATI representative put it this way: "The kids want to do well for him, they want to do well for him, they do, . . . They almost kinda see him like as a father figure and they want to do well for him. . . . I think that there is a sense of wanting to do well for him because he puts his faith in them and he tells them that, so they want to show him he made the right decision, and that also goes back to the fact that they know him better because he can spend more time with them."

In observing court interactions on calendar days, it was obvious that many of the kids did, over time, come to respect the judge, even when he had to be stern with them—or even remand them. As stoic as most of the kids attempted to be, body language and facial expressions often gave them away. I repeatedly witnessed genuine pride showing on a kid's face when the judge praised a good report card or some recent award. I saw more than one kid walk out of the court smiling with a bounce in his step after the judge had told him, "Keep up the good work, I'm proud of you," or "This is great, you've made my day." I also saw kids fidget nervously in the audience waiting for their turn when they knew that their ATI report wasn't going to be all positive. I saw regret slump kids' shoulders when they disappointed the judge. I witnessed some defendants grow impatient when the judge lectured them, and at times I saw them struggle to hide their negative reactions. I saw kids look sad, even hurt, when they were reproached by the judge. I also saw kids laughing and joking and being at ease with him. Most importantly, I saw kids who at first appeared highly intimidated develop, over time, the confidence to speak aloud and to have a voice in the court.

Although most people I spoke with stated that caring judges dedicated to rehabilitation goals could be found throughout New York's Family Court and criminal court, many indicated that Judge Corriero was a special case. As one ATI representative put it, "I don't want to single out Corriero, but he seems to have a particular attention to the issue of respect." Judge Corriero's exceptional personal dedication to the kids was obvious. His court attorney put it this way: "I am amazed, because he has so many kids coming in and out of here and he remembers their face, and he remembers their stories, and he'll remember things about them that I never wrote down in the file, but he knows it."

A framed black-and-white photo in the judge's chambers showed him hanging out with some of his teenage friends. In the photo, Corriero looks a bit like a tough guy, with a cigarette hanging out of his mouth. When I asked just how rough and tumble he was as a young man, he gestured toward the photo and said, "I looked rough and tumble, but . . . I walked with some very tough kids, let's put it that way. But I was never—I was who I am. They always said I was gonna be a lawyer, a negotiator." It was clear in talking with him and reading his writings that his memories of being a young man in a tough neighborhood remained vivid—the struggles to do good, the temptations to do bad, the need to protect one's honor, defend one's manhood, to not appear weak.[29] As one defense attorney said, these experiences made Corriero special: "He has a certain empathy that many judges lack." Another defense attorney explained it this way:

[The judge] comes from a conventional, Catholic, working-class family, so issues of family and traditional values are very important to him—and in a way it is a very good thing because it represents, like, stability to a kid, you know? And also what the kids see, the kids adore him because they see that he likes kids. They do, the kids know —it is an empathic thing—the kids respect him and adore him, and it's because in his heart he really likes kids and remembers what it is like to be a teenager and kids appreciate him.

When I asked her if they still felt that way when he put them back in jail, she replied, "Yes. They adore him, they adore him, and they understand that it is fair for the most part." Another seasoned defense attorney shared a story to illustrate how many of the kids in the Youth Part felt about Judge Corriero. She explained that she had a young defendant whose mother was mentally ill, and the boy couldn't get subway fare to come to court: "So he walked—from the Bronx! The judge was screaming 'I'm gonna issue a warrant,' and the kid showed up at two [o'clock]. I don't think he would have walked for most other [judges]."

Judge Corriero understood well how important the *process* kids and their families went through in his court was, not just the *outcomes* of their cases. He had a clear understanding of the force of procedural justice:

I mean, I represent society to them. If I appear biased or prejudiced or mean or arrogant or mean or uncaring, then what do they owe society? You know, again, I could be completely delusional, but I don't think so. And in any event, this is the way I'm going to live my life. This is the way I would want people who are in government, in bureaucracies, to behave when they're dealing with people who come into the system. . . . Do they ultimately feel that they have been treated fairly —even the kids that we send away? If I try to make an effort to make them feel that this is the only thing I can do, that this is fair, and you have to understand that you violated the rules and there is a consequence for it. Why? Because I don't want them to come out any angrier than they went in.

In terms of procedural justice, the Manhattan Youth Part was highly successful. The court's overt attempts to treat kids and families with respect, to allow them to have a voice in the court, to tailor responses based on knowledge of individual kids and the circumstances of their often difficult lives, created an atmosphere and case-processing style that seemed fair to most. Many of the kids and their family members lived in over-policed and over-surveilled communities of color. As young black and Hispanic urban males, many would have experienced being criminalized in their schools, in their neighborhoods, and in the streets. The Manhattan Youth Part, in its day-to-day handling of cases, did not replicate and reinforce these experiences, nor did it fuel the frustration they often foster. For that alone the court should be judged a success.

Judging Transfer

The transfer law boom of the 1990s ushered in a new era of legal responses to young offenders. It normalized the criminal prosecution of adolescents and moved unprecedented numbers of offending youths into the adult system. Did it work? After more than twenty years of harsh transfer laws on the books across the country, have these provisions proved useful as a response to adolescent offending? Does the criminal prosecution of adolescents reduce youth crime? In terms of specific deterrence (offenders not reoffending after prosecution), the research says no. In terms of general deterrence (sending a message to potential offenders that deters them from offending), the research says probably not. Studies comparing the reoffending rates for transferred youths to those for youths processed through the juvenile system have produced consistent results—either there has been no reduction in reoffending, or reoffending was higher among transferred youths.[30] A 2008 overview of extant research on recidivism and transfer policies produced by the U.S. Department of Justice's Office of Juvenile Justice and Delinquency Prevention (OJJDP) reported that six large studies using multiple methods in different jurisdictions with a variety of transfer mechanisms all came to the same conclusion:

> [H]igher recidivism rates among offenders who had been transferred to criminal court, compared with those who were retained in the juvenile system. . . . Thus, the extant research provides sound evidence that transferring juvenile offenders to the criminal court does not engender community protection by reducing recidivism. On the contrary, transfer substantially increases recidivism.[31]

A 2007 report put out by the Centers for Disease Control (CDC) reviewing available research on transfer came to similar conclusions: "The review provides sufficient evidence that the transfer of youth to the adult criminal justice system typically results in greater subsequent crime, including violent crime, among transferred youth; therefore, transferring juveniles to the adult system is counterproductive as a strategy for preventing or reducing violence."[32]

The clear takeaway from these reports is that trying youths as adults doesn't work—it doesn't reduce reoffending, especially violent reoffending, and may in fact increase it; and while general deterrent effects are harder to assess given the range of factors involved in decisions to offend, research has been inconclusive in determining any strong general deterrent effect for transfer.[33] Knowledge of potential negative sanctions is a prerequisite for general deterrence mechanisms to function, yet most young offenders who could be subject to criminal court prosecution were simply unaware of that possibility. Seven out of ten arrested juveniles in one study did not know, prior to their arrest, that they could be tried as adults.[34]

Thus, a growing body of reputable research strongly indicates that trying youths as adults does not have the intended deterrent effects and may, in fact, lessen public safety. As David Myers sums it up, the practice of trying youths as adults "is a very limited approach to dealing with serious and violent youthful offending and one that should not be fully relied upon by politicians and the general public as a way to prevent and reduce juvenile crime."[35] Jeffrey Butts and Ojmarrh Mitchell, authors of "Brick by Brick: Dismantling the Border between Juvenile and Adult Justice," put it more bluntly: "If expanded criminal court transfer policies do increase public safety, researchers have yet to find clear evidence of that effect."[36]

What affect does criminal prosecution have on notions of procedural justice? One study found that youths processed in the criminal courts have much more negative attitudes toward their experiences than those processed in the juvenile system. In their interviews with youths prosecuted in both systems, researchers found a high level of anger, resentment, and a sense of injustice among those criminally prosecuted.[37] Another study also found a high level of feelings of unfairness among transferred youths.[38] This sense of injustice, along with the stigma of criminal prosecution, the impact of a felony conviction, and the lack of rehabilitation-centered goals within the criminal court, may, in fact, lead to higher rates of reoffending among transferred youths.[39] All these studies, whether on general deterrence, specific deterrence, or procedural justice, strongly suggest the same thing—the criminal prosecution of youth does not make us safer. Put simply, it doesn't work. And yet it obtains.

Making the Case for the Differential Treatment of Juveniles

Public opinion can be easily manipulated by media misrepresentations and political maneuvering; thus, any assessments of public beliefs must be taken with caution. Nonetheless, a number of studies have shown that the public largely favors a nonretributive approach to the problem of youth offending, even serious violent offending, and that while public support for trying youths as adults does exist, it wanes in regard to the transfer of younger, first-time, and nonviolent offenders.

A 2007 study found that 81% of the public was against doing away with the juvenile court.[40] Another study found substantial public support for the transfer of serious, repeat juvenile offenders to the criminal system, but little for "transferring large numbers of juvenile offenders to the adult court," as is current practice in many places. Fully 73% of respondents in the study agreed with the statement that "juveniles who commit violent crimes" should be tried as adults, but when provided with short vignettes of individual cases of specific juveniles charged with violent offenses, their support for transfer waned—even when those vignettes included homicide charges. The researchers discovered that "people wanted transfer used selectively to handle the worst juvenile offenders."[41] Further, the study found strong support for rehabilitative goals in regards to youth offending—even violent offending.[42] Another 2007 poll found that "by more than a 15 to 1 margin (92% to 6%), the US voting public believes that decisions to transfer youths to the adult court should be made on a case-by-case basis and not be governed by a blanket policy."[43] A 2010 study found strong support for the adult prosecution of older repeat offenders and those charged with serious, violent crimes such as rape, but it also found decreasing levels of support for the transfer of younger, first-time, and nonviolent offenders.[44]

Taken together, these studies suggest that despite popular "tough on crime" discourse and fear-inducing media representations of violent juveniles, the majority of the public agrees that most adolescents are different from adults and therefore deserving of differential treatment under the law. This enduring idea, the very basis for the existence of our juvenile court system, is still commonly held by the general public. Current transfer laws contradict what the general public knows intuitively—that kids are different from adults and therefore deserve a different type of judicial response when they offend.

A large and compelling body of research on adolescent development and adolescent culpability supports the general public's attitudes.[45] This research indicates that the cognitive differences already acknowledged in children and young adolescents are present even in older adolescents.[46] In examining features of adolescent development relevant for understanding the efficacy of trying youths as adults—namely, psychosocial factors and cognitive development as they pertain to adolescent decision-making processes[47]—these developmental specialists make the important distinction between *cognition* and *judgment* in the adolescent mind. Whereas *cognition* refers to the act of knowing, *judgment* relates to such factors as peer influence, attitude toward risk, and temporal perspective. Adolescents, even older adolescents, are more likely to experience more direct peer pressure than adults, and are more likely to seek the approval of peers than adults are. In addition, perceptions of risk are different for adolescents than for adults, with adolescents more likely to have a present-time orientation and be less focused on the long-term outcomes of actions and decisions.[48]

In explaining the distinction between the development of cognitive abilities and judgment, Elizabeth Scott and Thomas Grisso, leading experts in the field of adolescent culpability, write: "Thus, adolescents on the street, who are making choices that lead to criminal conduct, may be less able than adults to consider alternative options that could extricate them from a precarious situation." They concluded that, although older adolescents may have "adult-like capacities for reasoning," they may lack the ability to "deploy these capacities" in an adult-like way, especially in "ambiguous or stressful situations."[49] Other development experts emphasize the importance of examining the interplay between cognition and psychosocial factors in understanding levels of competency in adolescent decision-making.[50] While adolescents may have the cognitive abilities to assess benefits and risks, they may lack the experience to make sound decisions.[51] This distinction between cognition and judgment is particularly salient given the commonly held belief that older adolescents have adult-like reasoning skills—a belief that allows for a general acceptance of trying youths, especially older adolescents, as adults. Development research shows, however, that while a 15-year-old may know right from wrong (cognition), his ability to make good decisions in stressful circumstances (judgment) may not be as well developed as that of an adult.

Advances in neurobiology that have shed light on adolescent brain development support these claims about the limitations of adolescent decision-making processes. Brain researchers are finding that brains are not fully physically mature until much later than originally thought.[52] There is strong evidence that the prefrontal cortex of the brain—where impulse control and other complex cognitive "executive" functions such as evaluating of risk and rewards are housed—is often still developing throughout and far beyond adolescence.[53] Psychology professor Laurence Steinberg and law professor Elizabeth Scott, who have researched and written extensively about adolescent decision-making and criminal culpability, summarize this brain research as follows:

> Patterns of development in the prefrontal cortex, which is active during the performance of complicated tasks involving long-term planning and judgment and decision making, suggest that these higher order cognitive capacities may be immature well into late adolescence.... There is good reason to believe that adolescents, as compared with adults, are more susceptible to influence, less future oriented, less risk averse, and less able to manage their impulses and behaviors and that these differences likely have a neurobiological basis.[54]

These findings support a strong connection between the neurobiological facts of brain development and adolescent, even late-adolescent, decision-making capabilities.

The experts contend that these limitations of adolescent decision-making processes have profound implications for adolescent legal culpability. In 2005, the Supreme Court cited this research in *Roper v. Simmons*, a case which could have implications for the future of trying youths as adults. In *Roper*, the Court, in a 5–4 decision, judged the imposition of the death penalty on those whose capital crimes were committed while under the age of 18 to be unconstitutional.[55] In its decision, the Court reaffirmed the basic principle that young people are qualitatively different from adults and thus entitled to differential treatment under the law.[56] The Court held three main reasons for its decision to revoke juvenile death penalty laws: (1) a majority of the states had already done away with a juvenile death penalty; (2) such a decision would bring the United States in line with international standards and practices; and (3) there are differences between juveniles and adults.[57] The Court cited the literature on adolescent development, brain science, and culpability at length and recognized three main differences between juveniles and adults. They cited the "comparative immaturity and irresponsibility of juveniles," noted that "juveniles are more vulnerable or susceptible to negative influences and outside pressures, including peer pressure,"[58] and that "the character of a juvenile is not as well formed as that of an adult."[59] In summing up their assessment of the relevant research, the Court stated, "Once the diminished culpability of juveniles is recognized, it is evident that the penological justifications for the death penalty apply to them with lesser force than to adults."[60]

This decision could potentially have serious implications for the future of transfer laws.[61] Many who work with or do research around youths who are tried as adults have been asking the same question since *Roper v. Simmons*: If, according to the Supreme Court, youth have a reduced level of culpability when facing a death penalty, would it not follow that they have a reduced level of culpability when facing criminal prosecution in general? Legal scholars Nina Chernoff and Marsha L. Levick argue that "the Court's . . . ultimate conclusion—that youth are categorically less culpable than adults—[has] implications for the prosecution, defense, and sanctioning of youthful offenders in the juvenile and criminal justice systems."[62] Enrico Pagnanelli, writing in the *American Criminal Law Review* on the potential impact of *Roper* on transfer law, states:

> Roper has signaled that the Supreme Court recognizes the diminished culpability of juveniles and believes that they are not deserving of the same punishment as adults. This recognition should transform juvenile jurisprudence and policymaking for violent offenders and allow the absolute failure of juvenile transfer in achieving objectives to be scrutinized for review and repair.[63]

Writing on the application of *Roper* to waiver proceedings in the *International Journal of Offender Therapy and Comparative Criminology*, clinical psychologist John Matthew Fabian also suggests that blanket waiver laws such as statutory exclusion and direct file provisions, as opposed to judicial waiver, may be particularly susceptible to claims of unconstitutionality under *Roper*.[64]

Another, more recent case has reinforced the Supreme Court's position on the reduced culpability of young offenders. In May 2010, the Supreme Court decided in *Graham v. Florida* that a sentence of life without the chance of parole for juveniles convicted of non-homicide offenses violated the constitutional protection against cruel and unusual punishment. The court, relying on *Roper*, again cited the "limited culpability" of juvenile offenders.[65] Noting that there was no reason to reconsider *Roper*, the court stated that "developments in psychology and brain science continue to show fundamental differences between juvenile and adult minds."[66] It remains to be seen whether any future Supreme Court cases will directly challenge the constitutionality of the practice of prosecuting youths as adults, but both *Roper v. Simmons* and *Graham v. Florida* have now affirmed the fundamental concept that youths are different from adults in important ways that should mitigate their legal culpability. In the article "Using *Graham v. Florida* to Challenge Juvenile Transfer Laws," published in the *Louisiana Law Journal*, Neelum Arya argues that "*Graham* is revolutionary in that it cuts to the heart of why we have a juvenile justice system, why it is separate from the adult system, and hopefully will make us rethink why we let the two bleed together so often."[67] The author goes on to say that "the diminished culpability of youth has been solidified by *Roper* and *Graham*."[68] In March 2012 the Supreme Court heard arguments in two other relevant cases, *Jackson v. Hobbs* and *Miller v. Alabama*. These cases question the constitutionality (again under the Eighth Amendment ban on cruel and unusual punishment) of sentences of life without parole for youths age 14 and under involved in homicides. As this book goes to press the Supreme Court has not ruled in these two cases, but, like *Roper* and *Graham*, they may prove significant in developing standards of adolescent culpability.[69]

Neither the developmental experts cited above nor the Supreme Court has indicated that young people should not be punished, or that young people involved in acts of transgression are blameless or lack responsibility for their actions. They claim only that adolescents have a diminished level of culpability and should be punished in ways different from adults, and that courts should act accordingly when handling their cases.[70] The Manhattan Youth Part embodied these basic principles in its everyday handling of cases. Working within the confines of the retributive intent of the Juvenile Offender Law, the court sought to hold youths accountable for their actions in ways that were in line with the reality of their adolescence.

Conclusion

Kids Will Be Kids

In late 2007, Judge Michael Corriero retired from the Supreme Court of New York. The work of the Manhattan Youth Part continues under the guidance of a new judge with new staff; another judge dedicated to the work of this specialized criminal court and, in his own unique way, to ideals of child-saving. In an interview a few months after his retirement, I asked Judge Corriero if he accomplished what he had set out to with the Manhattan Youth Part. He replied, "Yes, I think I did. I felt very good about what we were able to accomplish. But I recognize that it has a limitation and the limitation is the law, the legal structure. And that has to be changed. And there is no compromise on that—we have to adopt a transfer-up system."

Here the judge echoes one of Aaron Kupchik's most salient points—that the mechanisms that court actors may use to "filter" transfer laws cannot fully reverse the legal impact of those laws.[1] Regardless of how creative its case-processing mechanisms, or how many spaces within the law the court found to work within, the Youth Part could never fully nullify the impact of New York's statutory exclusion law. The creative mechanisms designed by the court to work around the edges of harsh, counterintuitive, and counterproductive law must be seen only as an interim measure until repeal of the Juvenile Offender Law is possible. Now retired from the bench, Corriero advocates freely for that repeal and for extending the jurisdiction of the Family Court in New York. He proposes that all defendants under 18 years of age be processed initially in the Family Court, with Family Court judges having the right to *transfer up* to criminal court the cases of those serious offenders deemed not amenable to treatment within the juvenile courts. With the exception of the representative from the Manhattan District Attorney's office—who thought the current system worked pretty well—all the folks involved with the Youth Part that I spoke with agreed with this proposal.

Many legal experts also suggest this model. Laurence Steinberg and Elizabeth Scott argue for "the adoption of, or renewed commitment to, a categorical approach, under which most youths are dealt with in a separate justice system, in which rehabilitation is the central aim."[2] Criminal justice scholar Joseph Sanborn suggests a transfer policy that allows for criminal prosecution of seriously violent and repeat offenders but leaves the bulk of cases in the juvenile court systems.[3] Under such a system, it would have been possible for Willie Bosket, in 1978, to have been transferred up to the criminal court, where he could have received a sentence more in line with his crimes and chronic offending history. At the same time, the less violent, less hardened, more rehabilitatable youths, like the vast majority of the kids I saw come through the Youth Part, could have their cases handled in the Family Court, and have the chance to avoid a lifetime felony record and all that comes with it. Such a system would be a serious alteration of how New York has done things historically. After my time in the part, it also seems like the only reasonable solution. So, while the work of the Manhattan Youth Part stands as a useful example of how court actors might best attempt to neutralize the impact of punitive transfer laws, it more importantly stands as a strong argument for the repeal of New York's Juvenile Offender Law and for extending the age of Family Court jurisdiction. True success for the work of the Manhattan Youth Part would be passage of new state legislation that would simply render the court unnecessary.

Reforming Transfer Laws

The last twenty years have seen a marked reduction in youth crime. The predicted generational onslaught of young urban superpredators never materialized.[4] A solid body of research indicates that prosecuting youths as adults does not reduce serious offending and may, in fact, increase it. Further evidence demonstrates that transfer laws have had a serious and consistently disproportionate effect on minority youth. The Supreme Court has reified the idea that youths are different from adults in ways that warrant their differential treatment under the law. Yet, retributive transfer legislation remains on the books in most states. These laws have not made us safer. What they have done is criminalize youth, particularly poor black and Hispanic youth, especially in urban areas. Serious consideration of the tenability of current transfer law is needed.

Many states are currently attempting various reform initiatives regarding the treatment of young offenders. These efforts are a strong indication that the pendulum may have begun to swing away from over-reactive, retributive policies and back toward more reasoned and rehabilitation-centered approaches to adolescent offending.[5] This is good news, and there is much to be hopeful about, but while a few states have acted to lessen the reach of transfer laws, the majority of current juvenile justice reform efforts have been focused more on what happens to kids after

NOTES

Epigraph: Nelson Mandela, *In the Words of Nelson Mandela*, edited by Jennifer Crwys-Williams (New York: Walker & Co., 2011), 25.

Notes to the Introduction

1 See Donna Bishop, "Juvenile Offenders in the Adult Criminal Justice System," in *Crime and Justice: A Review of Research*, vol. 27, ed. Michael Tonry (Chicago: University of Chicago Press, 2000); Eric Klein, "Dennis the Menace or Billy the Kid: An Analysis of the Role of Transfer to Criminal Court in Juvenile Justice," *American Criminal Law Review* 35 (1998): 371–410; David L. Myers, *Boys among Men: Trying and Sentencing Juveniles as Adults* (Westport, CT: Praeger, 2005); Howard N. Snyder, Melissa Sickmund, and Eileen Poe-Yamagata, *Juvenile Transfers to Criminal Court in the 1990s: Lessons Learned from Four Studies* (Washington, DC: U.S. Department of Justice, Office of Justice Programs, Office of Juvenile Justice and Delinquency Prevention, August 2000); David S. Tanenhaus, "The Evolution of Transfer out of the Juvenile Court," in *The Changing Borders of Juvenile Justice: Transfer of Adolescents to the Criminal Court*, ed. Jeffery Fagan and Franklin Zimring (Chicago: University of Chicago Press, 2000). The first juvenile court in Chicago, however, had no provision for transfer of cases to the jurisdiction of the criminal court; see Linda F. Giardino, "Statutory Rhetoric: The Reality behind Juvenile Justice Polices in America," *Journal of Law and Policy* 5 (1996): 223–76.

2 M. A. Bortner, Marjorie S. Zatz, and Darnell F. Hawkins, "Race and Transfer: Empirical Research and Social Context," in *The Changing Borders of Juvenile Justice: Transfer of Adolescents to the Criminal Court*, ed. Jeffery Fagan and Franklin Zimring (Chicago: University of Chicago Press, 2000).

3 See Neelum Arya, "Using *Graham v. Florida* to Challenge Juvenile Transfer Laws," *Louisiana Law Review* 71 (2010): 99–155, p. 143. As Arya writes, "While children adjudicated delinquent in the juvenile justice system have had a statutory and constitutional 'right to treatment' since the 1970s, children prosecuted in the adult system do not" (p. 123).

4 See Barry Feld, *Bad Kids: Race and the Transformation of the Juvenile Court* (New York: Oxford University Press, 1999); Robert M. Mennel, *Thorns and Thistles: Juvenile Delinquents in the United States, 1825–1940* (Hanover, NH: University Press of New England, 1973); Anthony M. Platt, *The Child Savers: The Invention of Delinquency* (Chicago: University of Chicago Press, 1969); David S. Tanenhaus, *Juvenile Justice in the Making* (New York: Oxford University Press, 2004).

5 See Feld, *Bad Kids*; Mennel, *Thorns and Thistles*; Platt, *The Child Savers*; Tanenhaus, *Juvenile Justice in the Making*.

6 Feld, *Bad Kids*; Barry Krisberg, "The Evolution of an American Institution," *Crime and Delinquency* 44 (1998): 5–8; Ira M. Schwartz, *(In)Justice for Juveniles: Rethinking the Best Interests of the Child* (Lexington, MA: Lexington Press, 1989); Howard N. Snyder and Melissa Sickmund, *Juvenile Offenders and Victims: 2006 National Report*

(Washington, DC: U.S. Department of Justice, Office of Justice Programs, Office of Juvenile Justice and Delinquency Prevention, 2006).

7   *Kent v. United States*, 383 U.S. 541 (1966), 555.

8   *In re Gault*, 387 U.S. 1 (1967); W. V. Stapleton and L. E. Teitelbaum, *In Defense of Youth: A Study of the Role of Counsel in American Juvenile Courts* (New York: Russell Sage Foundation, 1972).

9   Stapleton and Teitelbaum, *In Defense of Youth*, 29.

10 Fox Butterfield, *All God's Children: The Bosket Case and the American Tradition of Violence* (New York: Alfred A. Knopf, 1995); Klein, "Dennis the Menace or Billy the Kid"; *In re Gault* (1967).

11 *In re Gault* (1967), 13.

12 Feld, *Bad Kids*, 98.

13 Snyder and Sickmund, *Juvenile Offenders and Victims: 2006 National Report*.

14 *In re Winship*, 397 U.S. 358 (1970), 368.

15 Feld, *Bad Kids*; Simon I. Singer, *Recriminalizing Delinquency: Violent Juvenile Crime and Juvenile Justice* (New York: Cambridge University Press, 1996).

16 Patrick Griffin, *National Overviews: State Juvenile Justice Profiles* (Pittsburgh, PA: National Center for Juvenile Justice, 2002).

17 Giardino, "Statutory Rhetoric."

18 Melanie King and Linda Szymanski, *National Overviews: State Juvenile Justice Profiles* (Pittsburgh, PA: National Center for Juvenile Justice, 2006).

19 Laurence Winner et al., "The Transfer of Juveniles to Criminal Court: Reexamining Recidivism over the Long Term," *Crime and Delinquency* 43 (1997): 548–63; Patrick Griffin, Patricia Torbet, and Linda Szymanski, *Trying Juveniles as Adults in Criminal Court: An Analysis of State Transfer Provisions* (Washington, DC: U.S. Department of Justice, Office of Justice Programs, Office of Juvenile Justice and Delinquency Prevention, 1998); Jeffrey A. Butts and Ojmarrh Mitchell, "Brick by Brick: Dismantling the Border between Juvenile and Adult Justice," in *Criminal Justice*, vol. 2, *Boundary Changes in Criminal Justice Organizations*, ed. Charles M. Friel (Washington, DC: U.S. Department of Justice, Office of Justice Programs, 2000).

20 Griffin, Torbet, and Szymanski, *Trying Juveniles as Adults in Criminal Court*. See also Jeffrey A. Butts, *Youth Crime Drop* (Washington, DC: Urban Institute, Justice Policy Center, 2002); Butts and Mitchell, "Brick by Brick"; Patrick Griffin, *Trying and Sentencing Juveniles as Adults: An Analysis of State Transfer and Blended Sentencing Laws* (Pittsburgh, PA: National Center for Juvenile Justice, 2003).

21 See Benjamin Steiner and Craig Hemmens, "Juvenile Waiver 2003: Where Are We Now?" *Juvenile and Family Court Journal* 54 (2003): 1–24; Patrick Griffin, *National Overviews: State Juvenile Justice Profiles* (Pittsburgh, PA: National Center for Juvenile Justice, 2008).

22 See Bishop, "Juvenile Offenders in the Adult Criminal Justice System." The Office of Juvenile Justice and Delinquency Prevention (OJJDP) frequently reports on delinquency cases waived to criminal court and has documented a steady decline in judicially waved cases since 1993. See Benjamin Adams and Sean Addie, *Delinquency Cases Waived to Criminal Court, 2007*, OJJDP Factsheet (Washington,

DC: U.S. Department of Justice, Office of Justice Programs, Office of Juvenile Justice and Delinquency Prevention, 2010). This data can be misleading if not understood within the full context of changing transfer legislation—while judicial waivers were on the decrease since the early 1990s, transfers by all other means were on the increase. These non-judicially waived cases have not been adequately quantified.

23 Griffin, Torbet, and Szymanski, *Trying Juveniles as Adults in Criminal Court*, 13.

24 Griffin, *National Overviews*.

25 Michael M. Jacobson, *Downsizing Prisons: How to Reduce Crime and End Mass Incarceration* (New York: New York University Press, 2005); Myers, *Boys among Men*; Jonathan Simon, *Poor Discipline: Parole and the Social Control of the Underclass, 1890–1990* (Chicago: University of Chicago Press, 1993); Elizabeth S. Scott and Laurence Steinberg, *Rethinking Juvenile Justice* (Cambridge, MA: Harvard University Press, 2008).

26 Frank Zimring and Jeffrey Fagan, eds., *The Changing Borders of Juvenile Justice: Transfer of Adolescents to the Criminal Court* (Chicago: University of Chicago Press, 2000), 422.

27 Stanley Cohen, *Folk Devils and Moral Panics*, 3d ed. (London: Routledge, 2002), 1.

28 See Feld, *Bad Kids*; Alfred Blumstein and Richard Rosenfeld, *Assessing Recent Ups and Downs in U.S. Homicide Rates* (Pittsburgh, PA: National Consortium on Violence Research, 1998). It is worth noting that the majority of gun homicides that occurred during this time involved inner-city young black males not only as perpetrators, but as victims as well.

29 Thomas Bernard, *The Cycle of Juvenile Justice* (New York: Oxford University Press, 1992); Butts, *Youth Crime Drop*; Klein, "Dennis the Menace or Billy the Kid"; John J. Wilson and James C. Howell, *Comprehensive Strategy for Serious, Violent and Chronic Juvenile Offenders (Program Summary)* (Washington, DC: U.S. Department of Justice, Office of Justice Programs, Office of Juvenile Justice and Delinquency Prevention, 1993). According to FBI statistics, the percentage of violent crime attributable to juveniles (cleared by arrest) only increased by 4% between 1986 and 1996, the years in which we were supposedly witnessing a massive wave of youth violence. See Patricia Torbet and Linda Szymanski, *State Legislative Responses to Violent Juvenile Crime: 1996–97 Update* (Washington, DC: U.S. Department of Justice, Office of Justice Programs, Office of Juvenile Justice and Delinquency Prevention, 1998). In 1986, 9% of all violent crime was attributable to juveniles; in 1996, 13% was attributable to juveniles. See Howard N. Snyder, *Juvenile Arrests 1996* (Washington, DC: U.S. Department of Justice, Office of Juvenile Justice and Delinquency Prevention, 1997); Torbet and Szymanski, *State Legislative Responses*.

30 John DiIulio, "The Coming of the Super-Predators," *Weekly Standard*, November 27, 1995.

31 Quoted in Victor Rios, "The Racial Politics of Youth Crime," *Latino Studies* 6 (2008): 97–115.

32 Joyce Purnick, "Youth Crime: Should Laws Be Tougher?" *New York Times*, May 9, 1996.

33 Michael Welch, Eric A. Price, and Nana Yankey, "Moral Panic over Youth Violence: Wilding and the Manufacture of Menace in the Media," *Youth and Society* 34 (2002): 3–30.

34 Myers, *Boys among Men*, 96. See also Jesenia M. Pizarro, Steven M. Chermack, and Jeffrey A. Gruenewald, "Juvenile 'Super-Predators' in the News: A Comparison of Adult and Juvenile Homicides," *Journal of Criminal Justice and Popular Culture* 14 (2007): 84–111.

35 Frank Zimring, *American Youth Violence* (New York: Oxford University Press, 1998).

36 See Bortner, Zatz, and Hawkins, "Race and Transfer."

37 For an excellent analysis of this conflation in the political rhetoric surrounding California's Proposition 21, see Rios, "The Racial Politics of Youth Crime."

38 Zimring, *American Youth Violence*, xi.

39 Rios, "The Racial Politics of Youth Crime," 104.

40 Butts, *Youth Crime Drop*.

41 Laurence Steinberg and Elizabeth Cauffman, "A Developmental Perspective on Jurisdictional Boundary," in *The Changing Borders of Juvenile Justice: Transfer of Adolescents to the Criminal Court*, ed. Jeffery Fagan and Franklin Zimring Chicago: University of Chicago Press, 2000), 379.

42 See Bishop, "Juvenile Offenders in the Adult Criminal Justice System"; Donna M. Bishop, Charles E. Frazier, and John C. Henretta, "Prosecutorial Waiver: Case Study of a Questionable Reform," *Crime and Delinquency* 35 (1989): 179–201; Butts and Mitchell, "Brick by Brick"; Coalition for Juvenile Justice, *Childhood on Trial: The Failure of Trying and Sentencing Youth in Adult Criminal Court* (Washington DC: Coalition for Juvenile Justice, 2005); Patrick Griffin, *Different from Adults: An Updated Analysis of Juvenile Transfer and Blended Sentencing Laws, with Recommendations for Reform*, Models for Change (Pittsburgh, PA: National Center for Juvenile Justice, 2008); Griffin, Torbet, and Szymanski, *Trying Juveniles as Adults in Criminal Court*; Allison M. Grinnell, "Searching for a Solution: The Future of New York's Juvenile Offender Law," *New York Law School Journal of Human Rights* 16 (2000): 635–67; Thomas Grisso and Robert G. Schwartz, eds., *Youth on Trial: A Developmental Perspective on Juvenile Justice* (Chicago: University of Chicago Press, 2000); Jolanta Juszkiewicz, *Youth Crime / Adult Time: Is Justice Served?* (Washington, DC: Pretrial Services Resource Center, Building Blocks for Youth, 2000); Aaron Kupchik, "Prosecuting Adolescents in Criminal Courts: Criminal or Juvenile Justice?" *Social Problems* 50 (2003): 439–60; Aaron Kupchik, "Youthfulness, Responsibility and Punishment: Admonishing Adolescents in Criminal Court," *Punishment and Society* 6 (2004): 149–73; Aaron Kupchik, *Judging Juveniles: Prosecuting Adolescents in Adult and Juvenile Courts* (New York: New York University Press, 2006); Jodie Lane et al., "Adult versus Juvenile Sanctions: Voices of Incarcerated Youth," *Crime and Delinquency* 48 (2002): 431–55; Lonn Lanza-Kaduce et al., "Juvenile Offenders and Adult Felony Recidivism: The Impact of Transfer," *Journal of Crime and Justice* 28 (2005): 59–77; John H. Lemmon et al., "The Effect of Legal and Extralegal Factors on Statutory Exclusion of Juvenile Offenders," *Youth Violence and Juvenile Justice* 3 (2005): 214–34; David L. Myers, *Excluding Violent Youths from Juvenile Court: The Effectiveness of Legislative Waiver* (New York: LFB

20 Steven R. Weisman, "Crime—a Code for Winning Votes," *New York Times*, May 14, 1978, E5.

21 Butterfield, *All God's Children*.

22 Richard J. Meislin, "Carey, in Shift, Backs Trial in Adult Court for Some Juveniles," *New York Times*, June 30, 1978, 1.

23 Ibid.

24 Richard J. Meislin, "Albany Leaders Draw Tough Bill on Youth Crime," *New York Times*, July 15, 1978, 1.

25 "Criminals Yes, Adults No" (editorial), *New York Times*, July 14, 1978.

26 Singer and Ewing, "Juvenile Justice Reform in New York State."

27 E. J. Dionne, Jr., "Anticrime Bill Passed in Albany," *New York Times*, July 19, 1978; Richard J. Meislin, "Albany Legislature Votes Package of Stiff Youth and Adult Penalties," *New York Times*, July 20, 1978.

28 Edmund F. McGarrell, "The Ideological Bases and Functions of Contemporary Juvenile Law Reform: The New York State Experience," *Contemporary Crises* 13 (1989): 163–87, p. 173.

29 Quoted in McGarrell, "The Ideological Bases and Functions of Contemporary Juvenile Law Reform," 175.

30 Meislin, "Albany Legislature Votes Package of Stiff Youth and Adult Penalties."

31 Ibid.

32 Collier, "New York State's Juvenile Offender Law"; Singer and Ewing, "Juvenile Justice Reform in New York State."

33 For example, the maximum sentence for a Class B felony for those 16 and older was twenty-five years (compared to ten years of Juvenile Offenders), and for a Class C felony it was fifteen years (as opposed to seven years for JOs).

34 Marian Gewirtz, *Annual Report on the Adult Court Case Processing of Juvenile Offenders in New York City, January through December 2004* (New York: New York City Criminal Justice Agency, 2005); Eric Warner, *The Juvenile Offender Handbook* (Flushing, NY: Looseleaf Law, 2004). Also, the originally listed offense of "sodomy 1" has been renamed "criminal sexual act 1."

35 Citizens' Committee for Children of New York, *In Search of Juvenile Justice: An Interim Report on the 1978 Juvenile Offender Law* (New York: Citizens' Committee for Children of New York, 1979), 11.

36 Sobie, *The Juvenile Offender Act*, 31.

37 Association of the Bar of the City of New York Committee on Juvenile Justice, *New York Juvenile Offender Law*, Report of The Juvenile Justice Committee of the Association of the Bar of the City of New York, No. 2826 (New York: Association of the Bar of the City of New York, 1983), 5.

38 Butterfield, *All God's Children*, 227.

39 Citizens' Committee for Children of New York, *In Search of Juvenile Justice*, 6.

40 Sobie, *The Juvenile Offender Act*.

41 Data obtained from the New York City Division of Criminal Justice Services (DCJS). Problems with the DCJS data set for the years prior to 1984 preclude inclusion of numbers for those years. I have chosen to report data on JO indictments, rather than arrests, since indictment data more accurately reflect the

nature of youth seen in the criminal courts and more closely correlate with court observations.

42 Corriero, *Judging Children as Children*.

43 Collier, "New York State's Juvenile Offender Law."

44 Citizens' Committee for Children of New York, *In Search of Juvenile Justice*.

45 This "gender gap" in the practice of trying youth as adults is not unique to New York. See Robert O. Dawson, "Judicial Waiver in Theory and Practice," in *The Changing Borders of Juvenile Justice: Transfer of Adolescents to the Criminal Court*, ed. Jeffrey Fagan and Franklin Zimring (Chicago: University of Chicago Press, 2000). For a rare discussion of girls transferred to criminal court, see Emily Gaarder and Joanne Belknap, "Tenuous Borders: Girls Transferred to Adult Court," *Criminology* 40 (2002): 481–518.

46 Collier, "New York State's Juvenile Offender Law."

47 Sobie, *The Juvenile Offender Act*.

48 Joseph B. Sanborn, "Hard Choices or Obvious Ones: Developing Policy for Excluding Youth from Juvenile Court," *Youth Violence and Juvenile Justice* 1 (2003): 198–214.

49 New York Criminal Procedure Law, article 210, § 210.43 [1] [b].

50 Singer and Ewing, "Juvenile Justice Reform in New York State."

51 Sobie, *The Juvenile Offender Act*.

52 Ibid.

53 Part of the explanation for this may have to do with the ways in which certain details of criminal justice practices get labeled and quantified. For example, when prosecution "declines to prosecute" a case as a JO offense but recommends that it be charged in Family Court as a non-JO offense, that case may be considered "transferred to the Family Court," even though it is not technically a removal from criminal court after indictment. Often these two concepts—transfers by prosecution to Family Court via a lesser charge and removal by the criminal court—are conflated. It is difficult to assess whether these early studies included pre-indictment transfers and decline-to-prosecute decisions.

Notes to Chapter 3

1 Bernard C. Fisher, *Justice for Youth: The Courts for Wayward Youth in New York City* (New York: Bureau of Public Affairs, Community Service Society of New York, 1955).

2 Although the specific provisions for YO have shifted over the years, the current maximum incarcerative sentence is an indeterminate sentence of no more than one and a third to four years (New York Criminal Procedure Law, article 720, § 720.20). See also Marilyn A. Chandler, "New York State's Youthful Offender Statutes: An Empirical Investigation of Their Theoretical Basis and Their Operation" (PhD diss., State University of New York at Albany, 1982).

3 Simon I. Singer, Jeffrey Fagan, and Akiva Liberman, "The Reproduction of Juvenile Justice in Criminal Court: A Case Study of New York's Juvenile Offender Law," in *The Changing Borders of Juvenile Justice: Transfer of Adolescents to the Criminal Court*, ed. Jeffrey Fagan and Franklin Zimring (Chicago: University of Chicago

Press, 2000); Eric Warner, *The Juvenile Offender Handbook* (Flushing, NY: Looseleaf Law, 2004).

4 Singer, Fagan, and Liberman, "The Reproduction of Juvenile Justice in Criminal Court."

5 New York Criminal Procedure Law, article 1, §1.20 [41] [a–b].

6 The law does allow for some leeway if there are found to be mitigating factors in the nature of the offense.

7 New York Criminal Procedure Law, article 720, § 720.10.

8 New York Criminal Procedure Law, article 720, § 720.20[1] [a].

9 Chandler, "New York State's Youthful Offender Statutes," 89.

10 Joan McCord and Kevin P. Conway, "Patterns of Juvenile Delinquency and Co-Offending," in *Crime and Social Organization*, ed. Elin Waring and David Weisburd (New Brunswick, NJ: Transaction Publishers, 2002).

11 New York Penal Law, article 20, § 20.00.

12 As explained in chapter 1, youths up to the age of 16, whether being charged in the Family Court or the criminal court, are detained (pretrial) at one of the secure detention facilities in New York City run by the Department of Juvenile Justice. Youths 16–18 years of age, however, are detained on Rikers Island.

13 Legally, the People can appeal a decision the judge makes to grant YO over their objection. Although Judge Corriero stated that it had not happened to him, it is always a concern. More importantly, the judge knew that offering YO too often over the objection of the People could jeopardize the spirit of cooperation he had sought to cultivate since the inception of the Youth Part.

14 Edward J. Clynch and David W. Neubauer, "Trial Courts as Organizations: A Critique and Synthesis," *Law and Policy Quarterly* 3 (1981): 69–94.

15 As is clear from these numbers alone, things were done quite differently in each borough. More than one person involved with the courts said that each New York City borough is basically a completely separate system because of the differences in the culture of court administration and the philosophies and agendas of each borough's DA's office and judges.

16 Benjamin Cardozo (1921), quoted in Kent Greenawalt, "Discretion and Judicial Decision: The Elusive Quest for the Fetters That Bind Judges," *Columbia Law Review* 75 (1975): 359–99, p. 359.

17 See Celesta A. Albonetti, "An Integration of Theories to Explain Judicial Discretion," *Social Problems* 38 (1991): 247–66; Steven J. Cleveland, "Judicial Discretion and Statutory Interpretation," *Oklahoma Law Review* 57 (2004): 31–40; Malcolm M. Feeley, "Two Models of the Criminal Justice System: An Organizational Perspective," *Law and Society Review* 7 (1973): 407–25; Greenawalt, "Discretion and Judicial Decision"; Kenneth T. Moran and John L. Cooper, *Discretion and the Criminal Justice Process* (Port Washington, NY: Associated Faculty Press, 1983).

18 Malcolm M. Feeley, *The Process Is the Punishment: Handling Cases in a Lower Criminal Court* (New York: Russell Sage Foundation, 1979); Aaron Kupchik, *Judging Juveniles: Prosecuting Adolescents in Adult and Juvenile Courts* (New York: New York University Press, 2006).

19 Clynch and Neubauer, "Trial Courts as Organizations."

20 Frank H. Easterbrook, "Judicial Discretion in Statutory Interpretation," *Oklahoma Law Review* 57 (2004): 1–20; James Eisenstein, Roy Flemming, and Peter Nardulli, *The Contours of Justice: Communities and Their Courts* (Boston: Little, Brown, 1988); Greenawalt, "Discretion and Judicial Decision"; Stewart L. Macaulay, Laurence M. Friedman, and John Stookey, eds., *Law and Society: Readings on the Social Study of Law* (New York: W. W. Norton, 1995).

21 Clynch and Neubauer, "Trial Courts as Organizations."

22 Michael A. Corriero, "Youth Parts: Constructive Response to the Challenge of Youth Crime," *New York Law Journal*, October 26, 1990, 1.

23 Jeffrey T. Ulmer and John H. Kramer, "The Use and Transformation of Formal Decision-Making Criteria: Sentencing Guidelines, Organizational Contexts, and Case Processing Strategies," *Social Problems* 45 (1998): 248–67, p. 248.

24 Feeley, *The Process Is the Punishment.*

25 Unfortunately, Javier died from an asthma attack before he was able to receive his sentence of "YO + 5." Although he had apparently been drinking at the time of his death, there was no evidence of drug use.

26 Only occasionally does a case in the Youth Part go to trial. Kids tend to confess, evidence is easily gathered, and, as in every other arena of the criminal court, trials are time-consuming and expensive, so plea bargaining is the order of the day.

27 See Criminal Justice Agency, *Annual Report on the Adult Court Case Processing of Juvenile Offenders in New York City* (New York: Criminal Justice Agency, 1997–2001); Marian Gewirtz, *Annual Report on the Adult Court Case Processing of Juvenile Offenders in New York City* (New York: Criminal Justice Agency, 2002–6).

28 Marian Gewirtz, *Recidivism among Juvenile Offenders in New York City* (New York: Criminal Justice Agency, 2007).

29 Ibid.

Notes to Chapter 4

1 M. A. Bortner, *Inside a Juvenile Court: The Tarnished Ideal of Individualized Justice* (New York: New York University Press, 1982).

2 Even for those youths not eligible for YO, the court took time to learn something about them in order to impose appropriate sentencing as allowable under the law.

3 Caroline Joy DeBrovner, "Fridays in the Youth Part," in *Judging Children as Children: A Proposal for a Juvenile Justice System* by Michael Corriero (Philadelphia: Temple University Press, 2006), 114.

4 Ibid.

5 Ibid.

6 Passages is the New York City education department program inside the juvenile detention centers.

7 DeBrovner, "Fridays in the Youth Part."

8 See Aaron Kupchik, *Judging Juveniles: Prosecuting Adolescents in Adult and Juvenile Courts* (New York: New York University Press, 2006), for a full accounting of his mixed-methods research findings. For more on the ethnographic data he collected while conducting his research in the courts, see also Aaron Kupchik, "Prosecuting Adolescents in Criminal Courts: Criminal or Juvenile Justice?" *Social*

Problems 50 (2003): 439–60; Aaron Kupchik, "Youthfulness, Responsibility and Punishment: Admonishing Adolescents in Criminal Court," *Punishment and Society* 6 (2004): 149–73.

9 James Eisenstein and Herbert Jacobs, *Felony Justice: An Organizational Analysis of Criminal Courts* (Boston: Little, Brown, 1977); Edward J. Clynch and David W. Neubauer, "Trial Courts as Organizations: A Critique and Synthesis," *Law and Policy Quarterly* 3 (1981): 69–94.

10 Kupchik, "Youthfulness, Responsibility and Punishment," 151.

11 Ibid., 160–67.

12 Ibid., 155.

13 Clynch and Neubauer, "Trial Courts as Organizations."

14 Ibid.

15 Eisenstein and Jacobs, *Felony Justice*.

16 Kupchik, "Prosecuting Adolescents in Criminal Courts"; Kupchik, "Youthfulness, Responsibility and Punishment."

17 Kupchik, "Prosecuting Adolescents in Criminal Courts," 451; Kupchik, "Youthfulness, Responsibility and Punishment," 168.

18 Kupchik, "Youthfulness, Responsibility and Punishment," 162.

19 This attempt to assess a youth's attitude and demeanor through verbal engagement was also standard practice in Bortner's study of a juvenile court; Bortner, *Inside a Juvenile Court*.

20 Simon I. Singer, Jeffrey Fagan, and Akiva Liberman, "The Reproduction of Juvenile Justice in Criminal Court: A Case Study of New York's Juvenile Offender Law," in *The Changing Borders of Juvenile Justice: Transfer of Adolescents to the Criminal Court*, ed. Jeffrey Fagan and Franklin Zimring (Chicago: University of Chicago Press, 2000), 367–68.

21 Kupchik, "Youthfulness, Responsibility and Punishment," 167.

22 Kupchik, "Prosecuting Adolescents in Criminal Courts," 454.

23 Kupchik, Youthfulness, Responsibility and Punishment," 166

Notes to Chapter 5

1 Richard Barnum, "Clinical and Forensic Evaluation of Competence to Stand Trial in Juvenile Defendants," in *Youth on Trial: A Developmental Perspective on Juvenile Justice*, ed. Thomas Grisso and Robert. G. Schwartz (Chicago: University of Chicago Press, 2000).

2 Frank Zimring, *American Youth Violence* (New York: Oxford University Press, 1998).

3 Aaron Kupchik, *Judging Juveniles: Prosecuting Adolescents in Adult and Juvenile Courts* (New York: New York University Press, 2006).

4 See Barnum, "Clinical and Forensic Evaluation of Competence to Stand Trial in Juvenile Defendants; H. Ted Rubin, *Behind the Black Robes: Juvenile Court Judges and the Court* (Beverly Hills, CA: Sage Publications, 1985).

5 Joseph B. Sanborn, "Hard Choices or Obvious Ones: Developing Policy for Excluding Youth from Juvenile Court," *Youth Violence and Juvenile Justice* 1 (2003): 198–214. See also M. A. Bortner, *Inside a Juvenile Court: The Tarnished Ideal of Individualized Justice* (New York: New York University Press, 1982); Robert M. Emerson,

Judging Delinquents: Context and Process in Juvenile Court (Chicago: Aldine, 1969); Mark Jacobs, *Screwing the System and Making It Work: Juvenile Justice in the No-Fault Society* (Chicago: University of Chicago Press, 1990); Aaron Kupchik, "Prosecuting Adolescents in Criminal Courts: Criminal or Juvenile Justice?" *Social Problems* 50 (2003): 439–60.

6   Caroline Joy DeBrovner, "Fridays in the Youth Part," in *Judging Children as Children: A Proposal for a Juvenile Justice System* by Michael Corriero (Philadelphia: Temple University Press, 2006), 114.

7   Kupchik, *Judging Juveniles*, 63.

8   Ibid., 74.

9   DeBrovner, "Fridays in the Youth Part"; Ann Tobey, Thomas Grisso, and Robert G. Schwartz, "Youths' Trial Participation as Seen by Youths and Their Attorneys: An Exploration of Competence-Based Issues," in *Youth on Trial: A Developmental Perspective on Juvenile Justice*, ed. Thomas Grisso and Robert. G. Schwartz (Chicago: University of Chicago Press, 2000).

10   Barnum, "Clinical and Forensic Evaluation of Competence to Stand Trial in Juvenile Defendants."

11   Thirty-four states currently have some type of "once an adult, always an adult" law that requires that, once a young person has been convicted in the criminal courts, all subsequent cases brought against him or her are to be handled in the criminal courts. See Patrick Griffin, *National Overviews: State Juvenile Justice Profiles* (Pittsburgh, PA: National Center for Juvenile Justice, 2008). Such policies can reduce —but not eliminate—the likelihood, as happens in New York, of defendants having simultaneous adult and juvenile cases. "Once an adult, always an adult" laws differ across states, but it is possible for a youth with a prior, open case in the juvenile courts to encounter a simultaneous youth/adult status situation as well. For details on "once an adult, always an adult" statutes, see Griffin, *National State Overviews*; Sanborn, "Hard Choices or Obvious Ones."

12   Legal Aid Society, *Profile of a Juvenile Offender* (New York: Legal Aid Society, n.d.).

13   Another great irony within the Manhattan Youth Part was that Jorge, at age 16, was not a Juvenile Offender and had only found himself before Judge Corriero because one of his codefendants was less than 16 years of age. Had this not been the situation, Jorge's case would have been handled before some other criminal court judge. It is not known if another judge would have put Jorge in an ATI program or given him the benefit of the doubt because of his foster-care placement. Simply because of the age of a codefendant, Jorge's case was handled in a court uniquely equipped to deal with such a complex a set of circumstances.

14   Kupchik, *Judging Juveniles*.

Notes to Chapter 6

1   Marian Gewirtz and Elyse J. Revere, *Adult-Court Processing and Re-Arrest of Juvenile Offenders in Manhattan and Queens* (New York: Criminal Justice Agency, 2005); Marian Gewirtz, *Recidivism among Juvenile Offenders in New York City* (New York: Criminal Justice Agency, 2007).

2 Gewirtz and Revere, *Adult-Court Processing and Re-Arrest of Juvenile Offenders in Manhattan and Queens*, 2.

3 The authors of the 2007 CJA report note that "although too few juvenile cases are processed in the Supreme Court in Staten Island for comparisons to that borough to be stable, the data are included here so that the totals are truly citywide" (Gewirtz, *Recidivism among Juvenile Offenders in New York City*, 1).

4 "Citywide" for this data does not include Staten Island. Marian Gewirtz, *Annual Report on the Adult Court Case Processing of Juvenile Offenders in New York City* (New York: Criminal Justice Agency, 2002–6).

5 Gewirtz, *Recidivism among Juvenile Offenders in New York City*.

6 Ibid., 7.

7 Gewirtz, *Recidivism among Juvenile Offenders in New York City*, 37.

8 Ibid., 12. These cases were either "declined to prosecute" or were sent to the Family Court. See Gewirtz and Revere, *Adult-Court Processing and Re-Arrest of Juvenile Offenders in Manhattan and Queens*.

9 Gewirtz, *Recidivism among Juvenile Offenders in New York City*, 1. "Re-arrest data were collected for re-offenses that occurred between the date of the initial offense and January 31, 2005 for the juvenile offenders processed in the Supreme Court in any borough of New York City in 1997 through 2000" (p. 11).

10 Robert Martinson, "What Works? Questions and Answers about Prison Reform," *Public Interest* 35 (1974): 22–54.

11 Gewirtz, *Recidivism among Juvenile Offenders in New York City*, 14.

12 Gewirtz, *Recidivism among Juvenile Offenders in New York City*, 44.

13 Ibid., 41.

14 Ibid., 17.

15 Ibid., 27.

16 Marian Gewirtz, *The Risk of Re-Arrest for Serious Juvenile Offenders*, Research Brief No. 15 (New York: Criminal Justice Agency, 2007), 7.

17 Joel Copperman, Sarah Bryer, and Hannah Gray, *Community-Based Sentencing Demonstrates Low Recidivism among Felony-Level Offenders* (Kingston, NJ: Civic Research Institute, 2004), 29. The report does not indicate what percentage of those who enter the program actually graduate.

18 Andrew Glover Youth Program, *Annual Report 2005* (New York: Andrew Glover Youth Program, 2005). In conversations with AGYP personnel, I was told that for them recidivism means any new court involvement.

19 Michael A. Corriero, *Judging Children as Children: A Proposal for a Juvenile Justice System* (Philadelphia: Temple University Press, 2006), 13.

20 Task Force on Transforming Juvenile Justice, *Charting a New Course: A Blueprint for Transforming Juvenile Justice in New York State; A Report of Governor Paterson's Task Force on Transforming Juvenile Justice* (New York: Vera Institute of Justice, 2009), 14.

21 Ibid.

22 Correctional Association of New York, *Juvenile Detention in New York City* (New York: Correctional Association of New York, September 2007).

23 Some studies are just for JOs, some for youth in general processed through the Family Court or the criminal court; much of the data on recidivism from secure

facilities is quite old; some studies measure rearrest, while other measure reconviction, and still others reincarceration.

24 Correctional Association of New York, *Juvenile Detention in New York City* (New York: Correctional Association of New York, 2010); Task Force on Transforming Juvenile Justice, *Charting a New Course.*

25 Center for Alternative Sentencing and Employment Services (CASES), *Alternatives to Incarceration Programs: Cut Crime, Cut Cost, Help People and Communities* (New York: C AS ES, n.d.).

26 Tom R. Tyler, *Why People Obey the Law* (New Haven, CT: Yale University Press, 1990).

27 E. Allen Lind and Tom R. Tyler, *The Social Psychology of Procedural Justice* (New York: Plenum Press, 1988); Laurence W. Sherman, "Defiance, Deterrence, and Irrelevance: A Theory of the Criminal Sanction," *Journal of Research in Crime and Delinquency* 30 (1993): 445–73; Enrico Pagnanelli, "Children as Adults: The Transfer of Juveniles to the Adult Courts and the Potential Impact of *Roper v. Simmons*," *American Criminal Law Review* 44 (2007): 175–94; Alex R. Piquero et al., "Developmental Trajectories of Legal Socialization among Serious Adolescent Offenders," *Journal of Criminal Law and Criminology* 96 (2005): 267–98.

28 Piquero et al., "Developmental Trajectories of Legal Socialization."

29 Corriero, *Judging Children as Children.*

30 Donna Bishop, "Juvenile Offenders in the Adult Criminal Justice System," in *Crime and Justice: A Review of Research*, vol. 27, ed. Michael Tonry (Chicago: University of Chicago Press, 2000); Donna Bishop et al., "The Transfer of Juveniles to Criminal Court: Does It Make a Difference?" *Crime and Delinquency* 42 (1996): 171–91; Jeffrey Fagan, "Juvenile Crime and Criminal Justice: Resolving Border Disputes," *Future of Children* 18 (2008): 81–118; Jeffrey Fagan, Aaron Kupchik, and Akiva Liberman, *Be Careful What You Ask For: The Comparative Impacts of Juvenile versus Criminal Court Sanctions on Recidivism among Adolescent Felony Offenders*, Public Law Research Paper No. 03-61 (New York: Columbia University Law School, 2003); Jodie Lane et al., "Adult Versus Juvenile Sanctions: Voices of Incarcerated Youth," *Crime and Delinquency* 48 (2002): 431–55; Lonn Lanza-Kaduce et al., "Juvenile Offenders and Adult Felony Recidivism: The Impact of Transfer," *Journal of Crime and Justice* 28 (2005): 59–77; Craig A. Mason and Shau Chang. *Re-Arrest Rates among Youth Sentenced in Adult Court* (Miami: Juvenile Sentencing Advocacy Project, Miami-Dade County Public Defender's Office, 2001); David L. Myers, *Excluding Violent Youths from Juvenile Court: The Effectiveness of Legislative Waiver* (New York: LFB Scholarly, 2001); David L. Myers, "Adult Crime, Adult Time," *Youth Violence and Juvenile Justice* 1 (2003): 173–97; David L. Myers, *Boys among Men: Trying and Sentencing Juveniles as Adults* (Westport, CT: Praeger, 2005); Marcy R. Podkapacz and Barry Feld, "The End of the Line: An Empirical Study of Judicial Waiver," *Journal of Criminal Law and Criminology* 86 (1996): 449–92; Laurence Winner et al., "The Transfer of Juveniles to Criminal Court: Reexamining Recidivism over the Long Term," *Crime and Delinquency* 43 (1997): 548–63.

31 Richard E. Redding, *Juvenile Transfer Laws: An Effective Deterrent to Delinquency?* Juvenile Justice Bulletin (Washington, DC: U.S. Department of Justice, Office of

Justice Programs, Office of Juvenile Justice and Delinquency Prevention, August 2008), 6.

32 Centers for Disease Control and Prevention, *Effects on Violence of Laws and Policies Facilitating the Transfer of Youth from the Juvenile to the Adult System*, Morbidity and Mortality Weekly Report 56, no. RR-9 (Washington, DC: Centers for Disease Control and Prevention, 2007), 8.

33 Ibid.; Raymond R. Corrado, Irwin M. Cohen, and William Glackman, "Serious and Violent Offenders' Decisions to Recidivate: An Assessment of Five Sentencing Models," *Crime and Delinquency* 49 (2003): 179–200; Redding, *Juvenile Transfer Laws*; Simon I. Singer and David McDowall, "Criminalizing Delinquency: The Deterrent Effects of the New York Juvenile Offender Law," in *Representing Juvenile Offenders in New York* (Albany: New York State Bar Association, 1988); Benjamin Steiner, Craig Hemmens, and Valerie Bell, "Legislative Waiver Reconsidered: General Deterrent Effect of Statutory Exclusion Laws Enacted Post-1979," *Justice Quarterly* 23 (2006): 34–59; Benjamin Steiner and Emily Wright, "Assessing the Relative Effects of State Direct File Waiver Laws on Violent Juvenile Crime: Deterrence or Irrelevance?" *Journal of Criminal Law and Criminology* 96 (2006): 1451–77.

34 Richard E. Redding and Elizabeth J. Fuller, "What Do Juvenile Offenders Know about Being Tried as Adults? Implications for Deterrence," *Juvenile and Family Court Journal* 36 (2004): 35–44.

35 Myers, *Boys among Men*, 11.

36 Jeffrey A. Butts and Ojmarrh Mitchell, "Brick by Brick: Dismantling the Border between Juvenile and Adult Justice," in *Criminal Justice*, vol. 2, *Boundary Changes in Criminal Justice Organizations*, ed. Charles M. Friel (Washington, DC: U.S. Department of Justice, Office of Justice Programs, 2000), 197.

37 Donna Bishop and Charles E. Frazier, "Consequences of Transfer," in *The Changing Borders of Juvenile Justice: Transfer of Adolescents to the Criminal Court*, ed. Jeffrey Fagan and Franklin Zimring (Chicago: University of Chicago Press, 2000).

38 Redding and Fuller, "What Do Juvenile Offenders Know about Being Tried as Adults?"

39 See Corrado, Cohen, and Glackman, "Serious and Violent Offenders' Decisions to Recidivate"; Jeffrey Fagan, "The Comparative Advantage of Juvenile versus Criminal Court Sanctions on Recidivism among Adolescent Felony Offenders," *Law and Policy* 18 (1996): 77–114; Myers, "Adult Crime, Adult Time"; Sherman, "Defiance, Deterrence, and Irrelevance"; Winner et al., "Transfer of Juveniles to Criminal Court"; Richard E. Redding, "The Effects of Adjudicating and Sentencing Juveniles as Adults," *Youth Violence and Juvenile Justice* 1 (2003): 128–55.

40 Daniel P. Mears et al., "Public Opinion and the Foundation of the Juvenile Court," *Criminology* 45 (2007): 223–57.

41 Brandon K. Applegate, Robin King Davis, and Francis T. Cullen, "Reconsidering Child Saving: The Extent and Correlates of Public Support for Excluding Youth from the Juvenile Court," *Crime and Delinquency* 55 (2009): 51–77, p. 70.

42 Applegate, Davis, and Cullen, "Reconsidering Child Saving."

43 National Council on Crime and Delinquency, *Attitudes of US Voters toward Youth*

Crime and the Justice System (Oakland, CA: National Council on Crime and Delinquency, 2007), 1.

44 Laurence Steinberg and Alex Piquero, "Manipulating Public Opinion about Trying Juveniles as Adults: An Experimental Study," *Crime and Delinquency* 56 (2010): 487–506.

45 See Thomas Grisso, "Juveniles' Capacities to Waive Miranda Warnings: An Empirical Analysis," *California Law Review* 68 (1980): 1134–66; Thomas Grisso, "Society's Retributive Response to Juvenile Violence: A Developmental Perspective," *Law and Human Behavior* 20 (1996): 229–47; Thomas Grisso, *Clinical Evaluations for Juveniles' Competence to Stand Trial: A Guide for Legal Professionals* (Sarasota, FL: Professional Resource Press, 2005); Thomas Grisso, Michael O. Miller, and Bruce Sales,. "Competency to Stand Trial in Juvenile Court," *International Journal of Law and Psychiatry* 10 (1987): 1–20; Thomas Grisso and Robert G. Schwartz, eds., *Youth on Trial: A Developmental Perspective on Juvenile Justice* (Chicago: University of Chicago Press, 2000); Elizabeth S. Scott and Thomas Grisso, "The Evolution of Adolescence: A Developmental Perspective in Juvenile Justice Reform," *Journal of Criminal Law and Criminology* 88 (1997): 137–89; Elizabeth S. Scott, N. Dickon Reppucci, and Jennifer L. Woolard, "Evaluating Adolescent Decision Making in Legal Contexts," *Law and Human Behavior* 19 (1995): 221–44; Elizabeth S. Scott and Laurence Steinberg, "Blaming Youth," *Texas Law Review* 81 (2003): 799–840; Laurence Steinberg and Elizabeth Cauffman, "Maturity of Judgment in Adolescence: Psychosocial Factors in Adolescent Decision Making," *Law and Human Behavior* 20 (1996): 249–72; Laurence Steinberg and Elizabeth Cauffman, "A Developmental Perspective on Jurisdictional Boundary," in *The Changing Borders of Juvenile Justice: Transfer of Adolescents to the Criminal Court*, ed. Jeffery Fagan and Franklin Zimring (Chicago: University of Chicago Press, 2000); Laurence Steinberg and Robert G. Schwartz, "Developmental Psychology Goes to Court," in *Youth on Trial: A Developmental Perspective on Juvenile Justice*, ed. Thomas Grisso and Robert G. Schwartz (Chicago: University of Chicago Press, 2000); Laurence Steinberg and Elizabeth S. Scott, "Less Guilty by Reason of Adolescence: Developmental Immaturity, Diminished Responsibility, and the Juvenile Death Penalty," *American Psychologist* 58 (2003): 1009–18.

46 Steinberg and Scott, "Less Guilty by Reason of Adolescence."

47 Scott and Grisso, "The Evolution of Adolescence"; Scott, Reppucci, and Woolard, "Evaluating Adolescent Decision Making in Legal Contexts"; Steinberg and Cauffman, "Maturity of Judgment in Adolescence."

48 Scott and Grisso, "The Evolution of Adolescence."

49 Ibid., 165.

50 Scott, Reppucci, and Woolard, "Evaluating Adolescent Decision Making in Legal Contexts."

51 Scott and Grisso, "The Evolution of Adolescence."

52 Steinberg quoted in Erica Goode, "A Conversation with Laurence Steinberg: Are Young Killers Evil, or Works in Progress?" *New York Times*, November 25, 2003.

53 See "Inside the Teenage Brain," *Frontline*, written and directed by Sarah Spinks, aired January 2002 (Public Broadcasting System); Nina W. Chernoff and Marsha L.

Levick, "Beyond the Death Penalty: Implications of Adolescent Development for the Prosecution, Defense and Sanctioning of Youthful Offenders," *Clearinghouse Review, Journal of Poverty Law and Policy*, July–August 2005; Coalition for Juvenile Justice, *Childhood on Trial: The Failure of Trying and Sentencing Youth in Adult Criminal Court* (Washington, DC: Coalition for Juvenile Justice, 2005).

54 Steinberg and Scott, "Less Guilty by Reason of Adolescence," 1013.

55 At the time of the *Roper v. Simmons* decision, seventy-two people convicted of crimes committed when they were under 18 came off of death row. See Charles Lane, "5–4 Supreme Court Abolishes Juvenile Executions," *Washington Post*, March 2, 2005, A01.

56 *Roper v. Simmons*, 543 U.S. 551 (2005).

57 Ibid.

58 Ibid., 569.

59 Ibid., 570.

60 Ibid., 571.

61 Pagnanelli, "Children as Adults."

62 Chernoff and Levick, "Beyond the Death Penalty," 209.

63 Pagnanelli, "Children as Adults," 194.

64 John Matthew Fabian, "Applying *Roper v. Simmons* in Juvenile Transfer and Waiver Proceedings: A Legal and Neuroscientific Inquiry," *International Journal of Offender Therapy and Comparative Criminology* 55 (2011): 732–55.

65 *Graham v. Florida*, No. 08-7412, slip opinion at 23 (Supreme Court, May 17, 2010).

66 *Graham v. Florida*, No. 08-7412, slip opinion at 17.

67 Neelum Arya, "Using *Graham v. Florida* to Challenge Juvenile Transfer Laws," *Louisiana Law Review* 71 (2010): 99–155, p. 102.

68 Ibid., 139.

69 Adam Liptak, "Justices Will Hear 2 Cases of Life Sentences for Youths," *New York Times*, November 7, 2011.

70 Scott and Grisso, "The Evolution of Adolescence"; Elizabeth S. Scott and Laurence Steinberg, *Rethinking Juvenile Justice* (Cambridge, MA: Harvard University Press, 2008).

Notes to the Conclusion

1 Aaron Kupchik, *Judging Juveniles: Prosecuting Adolescents in Adult and Juvenile Courts* (New York: New York University Press, 2006).

2 Laurence Steinberg and Elizabeth S. Scott, "Less Guilty by Reason of Adolescence: Developmental Immaturity, Diminished Responsibility, and the Juvenile Death Penalty," *American Psychologist* 58 (2003): 1009–18, p. 1016.

3 Joseph B. Sanborn, "Hard Choices or Obvious Ones: Developing Policy for Excluding Youth from Juvenile Court," *Youth Violence and Juvenile Justice* 1 (2003): 198–214.

4 Howard N. Snyder and Melissa Sickmund, *Juvenile Offenders and Victims: 2006 National Report* (Washington, DC: U.S. Department of Justice, Office of Justice Programs, Office of Juvenile Justice and Delinquency Prevention, 2006); Charles M. Puzzanchera, *Juvenile Arrests 2007*, Juvenile Justice Bulletin (Washington, DC:

U.S. Department of Justice, Office of Justice Programs, Office of Juvenile Justice and Delinquency Prevention, April 2009).

5 Merril Sobie, "Pity the Child: The Age of Delinquency in New York," *Pace Law Review* 30 (2010): 1061–89.

6 Justice Policy Institute, *The Accelerating Pace of Juvenile Justice Reform*, Models for Change (Washington, DC: Justice Policy Institute, 2007), http://www.modelsforchange.net/publications/122.

7 Ibid.

8 Elizabeth Kooy, *The Illinois Success Story: Reducing Racial Disparity through Transfer Reform* (Washington, DC: Campaign for Youth Justice, 2009).

9 Neelum Arya, *State Trends: Legislative Changes from 2005 to 2010 Removing Youth from the Adult Criminal Justice System* (Washington, DC: Campaign for Youth Justice, 2011).

10 Ibid.

11 Task Force on Transforming Juvenile Justice, *Charting a New Course: A Blueprint for Transforming Juvenile Justice in New York State; A Report of Governor Paterson's Task Force on Transforming Juvenile Justice* (New York: Vera Institute of Justice, 2009), 12.

12 Ibid., 16.

13 Ibid.

14 William J. Brennan, "Reason, Passion and the Progress of Law: The Forty-Second Annual Benjamin N. Cardozo Lecture to the Association of the Bar of New York," September 17, 1987, published in *Benjamin Cardozo Law Review* 10, no. 3 (1988).

15 Michael A. Corriero, *Judging Children as Children: A Proposal for a Juvenile Justice System* (Philadelphia: Temple University Press, 2006), 2.

BIBLIOGRAPHY

Adams, Benjamin, and Sean Addie. 2010. *Delinquency Cases Waived to Criminal Court, 2007*. OJJDP Factsheet. Washington, DC: U.S. Department of Justice, Office of Justice Programs, Office of Juvenile Justice and Delinquency Prevention.

Albonetti, Celesta A. 1991. "An Integration of Theories to Explain Judicial Discretion." *Social Problems* 38: 247–66.

Amnesty International. 1998. *Betraying the Young: Human Rights Violations against Children in the US Justice System*. New York: Amnesty International.

Andrew Glover Youth Program. 2005. *Annual Report 2005*. New York: Andrew Glover Youth Program.

Applegate, Brandon K., Robin King Davis, and Francis T. Cullen. 2009. "Reconsidering Child Saving: The Extent and Correlates of Public Support for Excluding Youth from the Juvenile Court." *Crime and Delinquency* 55: 51–77.

Arya, Neelum. 2007. *Jailing Juveniles: The Dangers of Incarcerating Youth in Adult Jails in America*. Washington, DC: Campaign for Youth Justice.

———. 2010. "Using *Graham v. Florida* to Challenge Juvenile Transfer Laws." *Louisiana Law Review* 71: 99–155

———. 2011. *State Trends: Legislative Changes from 2005 to 2010 Removing Youth from the Adult Criminal Justice System*. Washington, DC: Campaign for Youth Justice.

Association of the Bar of the City of New York, Committee on Juvenile Justice. 1983. *New York Juvenile Offender Law*. Report of the Juvenile Justice Committee of the Association of the Bar of the City of New York, No. 2826. New York: Association of the Bar of the City of New York.

Austin, James, Kelly Dedel Johnson, and Maria Gregoriou. October 2000. *Juveniles in Adult Prisons and Jails: A National Assessment. Monograph*. Washington, DC: U.S. Department of Justice, Office of Justice Programs, Bureau of Justice Statistics.

Barnum, Richard. 2000. "Clinical and Forensic Evaluation of Competence to Stand Trial in Juvenile Defendants." In *Youth on Trial: A Developmental Perspective on Juvenile Justice*, edited by Thomas Grisso and Robert. G. Schwartz. Chicago: University of Chicago Press.

Bernard, Thomas. 1992. *The Cycle of Juvenile Justice*. New York: Oxford University Press.

Bishop, Donna. 2000. "Juvenile Offenders in the Adult Criminal Justice System." In *Crime and Justice, a Review of Research*, vol. 27, edited by Michael Tonry. Chicago: University of Chicago Press.

Bishop, Donna, and Charles E. Frazier. 2000. "Consequences of Transfer." In *The Changing Borders of Juvenile Justice: Transfer of Adolescents to the Criminal Court*, edited by Jeffrey Fagan and Franklin Zimring. Chicago: University of Chicago Press.

Bishop, Donna M., Charles E. Frazier, and John C. Henretta. 1989. "Prosecutorial Waiver: Case Study of a Questionable Reform." *Crime and Delinquency* 35: 179–201.

Bishop, Donna, Charles E. Frazier, Lonn Lanza-Kaduce, and Laurence Winner. 1996. "The Transfer of Juveniles to Criminal Court: Does It Make a Difference?" *Crime and Delinquency* 42: 171–91.

Blumstein, Alfred, and Richard Rosenfeld. 1998. *Assessing Recent Ups and Downs in U.S. Homicide Rates*. Pittsburgh, PA: National Consortium on Violence Research.

Bogira, Steve. 2005. *Courtroom 302: A Year behind the Scenes in an American Criminal Court*. New York: Alfred A. Knopf.

Bortner, M. A. 1982. *Inside a Juvenile Court: The Tarnished Ideal of Individualized Justice*. New York: New York University Press.

Bortner, M. A., Marjorie S. Zatz, and Darnell. F. Hawkins. 2000. "Race and Transfer: Empirical Research and Social Context." In *The Changing Borders of Juvenile Justice: Transfer of Adolescents to the Criminal Court*, edited by Jeffrey Fagan and Franklin Zimring. Chicago: University of Chicago Press.

Brennan, William J. 1987. "Reason, Passion and the Progress of Law: The Forty-Second Annual Benjamin N. Cardozo Lecture to the Bar Association of New York." September 17. Published in *Benjamin Cardozo Law Review* 10, no. 3 (1988).

Butterfield, Fox. 1995. *All God's Children: The Bosket Case and the American Tradition of Violence*. New York: Alfred A. Knopf.

Butts, Jeffrey A. 2002. *Youth Crime Drop*. Washington, DC: Urban Institute, Justice Policy Center.

Butts, Jeffrey A., and Adele V. Harrell. June 1998. *Delinquents or Criminals? Policy Options for Young Offenders*. Washington, DC: Urban Institute.

Butts, Jeffrey A., and Ojmarrh Mitchell. 2000. "Brick by Brick: Dismantling the Border between Juvenile and Adult Justice." In *Criminal Justice*, vol. 2, *Boundary Changes in Criminal Justice Organizations*, edited by Charles M. Friel. Washington, DC: U.S. Department of Justice, Office of Justice Programs.

"Carey Gets Report Urging More Power to Prosecute Youths Involved in Crime." 1978. *New York Times*, February 26, p. 33.

Center for Alternative Sentencing and Employment Services (CASES). N.d. *Alternatives to Incarceration Programs: Cut Crime, Cut Cost, Help People and Communities*. New York: CASES.

Centers for Disease Control and Prevention. 2007. *Effects on Violence of Laws and Policies Facilitating the Transfer of Youth from the Juvenile to the Adult System*. Morbidity and Mortality Weekly Report 56 (RR-9). Washington, DC: Centers for Disease Control and Prevention.

Chandler, Marilyn A. 1982. "New York State's Youthful Offender Statutes: An Empirical Investigation of Their Theoretical Basis and Their Operation." PhD dissertation, State University of New York at Albany.

Chernoff, Nina W., and Marsha L. Levick. 2005. "Beyond the Death Penalty: Implications of Adolescent Development for the Prosecution, Defense and Sanctioning of Youthful Offenders." *Clearinghouse Review, Journal of Poverty Law and Policy*, July–August.

Citizens' Committee for Children of New York. 1979. *In Search of Juvenile Justice: An Interim Report on the 1978 Juvenile Offender Law*. New York: Citizens' Committee for Children of New York.

Cleveland, Steven J. 2004. "Judicial Discretion and Statutory Interpretation." *Oklahoma Law Review* 57: 31–40.

Clynch, Edward J., and David W. Neubauer. 1981. "Trial Courts as Organizations: A Critique and Synthesis." *Law and Policy Quarterly* 3: 69–94.

Coalition for Juvenile Justice. 2005. *Childhood on Trial: The Failure of Trying and Sentencing Youth in Adult Criminal Court*. Washington, DC: Coalition for Juvenile Justice.

Cohen, Stanley. 2002. *Folk Devils and Moral Panics*. 3d ed. London: Routledge.

Collier, Walter V. 1984. "New York State's Juvenile Offender Law: An Analysis of Factors That Influenced Implementation of the Law." Master's thesis, New York University.

Copperman, Joel, Sarah Bryer, and Hannah Gray. 2004. *Community-Based Sentencing Demonstrates Low Recidivism among Felony-Level Offenders*. Kingston, NJ: Civic Research Institute.

Corrado, Raymond R., Irwin M. Cohen, and William Glackman. 2003. "Serious and Violent Offenders' Decisions to Recidivate: An Assessment of Five Sentencing Models." *Crime and Delinquency* 49: 179–200.

Correctional Association of New York. December 2006. *Youth Confined in OCFS Facilities*. New York: Correctional Association of New York.

———. September 2006. *Juvenile Detention in New York City*. New York: Correctional Association of New York.

———. September 2007. *Juvenile Detention in New York City*. New York: Correctional Association of New York.

———. N.d. *Juvenile Detention in New York City*. New York: Correctional Association of New York.

Corriero, Michael A. 1990. "Youth Parts: Constructive Response to the Challenge of Youth Crime." *New York Law Journal*, October 26.

———. 2006. *Judging Children as Children: A Proposal for a Juvenile Justice System*. Philadelphia: Temple University Press.

Coyle, Michael J. 2010. "Notes on the Study of Language: Towards a Critical Race Criminology." *Western Criminology Review* 11: 11–19.

Criminal Justice Agency. 1997. *Annual Report on the Adult Court Case Processing of Juvenile Offenders in New York City, January through December 1995*. New York: Criminal Justice Agency.

———. 1998. *Annual Report on the Adult Court Case Processing of Juvenile Offenders in New York City, January through December 1996*. New York: Criminal Justice Agency.

———. 1999. *Annual Report on the Adult Court Case Processing of Juvenile Offenders in New York City, January through December 1997*. New York: Criminal Justice Agency.

———. 2000. *Annual Report on the Adult Court Case Processing of Juvenile Offenders in New York City, January through December 1998*. New York: Criminal Justice Agency.

———. March 2001. *Annual Report on the Adult Court Case Processing of Juvenile Offenders in New York City, January through December 1999*. New York: Criminal Justice Agency.

———. October 2001. *Annual Report on the Adult Court Case Processing of Juvenile Offenders in New York City, January through December 2000*. New York: Criminal Justice Agency.

"Criminals Yes, Adults No." 1978. Editorial. *New York Times*, July 14.

Dawson, Robert O. 2000. "Judicial Waiver in Theory and Practice. In *The Changing Borders of Juvenile Justice: Transfer of Adolescents to the Criminal Court*, edited by Jeffrey Fagan and Franklin Zimring. Chicago: University of Chicago Press.

DeBrovner, Caroline Joy. 2006. "Fridays in the Youth Part." In *Judging Children a Children: A Proposal for a Juvenile Justice System* by Michael Corriero. Philadelphia: Temple University Press.

Dionne, E. J., Jr. 1978. "Anticrime Bill Passed in Albany. *New York Times*, July 19, p. 22.

DiIulio, John. 1995. "The Coming of the Super-Predators." *Weekly Standard*, November 27.

DiIulio, John, William J. Bennett, and John P. Walters. 1996. *Body Count: Moral Poverty . . . And How to Win America's War against Crime and Drugs.* New York: Simon and Schuster.

Easterbrook, Frank H. 2004. "Judicial Discretion in Statutory Interpretation." *Oklahoma Law Review* 57: 1–20.

Eisenstein, James, Roy Flemming, and Peter Nardulli. 1988. *The Contours of Justice: Communities and Their Courts.* Boston: Little, Brown.

Eisenstein, James, and Herbert Jacobs. 1977. *Felony Justice: An Organizational Analysis of Criminal Courts.* Boston: Little, Brown.

Emerson, Robert M. 1969. *Judging Delinquents: Context and Process in Juvenile Court.* Chicago: Aldine.

Fabian, John Matthew. 2011. "Applying *Roper v. Simmons* in Juvenile Transfer and Waiver Proceedings: A Legal and Neuroscientific Inquiry." *International Journal of Offender Therapy and Comparative Criminology* 55: 732–55.

Fabricant, Michael. 1981. *Juvenile Injustice: Dilemmas of the Family Court System.* New York: Community Service Society, Institute for Social Welfare Research.

Fagan, Jeffrey. 1996. "The Comparative Advantage of Juvenile versus Criminal Court Sanctions on Recidivism among Adolescent Felony Offenders." *Law and Policy* 18: 77–114.

———. 2008. "Juvenile Crime and Criminal Justice: Resolving Border Disputes." *Future of Children* 18: 81–118.

Fagan, Jeffrey, Aaron Kupchik, and Akiva Liberman. 2003. *Be Careful What You Ask For: The Comparative Impacts of Juvenile versus Criminal Court Sanctions on Recidivism among Adolescent Felony Offenders.* Public Law Research Paper No. 03-61. New York: Columbia University Law School.

Feeley, Malcolm M. 1973. "Two Models of the Criminal Justice System: An Organizational Perspective." *Law and Society Review* 7: 407–25.

———. 1979. *The Process Is the Punishment: Handling Cases in a Lower Criminal Court.* New York: Russell Sage Foundation.

Feld, Barry. 1999. *Bad Kids: Race and the Transformation of the Juvenile Court.* New York: Oxford University Press.

Fisher, Bernard C. 1955. *Justice for Youth: The Courts for Wayward Youth in New York City.* New York: Bureau of Public Affairs, Community Service Society of New York.

Gaarder, Emily, and Joanne Belknap. 2002. "Tenuous Borders: Girls Transferred to Adult Court." *Criminology* 40: 481–518.

Gewirtz, Marian. 2002. *Annual Report on the Adult Court Case Processing of Juvenile*

Offenders in New York City, January through December 2001. New York: Criminal Justice Agency.

———. 2003. *Annual Report on the Adult Court Case Processing of Juvenile Offenders in New York City, January through December 2002.* New York: Criminal Justice Agency.

———. 2004. *Annual Report on the Adult Court Case Processing of Juvenile Offenders in New York City, January through December 2004.* New York: Criminal Justice Agency.

———. 2005. *Annual Report on the Adult Court Case Processing of Juvenile Offenders in New York City, January through December 2004.* New York: Criminal Justice Agency.

———. December 2005. *Assessing the Impact of Differing Models of Youth Crime Prosecution.* Research Brief No. 10. New York: Criminal Justice Agency.

———. 2006. *Annual Report on the Adult Court Case Processing of Juvenile Offenders in New York City, January through December 2005.* New York: Criminal Justice Agency.

———. 2007a. *Recidivism among Juvenile Offenders in New York City.* New York: Criminal Justice Agency.

———. 2007b. *The Risk of Re-Arrest for Serious Juvenile Offenders.* Research Brief No. 15. New York: Criminal Justice Agency.

Gewirtz, Marian, and Elyse J. Revere. 2005. *Adult-Court Processing and Re-Arrest of Juvenile Offenders in Manhattan and Queens.* New York: Criminal Justice Agency.

Giardino, Linda F. 1996. "Statutory Rhetoric: The Reality behind Juvenile Justice Polices in America." *Journal of Law and Policy* 5: 223–76.

Gilliam, Frank D., and Shanto Iyengar. 1998. "The Superpredator Script." *Nieman Reports* 52: 45–46.

Goode, Erica. 2003. "A Conversation with Laurence Steinberg: Are Young Killers Evil, or Works in Progress?" *New York Times,* November 25.

Graham v. Florida, 7412 U.S. 8 (U.S. Supreme Court 2010).

Greenawalt, Kent. 1975. "Discretion and Judicial Decision: The Elusive Quest for the Fetters That Bind Judges." *Columbia Law Review* 75: 359–99.

Greenwood, Peter W., Joan Petersilia, and Franklin E. Zimring. 1980. *Age, Crime and Sanctions: The Transition from Juvenile to Adult Court.* Santa Monica, CA: RAND Corporation.

Griffin, Patrick. 2002. *National Overviews: State Juvenile Justice Profiles.* Pittsburgh, PA: National Center for Juvenile Justice.

———. 2003. *Trying and Sentencing Juveniles as Adults: An Analysis of State Transfer and Blended Sentencing Laws.* Pittsburgh, PA: National Center for Juvenile Justice.

———. 2008a. *Different from Adults: An Updated Analysis of Juvenile Transfer and Blended Sentencing Laws, with Recommendations for Reform.* Models for Change. Pittsburgh, PA: National Center for Juvenile Justice.

———. 2008b. *National Overviews: State Juvenile Justice Profiles.* Pittsburgh, PA: National Center for Juvenile Justice, www.ncjj.org/stateprofiles

Griffin, Patrick, Patricia Torbet, and Linda Szymanski. 1998. *Trying Juveniles as Adults in Criminal Court: An Analysis of State Transfer Provisions.* Washington, DC: U.S. Department of Justice, Office of Justice Programs, Office of Juvenile Justice and Delinquency Prevention.

Grinnell, Alison M. 2000. "Searching for a Solution: The Future of New York's Juvenile Offender Law." *New York Law School Journal of Human Rights* 16: 635–67.

Grisso, Thomas. 1980. "Juveniles' Capacities to Waive Miranda Warnings: An Empirical Analysis." *California Law Review* 68: 1134–66.

———. 1996. "Society's Retributive Response to Juvenile Violence: A Developmental Perspective." *Law and Human Behavior* 20: 229–47.

———. 2005. *Clinical Evaluations for Juveniles' Competence to Stand Trial: A Guide for Legal Professionals.* Sarasota, FL: Professional Resource Press.

Grisso, Thomas, Michael O. Miller, and Bruce Sales. 1987. "Competency to Stand Trial in Juvenile Court." *International Journal of Law and Psychiatry* 10: 1–20.

Grisso, Thomas, and Robert G. Schwartz, eds. 2000. *Youth on Trial: A Developmental Perspective on Juvenile Justice.* Chicago: University of Chicago Press.

Grisso, Thomas, et al. 2003. "Juveniles' Competence to Stand Trial: A Comparison of Adolescents and Adults' Capacities as Trial Defendants." *Law and Human Behavior* 27: 333–63.

Hume, Edward. 1996. *No Matter How Loud I Shout: A Year in the Life of Juvenile Court.* New York: Simon and Schuster.

In re Gault, 387 U.S. 1 (U.S. Supreme Court 1967).

In re Winship, 397 U.S. 357 (U.S. Supreme Court 1970).

"Inside the Teenage Brain." January 2002. Episode of *Frontline*, written and directed by Sarah Spinks. Public Broadcasting System.

Jacobs, Mark. 1990. *Screwing the System and Making It Work: Juvenile Justice in the No-Fault Society.* Chicago: University of Chicago Press.

Jacobson, Michael M. 2005. *Downsizing Prisons: How to Reduce Crime and End Mass Incarceration.* New York: New York University Press.

Justice Policy Institute. 2007. *The Accelerating Pace of Juvenile Justice Reform.* Models for Change. Washington, CD: Justice Policy Institute, http://www.modelsforchange.net/publications/122.

Juszkiewicz, Jolanta. 2000. *Youth Crime / Adult Time: Is Justice Served?* Washington, DC: Pretrial Services Resource Center, Building Blocks for Youth.

Kaiser, Charles. 1978. "Boy, 15, Who Killed 2 and Tried to Kill a Third Is Given 5 Years." *New York Times*, June 29.

Kent v. United States, 383 U.S. 541 (U.S. Supreme Court 1966).

King, Melanie, and Linda Szymanski. 2006. *National Overviews: State Juvenile Justice Profiles.* Pittsburgh, PA: National Center for Juvenile Justice.

Klein, Eric. 1998. "Dennis the Menace or Billy the Kid: An Analysis of the Role of Transfer to Criminal Court in Juvenile Justice." *American Criminal Law Review* 35: 371–410.

Kooy, Elizabeth. 2009. *The Illinois Success Story: Reducing Racial Disparity through Transfer Reform.* Washington, DC: Campaign for Youth Justice.

Krisberg, Barry. 1998. "The Evolution of an American Institution." *Crime and Delinquency* 44: 5–8.

Kupchik, Aaron. 2003. "Prosecuting Adolescents in Criminal Courts: Criminal or Juvenile Justice?" *Social Problems* 50: 439–60.

———. 2004. "Youthfulness, Responsibility and Punishment: Admonishing Adolescents in Criminal Court." *Punishment and Society* 6: 149–73.

———. 2006. *Judging Juveniles: Prosecuting Adolescents in Adult and Juvenile Courts.* New York: New York University Press.

Lane, Charles. 2005. "5–4 Supreme Court Abolishes Juvenile Executions." *Washington Post*, March 2, p. A01.

Lane, Jodie, Lonn Lanza-Kaduce, Charles E. Frazier, and Donna M. Bishop. 2002. "Adult versus Juvenile Sanctions: Voices of Incarcerated Youth." *Crime and Delinquency* 48: 431–55.

Lanza-Kaduce, Lonn, Jodie Lane, Donna M. Bishop, and Charles Frazier. 2005. "Juvenile Offenders and Adult Felony Recidivism: The Impact of Transfer." *Journal of Crime and Justice* 28: 59–77.

Laws of New York (1978).

Laws of New York (2005).

Legal Aid Society. N.d. *Profile of a Juvenile Offender*. New York: Legal Aid Society.

Lemmon, John. H., Thomas L. Austin, P. J. Verrecchia, and Matthew Fetzer. 2005. "The Effect of Legal and Extralegal Factors on Statutory Exclusion of Juvenile Offenders." *Youth Violence and Juvenile Justice* 3: 214–34.

Liberman, Akiva. 1996. *Minority Over-Representation among Juveniles in New York City's Adult and Juvenile Court Systems during Fiscal Year 1992*. New York: Criminal Justice Agency.

Liberman, Akiva, Bill Raleigh, and Freda Soloman. 1999. *Juvenile Offender Cases in Specialized and Non-Specialized Court Parts in New York City's Supreme Courts: 1994–95 and 1995–96*. New York: Criminal Justice Agency.

Lind, E. Allen, and Tom R. Tyler. 1988. *The Social Psychology of Procedural Justice*. New York: Plenum Press.

Ludwig, Frederick. 1955. *Youth and the Law: Handbook on Laws Effecting Youth*. Brooklyn, NY: Foundation Press.

Macaulay, Stewart L., Laurence M. Friedman, and John Stookey, eds. 1995. *Law and Society: Readings on the Social Study of Law*. New York: W.W. Norton.

Males, Mike, and Dan Macallair. 2002. *The Color of Justice: An Analysis of Juvenile Adult Court Transfers in California*. Washington, DC: Building Blocks for Youth.

Martinson, Robert. 1974. "What Works? Questions and Answers about Prison Reform." *Public Interest* 35: 22–54.

Mason, Craig A., and Shau Chang. 2001. *Re-Arrest Rates among Youth Sentenced in Adult Court*. Miami: Juvenile Sentencing Advocacy Project, Miami-Dade County Public Defender's Office.

Mathers, Lynn M. 1977. "Ethnography and the Study of Trial Courts." In *Public Law and Public Policy*, edited by John A. Gardiner. New York: Praeger.

McCord, Joan, and Kevin P. Conway. 2002. "Patterns of Juvenile Delinquency and Co-Offending." In *Crime and Social Organization*, edited by Elin Waring and David Weisburd. New Brunswick, NJ: Transaction Publishers.

McGarrell, Edmund F. 1989. "The Ideological Bases and Functions of Contemporary Juvenile Law Reform: The New York State Experience." *Contemporary Crises* 13: 163–87.

Mears, Daniel P. 2003. "A Critique of Waiver Research." *Youth Violence and Juvenile Justice* 1: 156–72.

Mears, Daniel P., Carter Hay, Marc Gertz, and Christina Mancini. 2007. "Public Opinion and the Foundation of the Juvenile Court." *Criminology* 45: 223–57.

Meislin, Richard J. 1978a. "Carey, in Shift, Backs Trial in Adult Court for Some Juveniles." *New York Times*, June 30, p. 1.

———. 1978b. "Albany Leaders Draw Tough Bill on Youth Crime." *New York Times*, July 15, p. 1.

———. 1978c. "Albany Legislature Votes Package of Stiff Youth and Adult Penalties." *New York Times*, July 20.

Mennel, Robert M. 1973. *Thorns and Thistles: Juvenile Delinquents in the United States, 1825–1940*. Hanover, NH: University Press of New England.

Moran, Kenneth T., and John L. Cooper. 1983. *Discretion and the Criminal Justice Process*. Port Washington, NY: Associated Faculty Press.

Myers, David L. 2001. *Excluding Violent Youths from Juvenile Court: The Effectiveness of Legislative Waiver*. New York: LFB Scholarly.

———. 2003. "Adult Crime, Adult Time." *Youth Violence and Juvenile Justice* 1: 173–97.

———. 2005. *Boys among Men: Trying and Sentencing Juveniles as Adults*. Westport, CT: Praeger.

National Council on Crime and Delinquency. 2007a. *And Justice for Some: Differential Treatment of Youth of Color in the Justice System*. Oakland, CA: National Council on Crime and Delinquency.

———. 2007b. *Attitudes of US Voters toward Youth Crime and the Justice System*. Oakland, CA: National Council on Crime and Delinquency.

National Juvenile Justice Network. 2009. *Turning It Around: Success and Opportunities in Juvenile Justice*. A Report of the National Juvenile Justice Network and the Connecticut Juvenile Justice Alliance. Washington, DC: National Juvenile Justice Network, http://www.njjn.org/uploads/digital-library/turning.pdf.

New York Criminal Procedure Law. Flushing, NY: Looseleaf Law.

New York Penal Law. Flushing, NY: Looseleaf Law.

New York State Division of Criminal Justice Services. 2005. Juvenile Offender Indictment Data, 1984–2005 (requested by author).

Pagnanelli, Enrico. 2007. "Children as Adults: The Transfer of Juveniles to the Adult Courts and the Potential Impact of *Roper v. Simmons*." *American Criminal Law Review* 44: 175–94.

Piquero, Alex R., et al. 2005. "Developmental Trajectories of Legal Socialization among Serious Adolescent Offenders." *Journal of Criminal Law and Criminology* 96: 267–98.

Pizarro, Jesenia M., Steven M. Chermack, and Jeffrey A. Gruenewald. 2007. "Juvenile 'Super-Predators' in the News: A Comparison of Adult and Juvenile Homicides." *Journal of Criminal Justice and Popular Culture* 14: 84–111.

Platt, Anthony M. 1969. *The Child Savers: The Invention of Delinquency*. Chicago: University of Chicago Press.

Podkapacz, Marcy R., and Barry Feld. 1996. "The End of the Line: An Empirical Study of Judicial Waiver." *Journal of Criminal Law and Criminology* 86: 449–92.

Purnick, Joyce. 1996. "Youth Crime: Should Laws Be Tougher?" *New York Times*, May 9.

Puzzanchera, Charles M. April 2009. *Juvenile Arrests 2007*. Juvenile Justice Bulletin. Washington, DC: U.S. Department of Justice, Office of Justice Programs, Office of Juvenile Justice and Delinquency Prevention.

Rainville, Gerald A., and Steven K. Smith. 2003. *Juvenile Felony Defendants in Criminal Courts: Survey of 40 Counties, 1998*. Washington, DC: U.S. Department of Justice, Office of Justice Programs, Bureau of Justice Statistics.

Redding, Richard E. 2003. "The Effects of Adjudicating and Sentencing Juveniles as Adults." *Youth Violence and Juvenile Justice* 1: 128–55.

———. August 2008. *Juvenile Transfer Laws: An Effective Deterrent to Delinquency?* Juvenile Justice Bulletin. Washington, DC: Department of Justice, Office of Justice Programs, Office of Juvenile Justice and Delinquency Prevention.

Redding, Richard E., and Elizabeth J. Fuller. 2004. "What Do Juvenile Offenders Know about Being Tried as Adults? Implications for Deterrence." *Juvenile and Family Court Journal* 36: 35–44.

Richie, Beth E. 2002. "The Social Impact of Mass Incarceration on Women." In *Invisible Punishment: The Collateral Consequences of Mass Imprisonment*, edited by Marc Mauer and Meda Chesney-Lind. New York: The New Press.

Rios, Victor. 2006. "The Hyper-Criminalization of Black and Latino Male Youth in the Era of Mass Incarceration." *Souls* 8: 40–54.

———. 2008. "The Racial Politics of Youth Crime." *Latino Studies* 6: 97–115.

Roper v. Simmons, 633 U.S. 3 (U.S. Supreme Court 2005).

Rubin, H. Ted. 1985. *Behind the Black Robes: Juvenile Court Judges and the Court*. Beverly Hills, CA: Sage Publications.

Sanborn, Joseph B. 1995. "How Parents Can Affect the Processing of Delinquents in Juvenile Court." *Criminal Justice Policy Review* 7: 1–26.

———. 2003. "Hard Choices or Obvious Ones: Developing Policy for Excluding Youth from Juvenile Court." *Youth Violence and Juvenile Justice* 1: 198–214.

Schiraldi, Vincent, and Jason Ziedenberg. 1999. *The Florida Experiment: An Analysis of the Impact of Granting Prosecutors Discretion to Try Juveniles as Adults*. Washington, DC: Justice Policy Institute, Center on Juvenile and Criminal Justice.

Schwartz, Ira M. 1989. *(In)Justice for Juveniles: Rethinking the Best Interests of the Child*. Lexington, MA: Lexington Press.

Scott, Elizabeth S., and Thomas Grisso. 1997. "The Evolution of Adolescence: A Developmental Perspective in Juvenile Justice Reform." *Journal of Criminal Law and Criminology* 88: 137–89.

Scott, Elizabeth S., N. Dickon Reppucci, and Jennifer L. Woolard. 1995. "Evaluating Adolescent Decision Making in Legal Contexts." *Law and Human Behavior* 19: 221–44.

Scott, Elizabeth S., and Laurence Steinberg. 2003. "Blaming Youth." *Texas Law Review* 81: 799–840.

———. 2008. *Rethinking Juvenile Justice*. Cambridge, MA: Harvard University Press.

Sherman, Laurence W. 1993. "Defiance, Deterrence, and Irrelevance: A Theory of the Criminal Sanction." *Journal of Research in Crime and Delinquency* 30: 445–73.

Simon, Jonathan. 1993. *Poor Discipline: Parole and the Social Control of the Underclass, 1890–1990*. Chicago: University of Chicago Press.

Singer, Simon I. 1996. *Recriminalizing Delinquency: Violent Juvenile Crime and Juvenile Justice*. New York: Cambridge University Press.

Singer, Simon I., and Charles P. Ewing. 1988. "Juvenile Justice Reform in New York

State: The Juvenile Offender Law." In *Representing Juvenile Offenders in New York*. Albany: New York State Bar Association.

Singer, Simon I., Jeffrey Fagan, and Akiva Liberman. 2000. "The Reproduction of Juvenile Justice in Criminal Court: A Case Study of New York's Juvenile Offender Law." In *The Changing Borders of Juvenile Justice: Transfer of Adolescents to the Criminal Court*, edited by Jeffrey Fagan and Franklin Zimring. Chicago: University of Chicago Press.

Singer, Simon I., and David McDowall. 1988. "Criminalizing Delinquency: The Deterrent Effects of the New York Juvenile Offender Law." In *Representing Juvenile Offenders in New York*. Albany: New York State Bar Association.

Snyder, Howard N. 1997. *Juvenile Arrests 1996*. Washington, DC: U.S. Department of Justice, Office of Juvenile Justice and Delinquency Prevention.

Snyder, Howard N., and Melissa Sickmund. 2006. *Juvenile Offenders and Victims: 2006 National Report*. Washington, DC: U.S. Department of Justice, Office of Justice Programs, Office of Juvenile Justice and Delinquency Prevention.

Snyder, Howard N., Melissa Sickmund, and Eileen Poe-Yamagata. August 2000. *Juvenile Transfers to Criminal Court in the 1990s: Lessons Learned from Four Studies*. Washington, DC: U.S. Department of Justice, Office of Justice Programs, Office of Juvenile Justice and Delinquency Prevention.

Sobie, Merril. 1981. *The Juvenile Offender Act: A Study of the Act's Effectiveness and Impact on the New York Juvenile Justice System*. New York: Foundation for Child Development.

———. 2010. "Pity the Child: The Age of Delinquency in New York." *Pace Law Review* 30: 1061–89.

Stapleton, W. V., and L. E. Teitelbaum.1972. *In Defense of Youth: A Study of the Role of Counsel in American Juvenile Courts*. New York: Russell Sage Foundation.

Steinberg, Laurence, and Elizabeth Cauffman. 1996. "Maturity of Judgment in Adolescence: Psychosocial Factors in Adolescent Decision Making." *Law and Human Behavior* 20: 249–72.

———. 2000. "A Developmental Perspective on Jurisdictional Boundary." In *The Changing Borders of Juvenile Justice: Transfer of Adolescents to the Criminal Court*, edited by Jeffrey Fagan and Franklin Zimring. Chicago: University of Chicago Press.

Steinberg, Laurence, and Alex Piquero. 2010. "Manipulating Public Opinion about Trying Juveniles as Adults: An Experimental Study." *Crime and Delinquency* 56: 487–506.

Steinberg, Laurence, and Robert G. Schwartz. 2000. "Developmental Psychology Goes to Court." In *Youth on Trial: A Developmental Perspective on Juvenile Justice*, edited by Thomas Grisso and Robert G. Schwartz. Chicago: University of Chicago Press.

Steinberg, Laurence, and Elizabeth S. Scott. 2003. "Less Guilty by Reason of Adolescence: Developmental Immaturity, Diminished Responsibility, and the Juvenile Death Penalty." *American Psychologist* 58: 1009–18.

Steiner, Benjamin, and Craig Hemmens. 2003. "Juvenile Waiver 2003: Where Are We Now?" *Juvenile and Family Court Journal* 54: 1–24.

Steiner, Benjamin, Craig Hemmens, and Valerie Bell. 2006. "Legislative Waiver

Reconsidered: General Deterrent Effect of Statutory Exclusion Laws Enacted Post-1979." *Justice Quarterly* 23: 34–59.

Steiner, Benjamin, and Emily Wright. 2006. "Assessing the Relative Effects of State Direct File Waiver Laws on Violent Juvenile Crime: Deterrence or Irrelevance?" *Journal of Criminal Law and Criminology* 96: 1451–77.

Sullivan v. Florida U.S. Supreme Court Docket # 08-7621 2009.

Tanenhaus, David S. 2000. "The Evolution of Transfer out of the Juvenile Court." In *The Changing Borders of Juvenile Justice: Transfer of Adolescents to the Criminal Court*, edited by Jeffery Fagan and Franklin Zimring. Chicago: University of Chicago Press.

———. 2004. *Juvenile Justice in the Making*. New York: Oxford University Press.

Tanenhaus, David S., and Steven A. Drizin. 2003. "Owing to the Extreme Youth of the Accused: The Changing Legal Response to Juvenile Homicide." *Journal of Criminal Law and Criminology* 92: 641–705.

Task Force on Transforming Juvenile Justice. 2009. *Charting a New Course: A Blueprint for Transforming Juvenile Justice in New York State. A Report of Governor Paterson's Task Force on Transforming Juvenile Justice*. New York: Vera Institute of Justice.

Thomas, Charles W., and Donna M. Bishop. 1984. "The Impact of Legal Sanctions on Delinquency: A Longitudinal Comparison of Labeling and Deterrence Theories." *Journal of Criminal Law and Criminology* 75: 1222–45.

Tobey, Ann, Thomas Grisso, and Robert G. Schwartz. 2000. "Youths' Trial Participation as Seen by Youths and Their Attorneys: An Exploration of Competence-Based Issues." In *Youth on Trial: A Developmental Perspective on Juvenile Justice*, edited by Thomas Grisso and Robert. G. Schwartz. Chicago: University of Chicago Press.

Torbet, Patricia, Patrick Griffin, Hunter Hurst, Jr., and Lynn R. MacKenzie. April 2000. *Juveniles Facing Criminal Sanctions: Three States That Changed the Rules*. Washington, DC: U.S. Department of Justice, Office of Justice Programs, Office of Juvenile Justice and Delinquency Prevention.

Torbet, Patricia, and Linda Szymanski. 1998. *State Legislative Responses to Violent Juvenile Crime: 1996–97 Update*. Washington, DC: U.S. Department of Justice, Office of Justice Programs, Office of Juvenile Justice and Delinquency Prevention.

Tyler, Tom R. 1990. *Why People Obey the Law*. New Haven, CT: Yale University Press.

Ulmer, Jeffrey T., and John H. Kramer. 1998. "The Use and Transformation of Formal Decision-Making Criteria: Sentencing Guidelines, Organizational Contexts, and Case Processing Strategies." *Social Problems* 45: 248–67.

Warner, Eric. 2004. *The Juvenile Offender Handbook*. Flushing, NY: Looseleaf Law.

Weisman, Steven R. 1978. "Crime—a Code for Winning Votes." *New York Times*, May 14, p. E5.

Welch, Michael, Eric A. Price, and Nana Yankey. 2002. "Moral Panic over Youth Violence: Wilding and the Manufacture of Menace in the Media." *Youth and Society* 34: 3–30.

West, Heather C., William J. Sabol, and Sarah J. Greenman. December 2010. *Prisoners in 2009*. Washington, DC: U.S. Department of Justice, Office of Justice Programs, Bureau of Justice Statistics.

Wilson, John J., and James C. Howell. 1993. *Comprehensive Strategy for Serious, Violent and Chronic Juvenile Offenders* (*Program Summary*). Washington, DC: U.S.

Department of Justice, Office of Justice Programs, Office of Juvenile Justice and
    Delinquency Prevention.
Winner, Laurence, Lonn Lanza-Kaduce, Donna M. Bishop, and Charles E. Frazier. 1997.
    "The Transfer of Juveniles to Criminal Court: Reexamining Recidivism over the
    Long Term." *Crime and Delinquency* 43: 548–63.
Wise, Daniel. 1992. "New Part Set Up for Cases against Violent Youth." *New York Law
    Journal*, October 26.
Young, Malcolm C. 2000. *Providing Effective Representation for Youth Prosecuted as
    Adults*. Washington, DC: U.S. Department of Justice, Office of Justice Programs,
    Bureau of Justice Assistance.
Ziedenberg, Jason. 2001. *Drugs and Disparity: The Racial Impact of Illinois' Practice of
    Transferring Young Drug Offenders to Adult Court*. Washington, DC: Justice Policy
    Institute, Center on Juvenile and Criminal Justice, Building Blocks for Youth.
Zimring, Frank. 1998. *American Youth Violence*. New York: Oxford University Press.
Zimring, Frank, and Jeffrey Fagan, eds. 2000. *The Changing Borders of Juvenile Justice:
    Transfer of Adolescents to the Criminal Court*. Chicago: University of Chicago Press.

INDEX

ABOUT THE AUTHOR

Carla J. Barrett is Assistant Professor of Sociology at the John Jay College of Criminal Justice in New York.